GHOSTBUSTERS™
THE ULTIMATE VISUAL HISTORY

Foreword by **DAN AYKROYD**
Introduction by **IVAN REITMAN**
Written by **DANIEL WALLACE**

INSIGHT EDITIONS

San Rafael, California

PREVIOUS PAGE Bill Bryan wears the full-sized Stay Puft suit on a miniature streetscape, with effects technicians hidden below.

THIS PAGE A concept illustration by artist Thom Enriquez for *Ghostbusters II*, in which the ghostbusters travel to a defunct subway system and encounter a car full of ghostly subway passengers.

CONTENTS

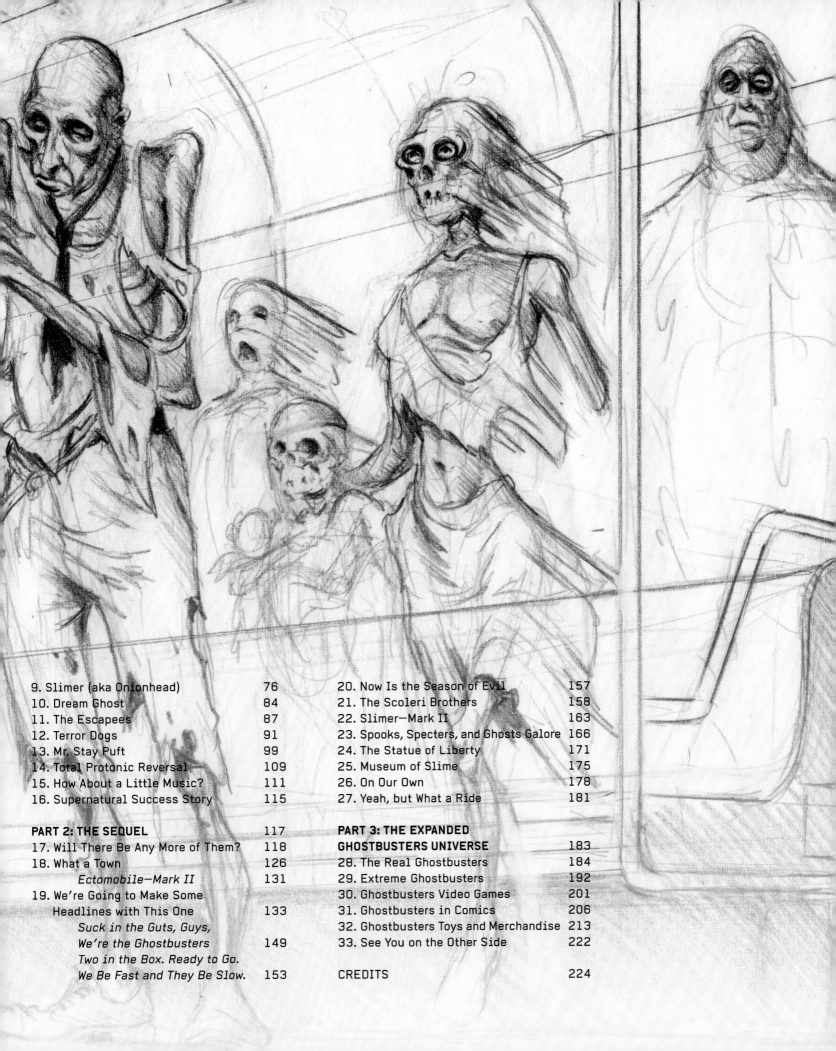

FOREWORD BY DAN AYKROYD

When Harold, Ivan and I were writing the early drafts of *Ghostbusters* we began work with my fellow Carleton University undergrad, artist John Daveikis. None of us imagined how well executed our graphic, design and scenic concepts would turn out to be.

We did give the various departments a pretty clear template and a full array of initial visual renderings to work with. But the skills and talents of the production designers and their staffs brought the concepts to life.

From little touches, like the clear plastic hoses on the jumpsuits (for incontinence due to fear) to the comic-realism of Slimer and Stay Puft to all the inspirations in between from props, costumes and make-up, the colander on Tully's head, the individual ideas and contributions of the people on the show made the film pop visually. Ivan, Bill, Harold's family, Ernie, John D., the movie crew and I know you will enjoy this book which presents the inside story of how *Ghostbusters* was originated and visually enlivened on screen.

OPPOSITE Dan Aykroyd as Ray Stantz shows off a ghost trap, one of the tools of the ghostbusting trade. **BELOW** Ray measures the psychic energy emanating from a portrait of Vigo the Carpathian in a scene from *Ghostbusters II*.

INTRODUCTION BY IVAN REITMAN

Dear Reader,

Here it is, thirty years after the initial release of *Ghostbusters*. I'm often asked if I had any idea that *Ghostbusters* would turn into the record-breaking financial success and worldwide cultural phenomenon that it became. I often answer by recalling the moment that I first witnessed Bill, Dan, Harold, and Ernie fully outfitted in ghostbusters gear, walking casually down Madison Avenue just as I was lining up the first shot of the movie. There was something remarkably iconic about the way they looked together on that street. It sent a shiver up my spine, and I instantly felt that something special was about to happen.

In fact, something special had been unfolding from the very beginning of my experience with this film.

It was April 1983, and I was sent Dan Aykroyd's inventive futuristic treatment that introduced the idea that a group of men, acting much like firefighters, would trap and catch ghosts as part of a new protective emergency service for the universe at large. I suggested to Dan that it might be more effective if we reset the story in modern-day Manhattan and frame the adventure as a "going into business" tale. It would center on a trio of clever postgrads who were studying and experimenting with the science of paranormal activity. Near the beginning of the film, they are thrown out of their comfortable university positions and forced to go into business "busting ghosts," eventually saving New York City from destruction.

Dan agreed with this story approach and with my suggestion to bring in Harold Ramis as a co-writer. And thus began the happiest creative experience of my life. Working within a remarkably short timeline, Aykroyd, Ramis, and I, with our families, went off to Martha's Vineyard for two weeks, where we hammered out the first draft of the movie. Production began in October 1983, and the finished movie opened in theaters across the country June 8, 1984.

The making of *Ghostbusters* brought together a fabulous array of very gifted comedy minds working at the top of their game. Most significantly, it brought me back together with the extraordinary Bill Murray for our fourth collaboration. In a funny, surprising, and wonderfully human performance, Bill joins Dan, Harold, and Ernie Hudson in a comedy quartet as intricately balanced and wonderfully funny as anything seen in

the movies. Adding to the comedy are the performances of the luminous Rick Moranis, the brilliant and beautiful Sigourney Weaver, and the masterful Bill Atherton playing the bureaucrat we all love to hate.

Matching the brilliance of the performers on-screen were a group of top professionals behind the camera. Comprising the best that Hollywood had to offer, cameraman László Kovács, production designer John DeCuir Sr., visual effects supervisor Richard Edlund, costume designer Theoni Aldredge, and composer Elmer Bernstein all contributed wonderful ideas that combined to make *Ghostbusters* the special movie that it became.

Enjoy this behind-the-scenes look at *Ghostbusters*, and thank you for holding my films, particularly *Ghostbusters*, so close to your heart. It makes me happy and proud to do what I do.

Enjoy!

OPPOSITE Bill Murray and Dan Aykroyd, suited up and ready for ghostbusting, take a break from saving the world with their director Ivan Reitman. **ABOVE RIGHT** A Slimer statue based on the original puppet from *Ghostbusters*, which is now displayed in Ivan Reitman's office.

PART 1

THE ORIGINAL
MOVIE

1. WHO YOU GONNA CALL?

During a breezy montage in 1984's *Ghostbusters*, a *Time* magazine cover flashes on screen. Its headline: "Ghostbusters: Supernatural Success Story." Even though it's just a movie mock-up, the line doubles as real-world commentary that's uncannily accurate in its clairvoyance.

Ghostbusters the movie is now Ghostbusters the institution. The answer to "Who you gonna call?" isn't so straightforward anymore, not when the spook-stoppers have plied their trade in movies, animation, comic books, and video games. Not a bad outcome for comedy heroes who, when confronted with irrefutable evidence of the supernatural, mused, "The franchise rights alone will make us rich beyond our wildest dreams."

In fact, the original *Ghostbusters* wears its business heart on its sleeve. Director Ivan Reitman wanted to filter the fantastic premise of the movie through a prism of realism, by focusing on the travails of entrepreneurs launching a start-up. In the film, we follow Peter Venkman, Ray Stantz, and Egon Spengler as they apply for loans, tour real estate sites, and film an ad campaign. When Winston Zeddemore answers a newspaper ad recruiting a fourth ghostbuster, his motive is suitably practical: "If there's a steady paycheck in it, I'll believe anything you say."

Along with the intriguing premise, *Ghostbusters* also benefitted from a cutting-edge cast. The off-the-cuff comedy style of *Ghostbusters* is arguably the ultimate expression of the late '70s–early '80s ensemble boom that saw the stars of *Saturday Night Live* and the Second City comedy troupe make the jump into box-office hits, including *Animal House*, *The Blues Brothers*, *Caddyshack*, and *Stripes*. With their finely honed improv skills and prior big-screen hits, the trio of Bill Murray, Dan Aykroyd, and Harold Ramis looked like a lineup that couldn't lose.

At the time, however, plenty of people were afraid of *Ghostbusters*. Aykroyd's original treatment seemed too epic in its scope, with an emphasis on the kind of big-budget effects that made studios nervous. But Aykroyd's secret weapon wasn't spectacle—it was the humor-meets-horror premise, founded upon his real-life belief in the supernatural.

"It wasn't a story about goofy guys who were chasing ghosts," says Ernie Hudson, who played Zeddemore. "For Danny, this was real to him. That gave it a certain integrity."

The matter-of-fact fashion in which the working stiffs snuffed out the phantoms sold the premise to audiences so convincingly that it seemed as if a local Ghostbusters office might be

PREVIOUS PAGE Ernie Hudson, Harold Ramis, Bill Murray, and Dan Aykroyd (clockwise from top left) pose within the Gozer temple set. **OPPOSITE** Dan Aykroyd, Bill Murray, and Harold Ramis behold something much more terrifying than their No-Ghost buddy in this publicity shot. **BELOW** Early sketch of a potential Ghostbusters logo.

spotted on the way home from the movie theater. "I think Dan's creation of a group that busts ghosts and the way they capture them, you somehow believe that it must have existed *before* the movie," says producer Joe Medjuck. "It's not so much a new phenomenon, as something that just enters the culture."

The blue-collar trappings helped too. Even though most of the ghostbusters have PhDs, they act like regular working stiffs, from the cigarette hanging off Ray Stantz's lower lip, to Venkman's fast-talking, salesman-like patter. The cast has a loose, "we're all in this together" camaraderie that invites the viewer to become their co-conspirator, something that never gets stale even after repeat viewings.

"It was such an original script, with so much heart and so much wit and so much goofy innocence," says Sigourney Weaver, who played Dana Barrett in *Ghostbusters* and its sequel. "It doesn't surprise me that they created something that was timeless."

A massive hit upon its initial release, *Ghostbusters* is a property that, like its array of colorful specters and ghouls, has proved to have a vibrant afterlife. You grow up with *Ghostbusters* but you never grow out of *Ghostbusters*.

"What I find exciting is now we have the third generation watching," says Dan Aykroyd. "We have the original parents who took their kids, and now those kids are grown up, and they have kids. We've got parents, kids, and grandkids."

WE'RE READY TO BELIEVE YOU

The ghosts are real in *Ghostbusters*, but the heroes quickly go from wide-eyed shock to shrugging acceptance. It's a perspective that could only come from someone steeped in the supernatural, and Dan Aykroyd comes from a long line of true believers.

Aykroyd grew up in a Canadian farmhouse owned by his family for five generations. By his account, paranormal phenomena filled the place from the cellar to the rafters. Aykroyd family ancestors participated in séances and summoned ghostly faces. Instead of *National Geographic* magazines, Aykroyd says the coffee tables in his home were littered with journals from the American Society for Psychical Research.

As a boy, Aykroyd thought he would join the Catholic priesthood, but ultimately he put those aspirations aside and followed the lure of comedy, performing in nightclubs where he sometimes filled in as a blues drummer.

He honed his ensemble skills with The Second City troupe in Toronto and later in Chicago, where he befriended fellow cast member Bill Murray. "Billy kind of took me under his wing when I first started in Chicago," he says. "He picked me up at the airport and made sure I had all the right things in the city to make me happy."

The improvisational comedy championed by The Second City found an eager audience in the '70s, and its practitioners discovered that the funniest material was often collaborative. "We learned a great process at Second City, which was never to say no," said Harold Ramis, another veteran of the troupe.[1] "If someone has an idea, you force yourself to say 'yes, and . . .' and then add something or put a spin on their idea that makes it better."

Ramis said he played "long-haired, freaked-out zanies" in Second City until newcomer John Belushi displaced him, leading Ramis to assume the role of the egghead. "We were told to always play from the top of your intelligence," he said.[2] "It's sort of a rule that I've always followed, that even if you're playing an idiot, the idiot can know a lot of things."

Aykroyd, Murray, and Belushi all parlayed their Second City success into starring roles on Lorne Michael's hit TV show *Saturday Night Live*. Aykroyd eventually won an Emmy for his work as a writer on *SNL*, but never forgot the eerie wonder of his experiences with the supernatural.

. . . IN A SPIRITUAL SENSE, OF COURSE

The notion of a "supernatural comedy" wasn't exactly unprecedented. Examples of the trend during the 1940s included Bob Hope's *Ghost Breakers,* Olson & Johnson's *Ghost Catchers,* and the Bowery Boys' *Ghosts on the Loose,* though no one had touched the genre in decades. Aykroyd saw an opportunity to update the idea for a new generation, shoring it up with actual parapsychological science, taking full advantage of the post–*Star Wars* leap in movie visual effects, and peppering the proceedings with *SNL*-flavored dialogue.

As a believer surrounded by skeptics, Aykroyd knew the frustration felt by those whose claims of paranormal experiences were automatically discarded. "What if you advertised on TV or in the yellow pages and said, 'Hey, we believe you, we understand you?'" he said.[3] "That was the birth of the commercial enterprise of ghostbusting."

He had a hook, but Aykroyd still needed a story. His first treatment included lead roles for himself and John Belushi as partners in ghost trapping. The two had gelled on *SNL*, even spinning their Blues Brothers characters into a hit film directed by John Landis. But in March 1982, at the age of thirty-three, Belushi died of a drug overdose.

Aykroyd persevered. Over the next year he refined his story, first with his eye on Eddie Murphy as a co-star, then with fellow *SNL* alum Bill Murray in the role.

Murray, the middle child in a family of nine, planned to become a doctor before he discovered his comedy niche. Specializing in playing unflappable oddballs, he could fire dry,

TOP Early design of a simple Ghostbusters "GB" logo.
OPPOSITE A simplified ghostly figure, showcasing the design basics that would be developed further in the iconic No-Ghost logo.

devastating ripostes in any situation. Though not involved with writing Aykroyd's script, he agreed to star if his friend could get the movie made. "Danny always said that Bill was going to be in it, and we never doubted it," recalls Joe Medjuck, who would later become an associate producer on *Ghostbusters*. "I don't know if he was legally attached at that point, and it's hard to get Bill to agree to do anything, but when Danny said, 'Bill says he's going to do it' we went forward on that basis."

Aykroyd's first-pass treatment, labeled "Ghost Smashers," threw audiences into the deep end of the pool, with a near-future setting and innumerable procedural details concerning high-tech parapsychological tactics. The heroes operated out of a converted New Jersey gas station and faced spectral threats including a skeletal biker who terrorized a small town, while Gozer appeared as a mysterious figure shrouded behind mosquito netting who collected the mounted trophy heads of bats, rats, and lobsters.

Optimistic about the treatment's appeal, Aykroyd brought it to his friend, filmmaker Ivan Reitman, who seemingly possessed a Midas touch for movie comedies.

"I was always a storyteller," says Reitman. "Even as a three-year-old I did puppet shows for my family in Czechoslovakia. As I was growing up in Toronto I was entertaining the kids on the block, organizing backyard circuses. "By the time I attended University [at Ontario's McMaster University] I was directing plays and writing for the student newspaper, and I directed my first film as part of the film club—an eighteen-minute comedy short [about] college orientation.

"That was when I realized that film is a combination of every kind of storytelling imaginable. From that moment, it was all I could think of doing. I directed for a start-up television station, and most importantly I did the movie *Cannibal Girls*—an improvised comedy horror that starred Eugene Levy and Andrea Martin long before Second City."

Cannibal Girls demonstrated Reitman's appetite for horror comedy, and he soon delved deeper into the culture that would birth *Saturday Night Live*. As producer of the off-Broadway stage comedy *The National Lampoon Show*, Reitman worked with Bill Murray, John Belushi, Gilda Radner, and more. "It was a hit, and my deal was that if I developed it as a film, I could produce and perhaps direct it," he says. "So I started working with Harold Ramis—who was also a part of that show—on a script that eventually became *Animal House*."

One of the biggest movies of 1978, *Animal House* made a star of John Belushi and cemented the rise of a new style of humor. "It was the first time people had seen comedy film expressed with a different voice," says Reitman. "A new comedic language representing the baby boom generation." He followed up with *Meatballs*, which he directed with Bill Murray, who had recently joined *Saturday Night Live*, in the lead. *Meatballs* became a sensation when it was released the year after *Animal House*, and the two movies contributed to a change in the American comedy landscape.

Reitman rounded out his comedy trifecta with the military outing *Stripes*, which also starred Murray and introduced Harold Ramis in his first big-screen role. When *Stripes* also turned out to be a hit, Dan Aykroyd approached Reitman with his own treatment for a supernatural comedy he had written that he

wanted to co-star in alongside John Belushi. Reitman's best films featured a sharp comic sensibility. In Aykroyd's ghost-busting story, he discovered the foundation for a movie that would hone this sensibility even further.

"I have amazing respect for Danny," explains Reitman. "We basically grew up together in Toronto—he was the announcer on a show called *Greed* I did for a UHF station. I got to know him and stayed in touch, and I started my film career while he was working on *Saturday Night Live* and doing *The Blues Brothers*."

Reitman delivered a mixed verdict on his friend's supernatural movie concept. "It was very expensive, and it didn't quite work as a story, but it had all these great ideas," he says. "I just felt it should be rewritten and placed into a real context."

Aykroyd admits his first draft wasn't fully baked. "It was set in multiple dimensions. There were teams of ghostbusters: some bad, some good. But it had a lot of elements [that ended up in] the first movie."

To help sell the visual aspect of his concept, Aykroyd recorded a video of himself in a jumpsuit wearing a proton pack made from Styrofoam. He also solicited conceptual illustrations from John Deveikis (nicknamed "the Viking"), an old college buddy. Included in Deveikis's first batch of artwork was an interpretation of a corporate emblem for supernatural exterminators: a classic bedsheet ghost inside a red, cross-barred circle.

"Danny had a friend in Canada, the Viking, and that 'no ghost' symbol was his idea," says Reitman. "Michael C. Gross, who was working with me at that time in my company, refined it later on. I always thought that was as great a logo as anything I had ever seen."

Within Aykroyd's sprawling treatment, Reitman found a lot to like in the concept of paranormal investigators who operate like firefighters. Reitman, joined at this stage by associate producer Joe Medjuck, brainstormed ways to ground the fantas-

enriquez

ABOVE A Thom Enriquez concept for a Stay Puft marshmallow man alternative. Enriquez came up with the idea that this monster could be Ray Stantz's pet lizard from his childhood. OPPOSITE An unused "pizza ghost" concept by Thom Enriquez for the montage sequence in *Ghostbusters*, showcasing a pizza delivery demon with cheesy flesh dripping from its face.

tical elements in a more familiar setting. He moved the action to a contemporary American city, and worked up a narrative that introduced the concept of ghostbusting before leading audiences through its evolution into a career. "Ivan turned to me and said, 'What if the ghostbusters were college professors?'" remembers Medjuck. "I said, 'I get that—I *was* a college professor. This could be good.'"

In a meeting with Aykroyd, Reitman proposed a new collaborator: Harold Ramis. "I pitched it as three ghostbusters, not two, and I suggested Harold," recalls Reitman. "Danny liked my ideas—he was very collaborative—and he had great respect for Harold as a writer."

"Ivan and Danny had lunch at Art's Deli [in LA]," says Medjuck. "When they came back they said, 'Do you think Harold would write this?' And I said, 'As long as he's in it, he will.' That same day, they walked across the street and got Harold."

Having co-written *Meatballs*, *Stripes*, and *Animal House*, Harold Ramis, a former *Playboy* joke editor, had earned Reitman's trust as a rock-solid story man. And by costarring with Murray in *Stripes*, Ramis had proven he could be funny in front of the camera too. With a flourishing directorial career of his own that included *Caddyshack* and *National Lampoon's Vacation*, Ramis could have afforded to pass on *Ghostbusters*. Fortunately, something drew him in.

Aykroyd remembers the recruitment as an open-and-shut case. "Ivan said to me, 'OK, what I'd like to do is make it more accessible, less dark. Let's get Ramis on it. Ramis looked at it and said, 'I get it. Let's go to work.'"

Though not quite on Aykroyd's true-believer level, Ramis (who had spent a year living on a Greek island rumored to be inhabited by vampires) wasn't unfamiliar with the paranormal. "When you live on an island where there's almost no media, tales of the supernatural seem to become kind of a pastime," he said.[4] I was always terrified to walk alone at night because there were so many ghost stories. What I loved about Dan's first script was that he took those things that had always been very chilling to me and made them seem perfectly mundane. The fact that the ghostbusters were like janitors who encountered such problems with casualness demystified a lot of it."

In Ramis, Reitman had a veteran writer, a third star to join Aykroyd and Murray, and the final piece of his comedy dream team. What he didn't have was a studio.

WE GOT ONE!

In May 1983, talent agent Michael Ovitz—who represented all four principal players, Reitman, Aykroyd, Ramis, and Murray—set up a meeting to discuss *Ghostbusters* with Columbia Pictures chairman Frank Price. Given the state of the script,

Reitman wisely avoided getting into story details, instead focusing his pitch on the movie's concept and its lineup of bankable comedy stars.

Reitman recalls being asked for his budget for the film by Price and, in a somewhat spontaneous gesture, the director proposed a number on the spot that was accepted. *Ghostbusters* was given the green light. The one catch was that the studio needed a big movie for release early the following summer, before July and the distraction of the 1984 Summer Olympics. That translated into a target release date of June 1, 1984. Reitman had just over one year to take the project from script to screen.

The risks were substantial. The box office hadn't been friendly to big-budget comedies, with Steven Spielberg's *1941*—starring Aykroyd and Belushi—having underperformed following its release in 1979. Furthermore, *Ghostbusters* would be an effects-driven comedy laced with genuine moments of terror. John Landis's *An American Werewolf in London* had deftly walked the line between comedy and horror two years earlier, but Reitman's blockbuster movie would need to play to bigger houses.

Buckling down for a major script rewrite, Aykroyd, Ramis, and Reitman retreated to Aykroyd's vacation home on Martha's Vineyard. There the trio disappeared into a camouflage-painted basement, nicknamed Dan's Bunker, to churn out screenplay pages on an old Royal typewriter.

"The writing process was Aykroyd, Ramis, and myself in Martha's Vineyard for about two-and-a-half weeks, where we basically knocked out what is now the movie that everybody knows," says Reitman. "I had always wanted to do a combination of big-time special effects that was genuinely scary and genuinely funny, and I pushed that as the central vision."

The character dynamics between the three leads became another area of attention. Reitman felt the trio should embody the concepts of "brains, heart, and mouth," with the archetypes filled by Ramis, Aykroyd, and Murray, respectively.

"In essence," said Ramis,[5] "that translated into one character being hipper and more verbal than the others—more of a huckster, the salesman of the team, someone who's weak on the technical side and probably didn't do all that well in school, but is smart enough to have hooked up with guys more intelligent than he is." That template coalesced into Peter Venkman, played by Bill Murray. Venkman is sometimes described as a cynical realist whose personality is a balance of acerbic wit, charm, and charisma.

Ray Stantz would be the team's true believer: optimistic and a little naïve. Ramis described Dan Aykroyd's character as "a mechanic, a nuts-and-bolts person—honest, straight-ahead, enthusiastic. And that really worked for Dan."[6]

Ramis himself would play the team's scientist, Egon Spengler, named after a high school classmate of Ramis's named Egon Donsbach and the German historian Oswald Spengler. "For my character, we went for a human computer—someone who has no emotional life whatsoever, who only deals in facts and information," said Ramis. In the script, Spengler is described as a "new wave Mr. Spock," with the added information that the character "single-handedly got Venkman through graduate school."

Elements retained from Aykroyd's original treatment included a gluttonous ghost and the colossal Stay Puft marshmallow man. Other pieces fell away during rewrites, including a climax in which the ghostbusters traveled to alternate dimensions. "It seemed almost like two different movies," Ramis noted. "And while I think most people can accept the notion of the supernatural as being one thing, interdimensional travel to them is sort of a shadow area that relates more to outer space. It just seemed too big a leap for the audience to make."

Ramis and Aykroyd continued to trim the fat from the story. A love interest for Peter Venkman seemed important, but one script made her a shape-shifting refugee from the supernatural realm. "Venkman's affair with the interdimensional creature was funny, but not very romantic," said Ramis.[7] "He wakes up with her one morning and she is this kind of warthog—which we realized was rather lacking in real human connection and love."

Despite the improvements to the story, Reitman still wasn't comfortable with the overall narrative flow. "For the longest time, the movie never really got going until the hotel scene," he says. "Then we added the library ghost, and then the ESP scene—which was very funny and got us moving right from the beginning."

The structure for the latter half of the movie proved to be a trickier puzzle. Eventually the menace of the ancient Sumerian god Gozer offered appropriately high stakes. Gozer's minions, Zuul and Vinz Clortho, brought the threat close to home when they possessed a pair of human mortals—including Venkman's love interest—and turned them into Terror Dogs. "The whole Keymaster-Gatekeeper idea came very late, and we struggled with it all the way," says Reitman.

Aykroyd and Ramis delivered their first coauthored script on June 6, and by October 7, the pair had locked down the final shooting script. "We wrote a little bit in LA and we wrote at Martha's Vineyard, and then two or three months after we finished the script, we were shooting it," recalls Aykroyd. "It was the fastest experience I've ever had making a film."

Due to an overseas movie-shoot commitment, Bill Murray had no input on the development of the *Ghostbusters* story. "Bill had committed to Danny, yet he wasn't around during preproduction," explains Joe Medjuck. "He was off in India making *The Razor's Edge*. But Harold knew Bill's voice."

Only weeks before the start of filming, Murray flew to New York for a script conference with Reitman. "Ivan wanted me with him, so we drove out to La Guardia," said Ramis.[8] "Bill flew in on a private plane, an hour late, and came through the terminal with a stadium horn—one of those bullhorns that plays eighty different fight songs—and he was addressing everyone in sight with this thing. We dragged him out of there and went to a restaurant in Queens. I've never seen him in higher spirits. We spent an hour together, and he said maybe two words about the whole script. Then he took off again. But it was trust.

"*Ghostbusters* was the first film he'd ever committed to without fighting like crazy, and he'd just decided we couldn't fail—which is certainly not to underestimate his part in the film. Bill's really great at thinking on his feet, and on the set he probably gives more than any comic actor around."

IF THERE'S A STEADY PAYCHECK IN IT . . .

In addition to his writers and his stars, Reitman had two lieutenants—associate producers Joe Medjuck and Michael C. Gross—who had earned his confidence as men who could get things done. Both had worked with Reitman before: Medjuck on *Stripes*, Gross on the animated film that Reitman produced, *Heavy Metal*.

BELOW Concept art by Ron Croci shows Dana Barrett and Louis Tully transformed into Terror Dogs at Gozer's temple.

STUDY FOR APPEARANCE OF MONSTERS "GHOSTBUSTERS" CROCI

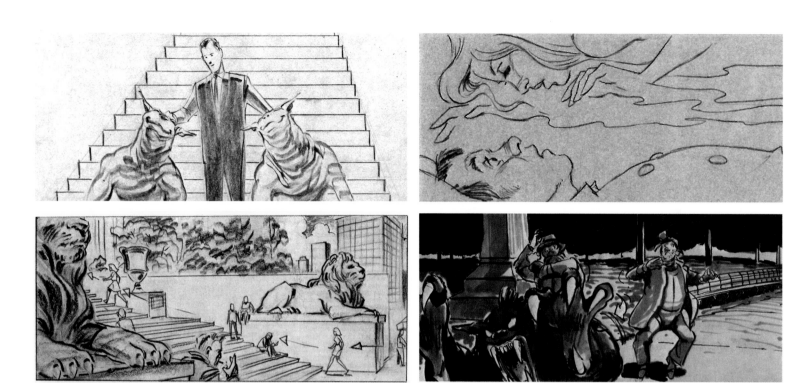

Frames from early storyboards including (clockwise from top left) a rejected design for Gozer, Ray's extended encounter with the Fort Detmerring ghost, a Terror Dog on the rampage in Central Park, and the iconic exterior of the New York Public Library. **ABOVE** Artist Brent Boates works on a storyboard for *Ghostbusters*.

"If Ivan was the heart and brains of the organization, then Joe and I were his left and right arms," says Gross. "We basically interpreted his needs, advised him, delivered what he wanted, argued with him, helped him, whatever it was. We were this team of two different people with two different skills and two different points of view."

With so much to do before the start of production, Medjuck assisted with script development and shooting, while Gross tackled the problem of visual effects. "I was Ivan's eyes, and Medjuck was his ears," says Gross.

"Even though we were still working on the script, we started working on the design and special effects at the same

time," explains Medjuck. Fortunately for *Ghostbusters*, Richard Edlund—the esteemed special effects designer of *Raiders of the Lost Ark* and the *Star Wars* trilogy—was ready to leave Industrial Light & Magic after seven years with the company.

"I had been down in LA after finishing *Return of the Jedi*," remembers Edlund. "I knew I was going to be leaving ILM, but I had injured my back because I'd lifted something too heavy off of my Land Rover, and I had to go into the hospital for minor surgery. While I was in the hospital, I got this call from Ivan to do *Ghostbusters*."

Looking to launch his own effects company, Edlund needed funding and film projects to put in the pipeline.

Study for the "alter" and scenic B.G. "Ghostbusters"

Two studios, Columbia and MGM, helped Edlund get things kicked off for his new venture, Boss Film Studios.

"Gary Martin at Columbia made a deal where Columbia paid for half of the money it took to set up Boss Films and MGM paid for the other half," says Joe Medjuck. "So Richard started with two films ready to go, *2010* and *Ghostbusters*, and he set up a completely new company from scratch."

The high-resolution equipment at Boss Films allowed for shooting at a 65mm film gauge, much sharper than the motion picture standard of 35mm. "All of our shots were done on a 65mm camera so we could make a reduction," says Edlund. "The reduction from 65mm to 35 anamorphic was more than double the film size, so we got incredibly high quality composites."

Concept artists soon began work on the ghosts and other psychic phenomena. Thom Enriquez recalls how he joined the team: "I was at a sushi bar with my portfolio, sitting next to Ivan Reitman and Michael Gross. I overheard them talking, showed them my work, and I got hired." Gross brought in other artists, including Bernie Wrightson and Italian illustrator Liberatore, but Enriquez remained close to the production.

"Everybody else was shipping [their designs] through the mail, and I was right there with Michael," he says. "My job was to draw storyboards, but I was also doing anything that he could think of. There was not a defined delineation of what the jobs were, and that was the fun part."

Meanwhile, Oscar®-winning art director John DeCuir (*The King and I, Cleopatra*) signed on as production designer—a coup for Reitman, who wanted his film to tell a visual story through unique architectural cues.

"When I started scouting the city I realized that there was this extraordinary group of gargoyles on these Art Deco and historical buildings throughout Manhattan," says Reitman.

"I thought that would be an interesting visual motif, in the telling of the architectural story. Architecture turns out to be a big thing in this film."

Other prominent hires included cinematographer László Kovács (*Easy Rider, Five Easy Pieces*), costume designer Theoni V. Aldredge (*Network*), and editor Sheldon Kahn (*One Flew Over the Cuckoo's Nest*).

"Ivan had never made a movie of that size before, and we were cocky," says Medjuck. "We didn't know enough to know that it would be difficult. We'd never done anything that required special effects like that, we just thought, 'Hey, we can do this.'"

Reitman shared the overall air of confidence, his spirits lifted by his movie's strong roster of talent. "I was fortunate I was surrounded by really brilliant people," he says, "like John DeCuir, and the stars who were also great writers. Things were coming at me very, very quickly. I just had a sense that it was going to work out."

TOP A concept rendering of the Gozer temple set by artist Ron Croci. **CENTER** Associate Producer Michael C. Gross during a storyboard session. **ABOVE** An alternate Thom Enriquez design for a creature seen within the extradimensional vastness of Dana's refrigerator.

2. BEAUTIFUL. YOU'RE HIRED.

The identities of the actors who would play the three founding ghostbusters were never in doubt. The script hinged on the participation of Murray, Ramis, and Aykroyd.

But the film couldn't squeak by with only a trio. Thanks to the efforts of casting director Karen Rea, *Ghostbusters* would hire a love interest, a neighbor, a secretary, and a nemesis—not to mention a fourth member of the 'busting crew.

Sigourney Weaver had already earned star status for her roles in *Alien* and *The Year of Living Dangerously* by the early 1980s. Although she had no experience with big-budget comedies, that didn't deter her when she saw an opportunity she couldn't pass up: the role of Dana Barrett.

"No one ever sent me comedy," she recalls. In *Ghostbusters*, Weaver saw the chance to play both a romantic interest and a demonic hellion—when it came time to audition for Reitman, she couldn't wait to prove what she could do.

"In the course of the audition I did something where I actually turned into a Terror Dog," she says. "And because I was from the theater, and [Ivan] didn't say cut, I started to turn *into* a dog. I growled, I ripped his cushions up in his office a little bit, and it

ended with me howling and shaking. I was doing it in earnest—to be funny of course—and he stopped the tape and said, 'Don't ever do that again. If the editor saw what you were doing he'd want to use it, because it's so grotesque.'

"I realized that he intended to have the Terror Dog as a special effect. I guess I was thinking that *I* would be the Terror Dog!"

Weaver's dedication to the part of Dana Barrett immediately made its mark on the story. At Weaver's suggestion, the character—originally conceived as a professional model—became a concert cellist.

In early storyboard illustrations, Dana's neighbor Louis Tully is drawn wide-bodied and full-faced. This portly version of the character is a leftover from Aykroyd and Ramis's original notion that Louis be played by comedian John Candy. Ramis and Murray had both starred with Candy in *Stripes*, and Louis was written in the same vein as Johnny LaRue, the showbiz lecher Candy had portrayed on Canadian comedy show Second City Television (SCTV).

"It was a different kind of character, much more flamboyant, more like the character John played on *SCTV*,"

BELOW Dan Aykroyd, Rick Moranis, and Ivan Reitman take a break during filming on the firehouse set. **OPPOSITE** Sigourney Weaver as Dana Barrett.

says Joe Medjuck. "I think he just didn't want to play it again, but he also had some strange ideas that Ivan didn't want to deal with." Candy's suggestions—including giving Louis a thick German accent and rottweilers as pets—seemed too out there for Reitman, who reached out to Candy's *SCTV* colleague Rick Moranis as a backup.

"Ivan knew Rick from Toronto and sent him the script," says Medjuck. "And Rick knew Harold from *SCTV*, and Danny from Toronto, so he was just one of the gang."

Moranis collaborated with Ramis to rewrite some scenes and penned other scenes on his own. "We let Rick form his own character," says Medjuck. "Sort of a nerd." Louis's dinner party, in which he invites clients instead of friends so he can claim the affair as a promotional expense, came from the mind of Moranis.

"Basically [Louis] was a thumbnail sketch, a template where any actor could have come in and said the lines," says Aykroyd. "But Rick Moranis took that part and ran with it. He basically rewrote it completely, and added all kinds of dialogue and elements that we never even thought of."

The ghostbusters' first hire is no-nonsense New Yorker Janine Melnitz, a part briefly considered for comedian Sandra Bernhard. Annie Potts won the role instead, exhibiting an admirable ability to remain unimpressed in the middle of chaos and wielding a famously brassy voice.

"I'm a Southerner, but I had a friend who had a very specific New York accent, so I thought I'd just do her," says Potts. "It's funny—after I did that part I actually lost out on

auditions because they said, 'Oh she's too ethnic, too New Yorky. Are you kidding me?'"

Janine's unflappable armor only cracks when she's close to Egon Spengler. Unfortunately, the oblivious scientist doesn't reciprocate her come-ons. Their subtly building romance was to have been a larger subplot in the film, though many scenes building up their connection (including Janine giving Egon her 1964 World's Fair "lucky coin") wouldn't survive the editing process.

The fourth ghostbuster, Winston Zeddemore, fills a critical role in the movie as the voice of the common man—able to ask questions that provide technical or plot information to the audience.

"In the process of writing, we realized that we needed someone who wasn't part of that initial college group," says Reitman. "Somebody who came in off the street who could ask the questions that a layperson would ask. Everyone thought that Winston was written for Eddie Murphy, but Eddie was really only going to costar with Danny in his original version of the story. I never spoke to Eddie about being in the film."

With each revision of the script, Winston's role evolved dramatically.

"We bent over backward to make Winston's character good, and in doing so we made him *so* good that he was the best character in the movie," said Ramis.[9] "We looked at it and said, 'Jesus! He's got all the good lines.'" Among the story beats originally given to Zeddemore were the initial confrontation with the hotel ghost and the mental conjuring that led to the creation of the Stay Puft marshmallow man.

ABOVE (left to right) Rick Moranis as Louis Tully; Annie Potts as Janine Melnitz; Ernie Hudson as Winston Zeddemore; William Atherton as Walter Peck.

"At the same time, everybody was saying Bill's character was a little weak," continued Ramis. "So, little by little, we started shifting Winston's attitude to Bill's character—which made perfect sense—and we ended up delaying Winston's introduction until much later in the film."

"When I first got the script it was a great character," says Hudson. "He came in at the very beginning when they left the university, and when they formed the ghostbusters organization he was a part of that. He was ex-military. He was the practical guy who ran things."

Hudson had worked with Reitman as one of the stars of *Spacehunter*, a sci-fi film on which Reitman served as executive producer, but he didn't land his first *Ghostbusters* audition for months. "By the time I went in, every actor that I knew—black, Hispanic, or otherwise—had gone in. But I made them laugh."

Says Reitman, "When Ernie came in I thought, *Wow, he'd be perfect*. I liked the way he looked—he had this lovely quality about him—and I thought he could be funny in a different way than the original ghostbusters."

Big changes didn't appear until the delivery of a new script, several weeks into rehearsal. "Suddenly Winston was coming in on page sixty-eight as opposed to page eight," says Hudson. "It was a real adjustment for me psychologically because I still had to show up and bring the best that I had, but there was a part of me that was really disappointed."

Although it wouldn't be apparent in the final film, Winston Zeddemore was written to be a man of many talents. "He was incredibly overqualified; it didn't make sense that

he was even trying out for the job," says Medjuck. As seen in unused dialogue from the shooting script, Winston is a veteran of the Strategic Air Command, an expert in small arms and electronic countermeasures, and a black belt in karate.

Despite his initial concerns, when the shoot was complete, Hudson was thrilled to be involved with the production. "I felt like once Winston was brought into the team that he was one of the ghostbusters," says Hudson. "I loved being a part of the movie, and in terms of my character development I give Harold credit—because the one guy who I could talk to was always Harold Ramis. Harold would take the time and he'd explain it from a perspective that I didn't have."

William Atherton, a classically trained stage actor and veteran of numerous films including Steven Spielberg's *The Sugarland Express*, won the role of the odious Walter Peck, hatchet man for the Environmental Protection Agency.

Given the comfortable comedic vibe between the core members of the cast, Atherton knew his villain would need to play as their polar opposite. "Here you had genius comics, the funniest people in America at the time," he says. "Am I supposed to try to be funny? It's absurd. What I felt, and what Ivan and I talked about, is that I had to be a male Margaret Dumont—[a comic foil like] Dumont was to Groucho Marx. I was going to play it as drama, like *Macbeth* or *Antigone*.

"My character didn't know why it was funny. My interpretation was: My purpose is to prevent disaster from [befalling] these incompetent, disrespectful people. And I would play it as if the lava was coming down Vesuvius."

WHAT ARE YOU SUPPOSED TO BE? SOME KIND OF A COSMONAUT?

A LEADING LIGHT IN THE FIELD of costume design, Theoni V. Aldredge had won an Academy Award® for Best Costume Design for *The Great Gatsby* (1974) plus numerous Tony Awards for her work for the Broadway stage. According to Ivan Reitman, Aldredge's *Ghostbusters* assignment brought with it a whole new set of challenges.

"The outfits were described as very simple, like a garbage man," says Reitman. "But it was her detailing that made them stand out. I liked that these guys were all PhDs, but they went into business for themselves. It was a blue-collar job and they were dressed in a blue-collar way."

Costume designer Suzy Benzinger worked on *Ghostbusters* as Aldredge's assistant. "Theoni never watched television and never paid attention to contemporary stars," she recalls. "When we got the script with Dan Aykroyd and Bill Murray's names on it, she said 'I don't even know these people.' She read the first couple pages and didn't understand the script: 'What do they mean, ghost *hunting*?' But we said, 'You *have* to do it.'"

Benzinger handled the day-to-day costume work throughout the length of the *Ghostbusters* production, measuring the stars, selecting outfits, and soliciting their feedback on the look of their

characters. "It was so much fun," she says. "Bill was wonderful, Dan was wonderful. Everyone in the cast was really extraordinary."

The iconic coveralls worn by the ghostbusters ultimately changed very little from Dan Aykroyd's original concept. "Theoni felt it was important that the uniform have a musty, kind of smoky, look—she wanted a taupe gray," says Benzinger. "The very first meeting that we had, Dan came in with a jumpsuit and that was almost exactly what they wound up wearing. He said, 'I wore this when I pitched it!'

"There was an element of wanting [the uniform] to look functional, wanting it to look nice, and wanting to have a funny element. They all looked great in it, in that sort of 'off-the-rack' feel. They didn't want it to look too costumey, but to come across like a real situation."

The characters wouldn't always be wearing jumpsuits, so Benzinger helped determine wardrobes by spending time with the actors who needed them. "Harold Ramis loved that gray suit he wore, which I got at a thrift store on St. Mark's Place," she says. "The first time I saw Harold, I thought, 'He really doesn't look like a professor. He doesn't have that scientist look.' So I took him to an eyeglass store on Seventh Avenue. I said, 'I really want to change

OPPOSITE Bill Murray as Dr. Peter Venkman in his distinctive ghostbusting uniform.
ABOVE The ghostbusters' costumes were designed for the kind of wear and tear that comes with fighting interdimensional evil.

your eyeglasses, is that OK?' and I knew just the glasses [he should wear]. He put them on, and I think he wore those forever."

Annie Potts, who played Janine Melnitz, had a great deal of influence over her personal style. "Theoni gave everybody total rein over how they wanted to present themselves," she recalls. Suzy Benzinger collaborated with Potts by taking a page out of her own sartorial playbook. "When Annie came in for her measurements, she said to me, 'Oh my God, I think *you're* the character.' So I actually did her up like me."

By contrast, Sigourney Weaver's character of Dana Barrett bore a heavy Theoni Aldredge influence. "Sigourney was totally based on Theoni," admits Benzinger. "Theoni was also a very tall woman, so when she saw Sigourney she started to name off designers that she loved. Sigourney loved those designers too. Theoni said, 'We're going to dress her basically like me.' She wore a lot of sweaters, long skirts, and boots."

Dana's transformation into the demonic Zuul is advertised with a seductive, flame-hued dress—an alarming contrast to her everyday wear. "Bill picked out the color," reveals Benzinger. "Theoni wanted to put her in a lavender dress, but Bill said, 'I think

it should be orange.' We were trying to use a dress that looked sort of dated and weird and strange. *Flashdance* had been out for a while, and it was very outré to have that off-the-shoulder look. We did it as a Jennifer Beals sort of dress."

Sigourney Weaver completed her bizarre look with assistance from makeup artist Leonard Engelman. "When it came time to do Zuul, I wanted to turn nice Dana on her head," Weaver says. "I said, 'I want my hair to be like I've been electrified, like I put my finger in a socket.' I wanted my make up to be—not really *Bride of Frankenstein*—but to be other-earthly, and unlike anything that would logically happen to Dana."

William Atherton knew Aldredge from the New York Shakespeare Festival, and collaborated with her to craft the buttoned-up bearing of EPA agent Walter Peck.

"[Peck] has a very specific purpose, and visually we didn't want to vary it," says Atherton. "Every time you see him, you have to know what he represents. I only had one suit—a dark navy suit with a vest—and I added a Phi Beta Kappa pin to show that he was one of those starchy, heavy bureaucrats: a wannabe good-old boy."

BELOW Close-up view of the belt equipment and fuses.
OPPOSITE Front view of Egon Spengler's jumpsuit and gear.

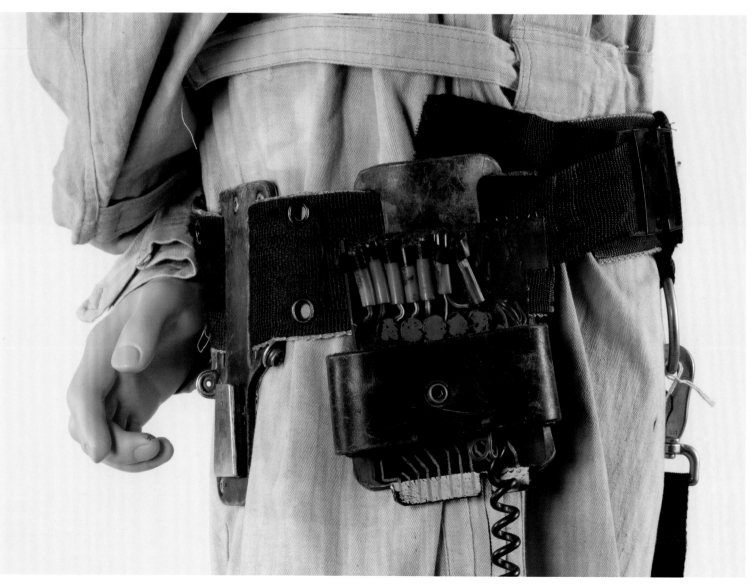

3. NICE SHOOTIN', TEX

With a finalized script in hand, Ivan Reitman and his production team descended on New York City in late October 1983. Their shooting schedule included one week of preliminary second unit work and three-and-a-half weeks of principal photography. *Ghostbusters* would be Reitman's first New York shoot.

The city, reeling from years of financial mismanagement and street violence, was a long way off from the rebound that would later enshrine it as a tourist mecca. *Ghostbusters* reveled in the culture of the city and proudly poked fun at its flaws. The movie's final line—a triumphant shout of "I love this town"— was a four-word ode to the Big Apple.

Reitman began filming with a bottomless reservoir of self-assurance—he'd found success with similar comedies,

and here he hoped to hit another home run. "I was living in kind of an alternate universe already, because at this point I had done *Animal House*, *Meatballs*, and *Stripes*," he says. "So that first time I saw the Ghostbusters walk down the street I said, 'Oh my god, this should work somehow.' I don't know what it was, but the combination of the guys in those almost ridiculous outfits made a kind of visual sense."

I LOVE THIS TOWN

Location shooting in New York City included filming at the New York Public Library, Columbia University, Lincoln Center, Central Park West, Columbus Circle, and the Tavern on the Green restaurant in Central Park where Louis Tully falls prey to a Terror Dog.

OPPOSITE Coated in simulated marshmallow, Harold Ramis, Dan Aykroyd, and Bill Murray pose for a publicity still. **BELOW** Reitman directs his actors during location shooting in New York's Central Park West.

Columbia University complied on the condition that the school not be identified by name, though Joe Medjuck points out that "now they sort of brag about it." Columbia's Havemeyer Hall became the fictitious "Weaver Hall," home to the Department of Psychology where Peter Venkman—the wiseass counterpoint to his head-in-the-cloud colleagues—performs his sadistic ESP test.

The New York Public Library's grand entrance—with its famed marble lions flanking the staircase—announced the importance of sculpture in a film littered with architectural icons, while the scene where Stantz takes out a third mortgage to fund the ghostbusters enterprise was shot at the Irving Trust Bank on Fifth Avenue.

"Building the business, that was the idea," says Medjuck. "People would get excited when they went to the bank and got the loan. It's always fun to see a group get together."

Ivan Reitman felt that financial risk and bureaucratic paperwork would root the characters in a reality the audience could identify with, despite the company's outlandish premise. Similar logic informed the team's purchase of a deserted firehouse as their corporate headquarters. Hook & Ladder Company No. 8 in the city's Tribeca neighborhood starred in shots of the firehouse's exterior.

"I saw it structurally as a 'going-into-business' film," says Reitman. "It had this great idea that there were people acting like firemen whose job it was to get rid of ghostly beings."

Sigourney Weaver joined the production during the New York shoot. The conversation between Dana Barrett and Peter Venkman at the edge of the Lincoln Center fountain was Weaver's first scene with Murray.

"I was thrown from my world into the world of Second City, which was wonderfully chaotic and generous and improvisational," says Weaver. "Ivan had to wrangle these huge energies, and Bill wouldn't let me take myself seriously for one second. I would be off in the corner trying to think Dana thoughts and he'd come up and put his arms around me and make fun of my hair. I just adored him from the very beginning. When I met him I introduced myself as Sigourney, and he said, 'I believe your name is Susan,' and picked me up and threw me over his shoulder and walked down Fifth Avenue with me laughing hysterically. No one ever picked me up, because I was six feet tall!"

The Lincoln Center site offered wide shots of streets teeming with New Yorkers and stood adjacent to Avery Fisher Hall, home of the New York Philharmonic and presumably Dana's workplace as a concert cellist. The conversation between Dana and Venkman at Lincoln Center was one of the only scenes with dialogue that had to be looped in post, due to the noise of the fountain visible in long shots.

The playfulness between the two performers set the tone for their interactions throughout the remainder of filming.

"I always felt with Bill, he's either there or he's not, and if he doesn't feel like being there he'd be bicycling around or something," says Weaver. "But when he was there in those scenes he was very present. He made it easy for me to love him as Venkman and to hate him as Venkman."

BELOW Reitman shoots on the steps of the New York Public Library, with a crowd of spectators gathered behind him.
OPPOSITE Annie Potts, seated, takes a break during filming of the firehouse explosion scene, with Bill Murray, Harold Ramis, Rick Moranis, and Dan Aykroyd arrayed around her.

ABOVE Ramis, Aykroyd, and Murray shoot the scene in which their characters discuss going into business together. OPPOSITE TOP Associate producer Joe Medjuck (seated) with Ramis, Murray, Aykroyd, Moranis, and Potts. OPPOSITE BOTTOM Bill Murray and Dan Aykroyd in costume as New York City bums, characters ultimately cut from the final film.

Another key scene shot on location saw Louis Tully running for his life from a snarling Terror Dog. His path takes him through Central Park, before he ends up against the tall glass windows of Tavern on the Green, where his distress is amusingly overlooked by the diners inside.

Production designer John DeCuir added two stone figures near the restaurant's entrance, subliminally emphasizing the film's equivocation of statues with the supernatural. "We were putting sculptures everywhere," says Medjuck. "We were sort of turning New York into a Gothic city."

Shooting in Central Park would yield scenes that were ultimately deleted where Bill Murray and Dan Aykroyd

played homeless men who delivered an absurd commentary on unfolding events. In the script, upon spotting the Terror Dog, Aykroyd's character confidently identifies the creature as "definitely some kind of fighting spaniel." Harold Ramis felt the duo could have served as "Shakespearean fools or gravediggers" by making appearances throughout the film.

"We did a thing of Danny and Bill pretending to be bums," says Joe Medjuck, who recalls that the concept seemed funny on its own merits but would have confused audiences who would easily spot the moonlighting actors. "It got thrown out very early," he concedes.

Other Manhattan filming locations included a jail cell interior, where the ghostbusters are held after the city finds them

liable for an explosion that tears the roof off their firehouse. Filming took place in an abandoned prison, which Aykroyd promptly declared to be haunted.

DOGS AND CATS, LIVING TOGETHER...
MASS HYSTERIA

Due to worrying signs that the city is facing a disaster of biblical proportions, the ghostbusters are hauled before the mayor of New York to deliver an explanation. Reitman shot the scene at City Hall in lower Manhattan, inside the office of City Council President Carol Bellamy. In a fitting piece of set dressing, a plaque on the mayor's desk reads "BE NOT AFRAID."

The critical confrontation in this office brings together all the factions that shape the city, including politicians, the police, government agencies such as Walter Peck's EPA, and organized religion (in the form of the archbishop of New York). David Margulies, who played the mayor, reveals that much of the dialogue was ad-libbed on the spot.

"A lot of the improvisatorial quality of the scene was because of Bill Murray, and his suggestions were wonderful," he says. "He's the one who suggested that I should be on a first name basis with the cardinal. That's terrific stuff. That's really New York savvy, about how tight [mayor] Koch was, for example, with O'Connor. So the use of the names Lenny and Mike, or whatever I call the cardinal, all of that was Bill's suggestion on the set."

Ramis suggested[10] the scene held a "particular resonance for Bill, who comes from a large Catholic family. There was a Murray archbishop of New York in their family."

The tide turns in the ghostbusters' favor when Venkman puts the stakes in terms the mayor can understand. If he acts he won't just save lives, he'll save the lives of "millions of registered voters."

"There's a shot of me changing my mind when I realize the political advantage," says Margulies. "You can see it in my eyes and my smile. It's all smart. It's smart, New York–knowledge writing."

But Walter Peck isn't about to go down without a fight, especially when Venkman fires off his famous "dickless" insult. "'This man has no dick,' was probably the biggest laugh in the movie," says Margulies. During one take, Aykroyd referred to Peck as "wee weenie winkle"—triggering a rare laughing fit from Murray.

RIGHT In prison, the ghostbusters deduce the nature of the threat facing the city. BELOW David Margulies, as the mayor of New York City, gets brought up to speed by the ghostbusters.

GHOST FEVER GRIPS NEW YORK

A FLURRY OF MANHATTAN HOT SPOTS appears in the montage sequence that conveys the ghostbusters' rapid rise to fame. From Rockefeller Plaza to Little Italy to Saks Fifth Avenue to Chinatown, these short scenes are high on energy while showcasing their car, the Ectomobile, and the crew's ghost-catching gear.

"Ivan loves shooting in crowds," says Joe Medjuck. "We had a fair amount of cooperation from the city and the police. Our biggest problem was causing traffic jams, because we were putting so many people on the street."

Much of the montage is told through newspaper headlines and magazine covers. The tabloid-trashy *Globe* touts a ghostbusters celebrity diet, while *The Atlantic* frets over civil rights issues concerning the recently deceased.

In-jokes abound: the corner flap on the *Time* cover (labeled "The New Poets") bears a photo of producer Michael Gross, while a story on *USA Today*'s front page about a new golf champion ("A Winner Without Practice") mentions *Ghostbusters* graphic

designer Michael McWillie, who created most of the mock covers. The *New York Post* story about a Chinatown ghost was to have featured an airbrushed illustration of the phantom in question, but Reitman wasn't happy with the artist's rendition.

One scratched scene for this sequence was to have shown the ghostbusters parking their vehicle at home plate and walking into a baseball dugout. A cut to an illuminated Times Square sign would have advertised their success: GHOSTBUSTERS NAB PHANTOM BAT BOY AT YANKEE STADIUM.

Another dropped idea concerned Egon's conversation with a street punk. When asked if a proton stream could hurt Superman, Dr. Spengler takes the question seriously. "On Earth, no," he answers. "But on Krypton, we could slice him up like Oscar Mayer bologna."

"I like montage," says Reitman, reflecting on the sequence. "It's a great visual and editorial tool, and it was a very efficient way to get a lot of information out in a relatively short period."

ABOVE Murray, Aykroyd, and Ramis pose in front of the firehouse HQ, holding paranormal equipment as they prepare to shoot the TV commercial sequence.

SPOOK CENTRAL

When business starts booming for the ghostbusters, Ray Stantz discovers that profit comes with a price. The city's heightened spiritual activity is nothing less than a sign of the apocalypse, thanks to architect Ivo Shandor, who designed a building to focus infernal energy and bring about the end of the world at the hands of the Sumerian deity Gozer. Though Stantz calls Shandor "either a certified genius or an authentic wacko," he's definitely both—and his masterwork is the formidable apartment building at 55 Central Park West.

For a time, a building in Greenwich Village at 1 Fifth Avenue stood as the top candidate for Shandor's edifice, bolstered by the fact that the Stay Puft marshmallow man, who attacks the building in the film's climax, could be photographed against the distinctive Washington Square arch. When plans to film there fell through, the production turned its attention uptown where the monument in Columbus Circle could perform a similar function.

"We found this building on Central Park West that seemed like the perfect location," says Reitman. "It was just a little stumpy in terms of height, so John DeCuir added eight stories to

the building [with a matte painting], and he took the visual motif of the gargoyles and worked them into this magical rooftop. We put those dog statues up there as if they were guarding the gate. It all had a lovely historical sensibility filtered through DeCuir's classical design background."

John DeCuir Jr., who worked on *Ghostbusters* as an art director, recalls how his father crafted numerous aspects of the building: as a physical location, the upper stories of which were augmented by a matte painting; as a rooftop set on a soundstage; as a miniature model for the FX crew to explode; and as a street-level entrance duplicated on a studio back lot.

"His job was to find a place in New York, but they couldn't find a building that was dramatic enough to do what he felt the story demanded," he says. "That's when he came up with the concept of creating a transitional element with the matte shot, the miniature, and the live, full-sized set on top of the tower. His sketches developed that, and the drawings were taken by a team who built the top of the building on Stage 16 in LA. [Visual effects director] John Bruno and the special effects people took the miniature building and [construction supervisor] Don Noble and I took the lower street section."

Location shooting also needed to take place outside the building's entrance to capture the rapturous, terrified crowds gathered at 55 Central Park West during the movie's climax.

The production crew closed north and south traffic on Central Park West and all crosstown traffic between 61st and 67th Streets. "It was the most extraordinary location," remembers William Atherton, of the long stretch of improbably deserted New York pavement. "Central Park West for like, five blocks. And with all the lights, it looked like *Triumph of the Will*."

The assembled crowds cheered the heroes by name, chanting "ghostbusters, ghostbusters!" Yet at that point in the production, the name of the movie was far from settled. The existence of the 1975 live-action children's television program *The Ghost Busters* meant that first dibs on the title could be claimed by the show's production company, Filmation. Columbia began talks with Filmation, but prepped backup titles should things fall through, including "Ghoststoppers" and "Ghostblasters." Joe Medjuck reveals that when the crowd extras were chanting "ghostbusters" he called Columbia and held up the receiver, urging them to secure the title and avoid the need for reshoots. Columbia locked up the rights, and the replacement options were never needed.

In the finished film, a tremor shakes the foundations of the building when the ghostbusters arrive at the scene. The earthquake effect would be achieved through hydraulics during the studio shoot in LA, but its simulated aftermath was filmed in New York. "When we did the results of the earthquake we just laid things on top of the street," says Medjuck, in reference to the jagged, broken segments of road and the rear section of a police car that appears to protrude from a sinkhole. "It looked very, very real when you were there."

"They had one night to dress the street," says John DeCuir Jr. "When people went home early in the evening everything was normal, and when the little old ladies came out to walk their dogs in the morning, the whole street had erupted. Apparently people complained to the New York police department and their switchboard lit up."

During filming, Aykroyd approached one of his idols, legendary science fiction author Isaac Asimov. The writer demanded to know whether Aykroyd was responsible for the traffic jam surrounding Central Park West. When he answered in the affirmative, Asimov shot back witheringly: "It's disgusting."

While not every Manhattanite was enthusiastic about the shoot, infectious energy was everywhere. The upbeat vibes seemed to buoy the production schedule, and the New York shoot finished two-and-a-half days earlier than expected.

"I think it was a love letter to New York and New Yorkers," says Weaver. "Central Park West, and Tavern on the Green, and the horses in the park, and the doorman saying, 'Someone brought a cougar to a party'—that's so New York. When we come down covered with marshmallow, and there are these crowds of New Yorkers of all types and descriptions cheering for us—as a New Yorker it was one of the most moving things I can remember. I thought, 'This film has its finger on the pulse of something that's happening in the zeitgeist,'" continues Weaver. "The energy was irresistible."

BELOW A matte painting by artist Matthew Yuricich shows the devastation wreaked on Dana Barrett's apartment by the coming of Gozer.

I FOUND THE CAR

IT'S BOTH A MOBILE HEADQUARTERS and a highly effective advertisement—all the way from the No-Ghost logos on its doors to the license plate reading ECTO-1. The Ectomobile, a $4,800 steal when Dr. Ray Stantz ponies up the cash for the retro ride, is a 1959 Cadillac Miller-Meteor with an aftermarket ambulance conversion.

In the movie, the four-wheeled slab of Detroit steel barely rolls into the firehouse under its own power, badly in need of "suspension work and shocks, brakes, brake pads, lining, steering box, transmission, rear end, new rings, mufflers, and a little wiring." In short order the Ectomobile gets a shiny white-and-red skin and a chassis full of ghost-hunting gadgets.

Design consultant Stephen Dane designed and modified the Ectomobile for filming, but the vehicle existed in ghostbusters mythology since Aykroyd's first script and the concept drawings of John Daveikis. Early drafts gave the vehicle a more fantastical edge, with the Ectomobile able to dematerialize and evade police pursuit. It was also painted jet black—a menacing quality jettisoned when cinematographer László Kovács pointed out that the car would be nearly invisible on camera when shot at night.

Special modifications to the final version of the Ectomobile included a high-tech roof array packed with equipment. "I'd seen the roof rack on fire trucks and things like that," says Dane. "I put a TV antenna on it, a directional antenna, an air-conditioning unit, storage boxes, a radome—I just filled it up with bullshit. I showed Ivan the pictures in my military magazines and then sketched it up."

The dark-beige ambulance that would become the Ectomobile sat on the Columbia back lot for weeks as Dane took measurements and drew sketches. Shortly before shooting was scheduled to begin, production realized that the vehicle wasn't ready. "It was one of these things where the prop master says, 'I don't have the ambulance—I thought the decorator was going to make it,' and the decorator says, 'I thought props was going to do it,'" recalls Dane. "They needed to get something done fast, and I turned the thing around in about a week and a half.

"We did the paint and application, but we couldn't ship it on an airplane because it was so big. It got shipped by railroad instead. The roof rack we built separately and that got put on an airplane. There were probably at least four or five days where the vehicle was in transit between Hollywood and Manhattan."

In a scene cut from *Ghostbusters*, a New York City policeman tries to stick a parking ticket on the Ectomobile's windshield. The officer starts to sweat when the car's sensors appear to be tracking him, and he gets really rattled when the parking ticket superheats and burns up in a flash of fire.

OPPOSITE The Ectomobile, or Ecto-1, currently stored within Sony's archives. **BELOW** Dan Aykroyd and Ernie Hudson step out of the Ectomobile on their arrival at Fort Detmerring.

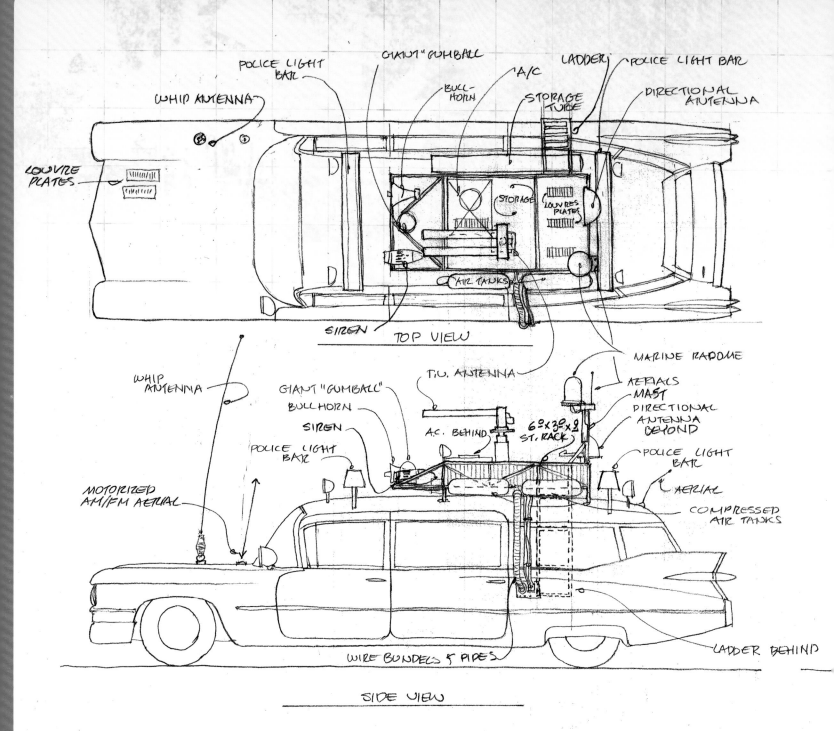

WHIP ANTENNA

POLICE LIGHT BAR

GIANT "GUMBALL"

A/C

BULL-HORN

LADDER

STORAGE TUBE

POLICE LIGHT BAR

DIRECTIONAL ANTENNA

LOUVRE PLATES

STORAGE

LOUVRES PLATES

AIR TANKS

SIREN

TOP VIEW

WHIP ANTENNA

GIANT "GUMBALL"

BULLHORN

SIREN

T.V. ANTENNA

MARINE RADOME

AERIALS MAST

DIRECTIONAL ANTENNA BEYOND

A.C. BEHIND

6°x3°x2 ST. RACK

POLICE LIGHT BAR

POLICE LIGHT BAR

AERIAL

MOTORIZED AM/FM AERIAL

COMPRESSED AIR TANKS

WIRE BUNDLES & PIPES

LADDER BEHIND

SIDE VIEW

S.DANE / 12 SEP 83   SCALE: ½" = 1FT.   ECTO I - CADDY REVAMP

ABOVE Stephen Dane's illustrations of the top and side of the Ectomobile, featuring Dane's handwritten labels identifying the car's gadgetry. **OPPOSITE TOP LEFT** Stephen Dane's illustrations of the front and rear views of the Ectomobile. **OPPOSITE TOP RIGHT** The unretouched vehicle before remodeling work began. **OPPOSITE CENTER RIGHT** The finished Ectomobile photographed during the production.

These hints that the Ectomobile possessed paranormal abilities fell victim to the editor's knife. Reitman decided it slowed down the pace of the "ghostbusting around town" montage, and that audiences might find it similar to the outrageous aspects of the vehicle in *The Blues Brothers*, Aykroyd's earlier blockbuster.

One of the most recognizable qualities of the Ectomobile is its siren, which delivers an eerie, descending wail. "I spent a fair bit of time on it, but in a way it was one of the simplest things I came up with," explains sound designer Richard Beggs, an Academy Award–winner for his work on *Apocalypse Now*. "It was a leopard snarl that I had done a number of things to. I looped it, cut it in quarter-inch tape, and played it backward.

"Usually I am very loath to play things backward, because they have a very telltale characteristic and I think it's sort of a cop out. I played it backward and it did that *err-reearr-err-reearr*—the exact opposite of an animal going *arghh*. It lost some of its organic sound and it became this 'mechanical animal' claxon."

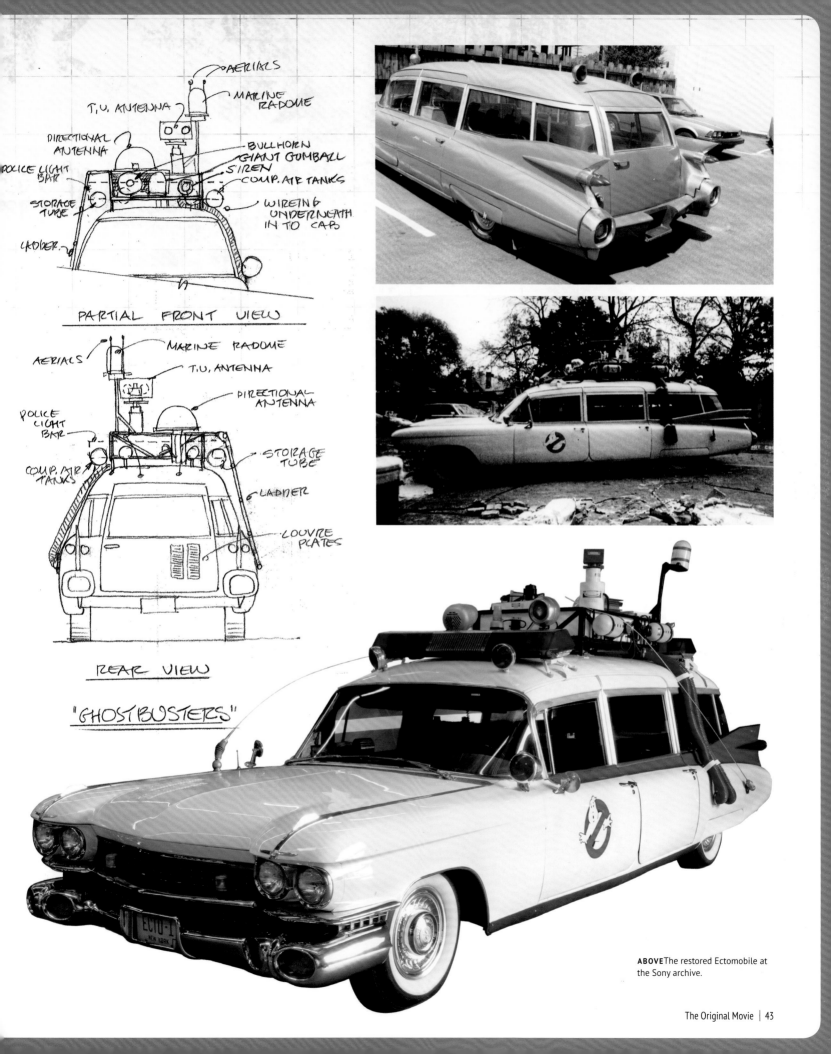

AERIALS

MARINE RADOME

T.U. ANTENNA

DIRECTIONAL ANTENNA

POLICE LIGHT BAR

BULLHORN GIANT GUMBALL SIREN

COMP. AIR TANKS

STORAGE TUBE

WIRING UNDERNEATH IN TO CABS

LADDER

PARTIAL FRONT VIEW

AERIALS

MARINE RADOME

T.U. ANTENNA

DIRECTIONAL ANTENNA

POLICE LIGHT BAR

STORAGE TUBE

COMP. AIR TANKS

LADDER

LOUVRE PLATES

REAR VIEW

"GHOSTBUSTERS"

ABOVE The restored Ectomobile at the Sony archive.

LEFT Close-up detail of the rear tailfin and taillights, with the No-Ghost logo on the rear door. **TOP** Detail of the car's roof equipment. **CENTER** Front view of the Ectomobile's roof rack. **BOTTOM** Inside view of the car's equipment and its hospital gurney racks.

4. DON'T CROSS THE STREAMS

All the momentum built up during the New York filming sputtered out when *Ghostbusters* shifted coasts for a nine-week shoot in LA. While on the East Coast, the crew notched a record of twenty-six shots in a single day, but during their first day in LA, they finished only one shot. The second day bagged only three. Almost immediately, the production fell seven days behind schedule.

Much needed to be done. In addition to extensive sound-stage work scheduled for The Burbank Studios [now known as the Warner Bros. studios], the crew needed to film interiors on location at local sites including the LA Central Library, an abandoned firehouse, and the lobby of the Biltmore Hotel.

Assistant director Gary Daigler joined the production upon its arrival in LA. It fell to Daigler to coordinate the daily actions of the crew, the actors, and the camera to keep the shooting schedule on track. Daigler quickly encountered a rogue element in the form of Bill Murray.

"Bill hated to be called to the set when we weren't ready," he says. "I said to the cameraman, 'Look, I can't bring these guys back—especially Bill—and do ten minutes of relighting. I wound up giving Bill a two-way radio. He and Danny would go to a nearby sushi restaurant, and I'd call them on the radio and say 'Dan, Bill, we're ready for you now.' He respected that, and it wound up being a good relationship."

... AND THE NEIGHBORHOOD IS LIKE A DEMILITARIZED ZONE

The interior of the Los Angeles Central Library stood in for its New York counterpart as the basement location where the heroes face their first specter. Physical effects supervisor Chuck Gaspar coated the book stacks in slime and rigged a card catalog with air hoses to send its contents airborne in a shower of paper.

"Things like the books floating across, those were on a wire and shot in camera," says Joe Medjuck. "More of the effects were done practically than you would think."

The interiors of the ghostbusters' firehouse headquarters needed to sync up with the exterior, which had been shot in

OPPOSITE Harold Ramis, Dan Aykroyd, Bill Murray, and Ernie Hudson pose outside Ghostbusters HQ. **BELOW** Bill Murray goofs off during filming of the scene in which the ghostbusters question the shaken librarian about her close encounter.

New York. Luckily, John DeCuir found an almost perfect match in downtown LA's Fire Station No. 23.

"He was very fortunate that we found two firehouses, one in New York, one in Los Angeles, that were quite similar in design, configuration, and proportion," says John DeCuir Jr. "So the connectivity between the interior in Los Angeles and the exterior in New York worked very well.

"It was a decommissioned firehouse. It had not been used as anything else and was in pretty pristine shape. We had to build the offices on the lower floor which did not exist—the secretarial desk and [Venkman's] office downstairs."

John DeCuir constructed a foam-core mock-up of the firehouse interior to help Reitman determine blocking and camera angles. "John DeCuir was a master builder," says Michael C. Gross. "He built Rome three times for *Cleopatra*. He was constantly wanting to build everything."

Set decorator Marvin March dressed up the firehouse's interior, including the gadgets and miscellaneous junk that cluttered the upstairs laboratory. The scenes shot there needed very little editing trickery, the firehouse having almost exactly the right physical spaces for the planned scenes. For example, shots of the ghost containment unit in the firehouse's basement were actually filmed in the basement of the firehouse location.

WE CAME, WE SAW, WE KICKED ITS ASS!

The entrance of the Sedgewick Hotel, where our heroes bag their first ghost, originally looked like a fit for New York's Waldorf Astoria, but Reitman opted for LA's Biltmore Hotel and its spacious, elegant lobby instead.

A tracking shot following the ghostbusters as they step inside the hotel is the first time the audience sees them in full uniform, proton packs strapped to their backs. Almost immediately, the characters are intercepted by the uptight hotel manager, played by Michael Ensign.

"I had read for the William Atherton [Walter Peck] part," says Ensign, "and one day I got a phone call saying, 'Do you want a consolation prize?'" Ensign, who came from a mixed British-American family and had spent three years in the Royal Shakespeare Company, knew just how to inject the right dose of upper-crust rigidity. "I keyed in intuitively to that part," he says. "The fussy little man in the bow tie."

The shoot at LA's Biltmore, originally scheduled for multiple days, got compressed to a single night. Pressure and tempers were high.

"There's a long shot where I get them at the door, lead them into the hotel, and then we turn," says Ensign. "That was a tricky camera move that had to be timed very precisely, and I had to deliver lines at very specific times. But the guys started

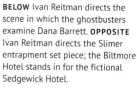

BELOW Ivan Reitman directs the scene in which the ghostbusters examine Dana Barrett. **OPPOSITE** Ivan Reitman directs the Slimer entrapment set piece; the Biltmore Hotel stands in for the fictional Sedgewick Hotel.

making up everything—they weren't on script at all! So I said, 'When am I supposed to say anything? What they're saying doesn't match my cue lines!'"

Joe Medjuck confirms that the core cast members had slipped into an improvisational groove by the time they arrived in Los Angeles. "Ivan's methodology is to rehearse the scene then let people make dialogue changes while they're doing it," he says. "With these guys, they don't make jokes for themselves—they do what's funniest. And sometimes Ivan would push them. In the scene when they've captured their first ghost at the hotel, Bill says, 'We came, we saw, we kicked its ass.' Ivan said, 'You can do better than that—go back and do it again.' The door would swing open and we never knew what Bill was gonna say. He did about ten things, and I'd say seven of them were great."

Among Murray's alternate lines was, "What a knockabout of pure fun *that* was!" This rejected take found a curious second life on television, where it was spliced into the hotel scene to placate broadcast censors who objected to the use of "ass."

Murray's snarky boast heralds a second encounter with the hotel manager, who is spitting mad about their reckless property

START PAN HERE

THE METAL BOX FLIPS OPEN. CAM. PANS UP WITH A
FIXED MULTI-DIMENSIONAL INVERTED PYRAMID OF BRIGHT,
BEADED WHITE LIGHT

of man, that would be seething rage. That would be as far as he would ever go."

The ballroom blitz preceding this scene was shot inside the Biltmore's actual ballroom, as the ghostbusters attempt to bag their first ghoul, the gluttonous ghost who would later come to be known as "Slimer." Physical effects supervisor Chuck Gaspar oversaw the installation of fake walls embedded with fuses and pyrotechnics. The resultant light show accompanied the messy capture of the renegade spirit, a process described in the shooting script as "like trying to push smoke into a bottle with a baseball bat."

Often overlooked is a sign outside the ballroom doors, announcing the room's imminent use as a midnight buffet for the members of a theater association. This tiny bit of set dressing provided justification for the table settings and fully loaded banquet offerings despite the lateness of the hour.

The hallways of the Sedgewick Hotel, in which the ghostbusters first encounter the greedy green ghost, weren't real. Production manager John DeCuir purchased the set from MGM, which had built it for George Cukor's 1981 film *Rich and Famous*. Its décor resembled that of New York's famed Algonquin Hotel.

During soundstage shooting inside DeCuir's set, the trigger-happy ghostbusters unleash their proton streams on the first thing that moves—a hotel maid pushing a cart of cleaning supplies. Reitman likened the characters in the scene to "rookie cops with loaded weapons."

damage. But when the ghostbusters threaten to release their captive phantom, they land a $5,000 payday.

"The last thing in the world that he would have wanted was ghosts in his hotel," says Ensign. "And secondly, to have *these* guys in there was just beyond the pale. When they announced that they would let the whole mess loose again, that's where I allowed myself to lose my temper. For this kind

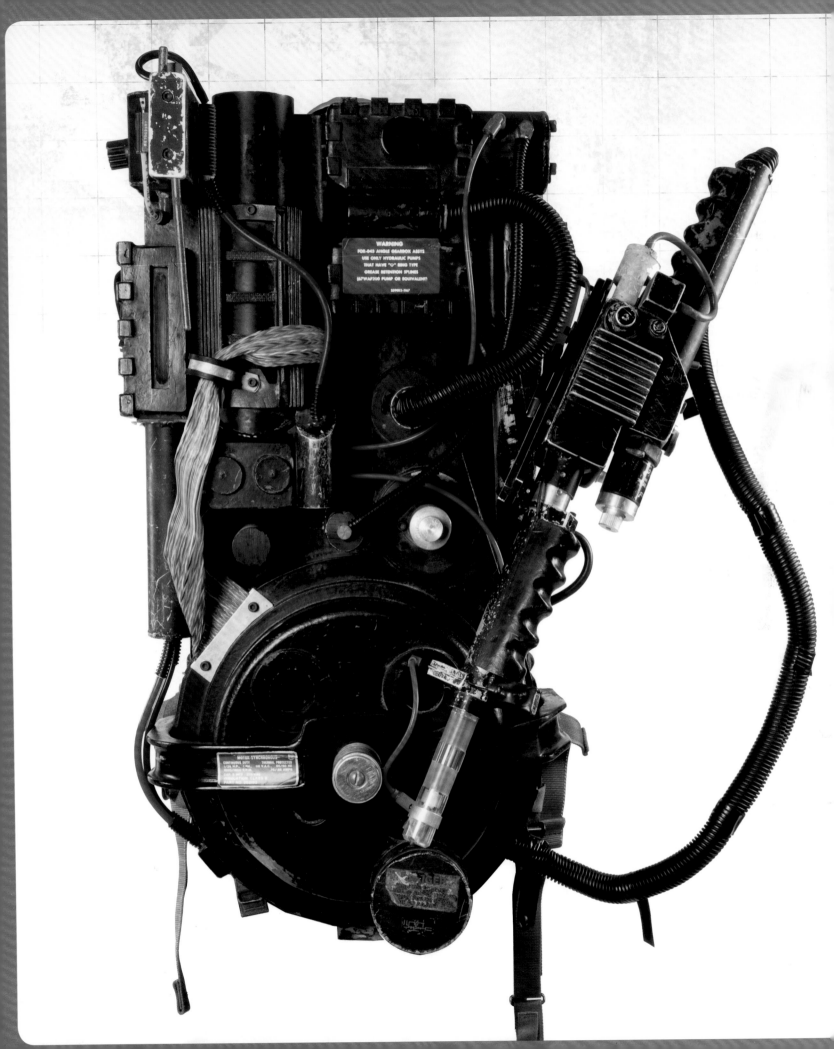

Visual effects director John Bruno recalls the mishap that led to one of the movie's funniest moments: "For the woman who was playing the maid, they said, 'OK, push this cart, and at the end of the hallway it's going to blow up, because they're going to shoot at you.' The cart was all prerigged with pyro work. So she pushes the cart out, strobe lights go off, the cart exploded—and it scared the hell out of her. She fell to the ground, looked up, and was like, 'What the hell are you doing?' It wasn't scripted. It's just what happened."

Many short comedy vignettes were to have taken place in the hotel, though none survived the final cut. In one, a newlywed couple played by Charles Levin and Wendy Goldman bicker during their post-coitus disappointment until they encounter a green ghost in the bathroom. "It was like a sketch on *Saturday Night Live*," Reitman recalled.[11] "Funny in itself, but out of tone with the rest of the film. Cutting it was one of the tougher decisions I had to make."

In the film, Venkman becomes a believer when the ghost knocks him flat and leaves behind a goopy sheen of ectoplasm. The slime used on set consisted mostly of methylcellulose ether, a powdered thickening agent.

Harold Ramis wasn't entirely surprised when Venkman's line, "He slimed me," became an audience catchphrase. "We knew it would get a good response," he said in 1985.[12] "I'd had a lot of people read the script to get their reactions, and everybody loved that line—even though it was fairly simple. Dan had coined the term 'ecto-slime' and so 'He slimed me' was kind of a natural progression from that."

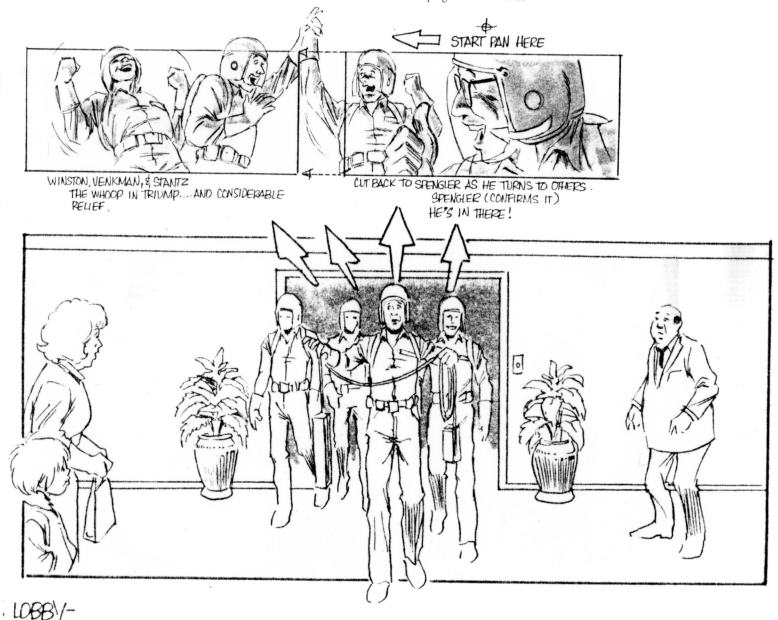

WE HAVE THE TOOLS, WE HAVE THE TALENT.

"THE WHOLE PREMISE was that this is dirty work," says Dan Aykroyd. "Work that no one else wants to do, and that no one else knows how to do. It was a tough job, very industrial, like waste management. From that point it was easy to devise the look of the equipment, because we were operating on the premise of sanitizers."

Aykroyd used this design philosophy to guide the creation of proton packs and neutrona wands, essential ghostbusting equipment present in every incarnation of the script going back to the very first draft.

Ivan Reitman remembers his first exposure to the ghostbusters' paraphernalia. "I knew the look I wanted for the equipment was a home-made hobbyist approach," he says. "None of this stuff should have the finished gloss that most science-fiction gadgets had. I wanted to believe that somehow these men were working with, like, hi-fi equipment from the '70s. I wanted to feel the nuts and bolts. I thought it should impart the sensibility of guys working in their garages."

PROTON PACKS

"Each of us is wearing an unlicensed nuclear accelerator on his back," observes Peter Venkman to his two colleagues during their hotel bust. Venkman isn't exaggerating. Within the reality of the film, each proton pack is a portable cyclotron capable of releasing a stream of directed protons through a neutrona wand (also called a proton gun). This scientific firepower is sufficient to counter the negatively charged ectoplasmic energy of a phantom, specter, or spook.

In one early draft, the heroes wielded particle throwers that seemed more like magic wands than infantryman rifles—they were strapped to an operator's wrist and aimed through gestures.

In creating the final weapon, design consultant Stephen Dane created numerous sketches for Ivan Reitman's review, including designs where the projecting mechanism folded out from the pack and included labels like "ecto sucker." Even as late as the final shooting script, the ghostbusting gear carried a slicker, more modern connotation, with descriptions of "matching blue futuristic jumpsuits" and "brushed-metal, flip-down ecto-visors worn on the head like a welder's mask." Those ideas fell aside when concepts gave way to construction.

Stephen Dane built the proton pack prototype. "It all started with the backpack," says Dane. "I went home and got foam pieces and just threw a bunch of stuff together to get the look. It was highly machined but it had to look off-the-shelf and military surplus. When I was working on *Blade Runner*, I went out to the Tucson airplane wrecking area and came back with two forty-foot flatbeds full of aircraft junk, and that sensibility showed up in *Ghostbusters*."

Chuck Gaspar used Dane's design to construct the "hero props" to be worn by the stars. A rubber mold allowed Gaspar's crew to create identical fiberglass shells, which they attached to aluminum back plates and Army surplus ALICE (all-purpose lightweight individual carrying equipment) frames. Resistors,

OPPOSITE Detailed view of a ghostbusters proton pack. **ABOVE** A Polaroid snap shows the first prototype proton pack constructed by Stephen Dane. **BELOW LEFT AND RIGHT** Close-up details of proton pack labels and fittings.

ABOVE An original ghost trap prop, complete with control knobs, indicator lights, and caution markings.

hoses, cables, metal fittings, warning labels, and other miscellaneous gizmos added authenticity during prop dressing.

Each pack weighed about thirty pounds—nearly fifty pounds with batteries installed—which strained the actors' backs during long shoots. Lightweight packs made of foam rubber were used for stunt work. In the tip of each neutrona wand, a tiny strobing light acted as a visual cue for the postproduction synchronization of visual effects.

Ghostbusters sound designer Richard Beggs created the distinctive sounds associated with the ghostbusting hardware. "You get these assignments and you start sweating, like, 'I've got to come up with something that justifies their hiring me,'" he says. "For the proton pack, the idea was that it was small but dangerous. I didn't want it to sound cartoony. You could get hurt with these things, so the start-up sound was a big deal. There was a click and there was a low thrum, and it would sweep up like there was a start-up period. It would come up to speed and reach critical energy, and then when they pulled the trigger it would unleash."

The neutron stream's chaotic blast of energy seemed less like a laser and more like the barely controlled spray of a fire hose. And according to Egon, combining more than one burst—"crossing the streams"—is enough to cause every molecule of the operator's body to explode at the speed of light. The proton-pack blasts also seemed to anchor themselves to walls and furnishings, requiring the ghostbusters to "drag" the streams along.

Effects designer John Bruno speculated that the process could be a two-way energy exchange, with protons shooting out and a counter-flow of particles pulled back into the gun's barrel—an effect achieved in animation by sliding orange- and blue-colored flows in opposite directions. It fell to Richard Beggs to figure out what such a sloppy stream might sound like.

"There was a liquid part to the sound," he says. "I wanted something that sounded splashy but electronic, like a plasma flow. I'd gotten the base sound of it down, but it was too uniform and not very dynamic. So I did a feedback loop in the harmonizer

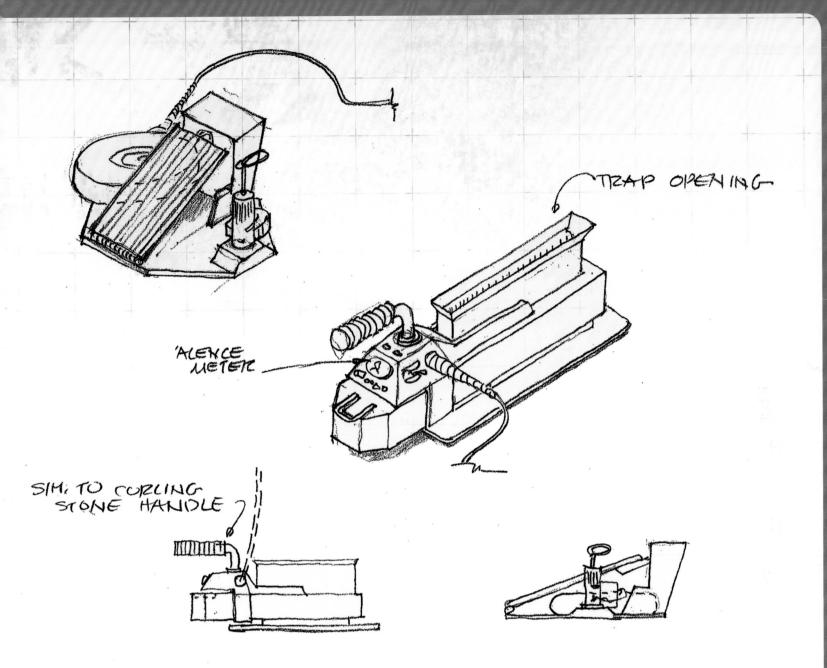

TRAP OPENING

'ALENCE
METER

SIM; TO CURLING
STONE HANDLE

and got this sort of rhythmic, pulsing thing between it and the Moog. I made the sound of the neutrona wand depend on the violence of the shot or the impact. Some were a little whimpery, like what happens when they start up, and at low, medium, and high intensity. I created this library of raw stuff in six or seven different families of sounds, then I would choose one for Bill Murray, one for Dan, and so on, and that would be theirs."

Ernie Hudson and his fellow ghostbusters spent time getting comfortable with their equipment. "It was like doing cop shows where we would go out and shoot the guns," says Hudson. "Because this is your world, you want to make that as believable as possible—you have to know it. So when we went to the props it was, 'This is how this works, this is what happens when the ghosts are contained, this is where they're contained.' It was a world I had no trouble believing, and so what we were doing was easy to sell."

GHOST TRAP

The ghost trap is a metal box conspicuously marked with yellow and black caution stripes. When opened, it draws an immobilized ghost into its depths with a satisfying vacuum suck, allowing the ghostbusters to transport the captive back to the firehouse headquarters and transfer it into the main holding tank. Each ghost trap has rolling wheels and a cable that connects to a foot-operated activation pedal. A blinking light on its upper surface indicates a successful capture.

"It was like an upside-down set of bomb-bay doors, except instead of the bombs coming out, something gets sucked in," says Dane, who designed the ghost trap. Some early designs lacked the doors, and instead relied on a narrow vacuum slot. Dane conceived of the handle as being similar to that found on a curling stone. "It's all hardware that that I've seen somewhere," he says, "but never in this combination."

When the heroes triumphantly emerge from the ballroom of the Sedgewick Hotel, they hold up a smoking trap containing their first bust. Fabric strips soaked in smoke-generating liquid produced the effect during filming.

ABOVE Stephen Dane's original concept sketches for the ghost trap.

"MONACLE" STYLE
ECTO VISOR

ECTO-GOGGLES

When Ray Stantz isn't peering through the lenses of his ecto-goggles, they're probably pushed up on his forehead. *Ghostbusters* implies that ecto-goggles allow the wearer to detect anomalies in the psychokinetic energy field and to track the nonvisible traces of ghostly movement.

The ecto-goggles in the film were modified versions of the U.S. Army's AN/PVS-5a night-vision goggles, which were introduced in 1972 and still in widespread use at the time the movie was made.

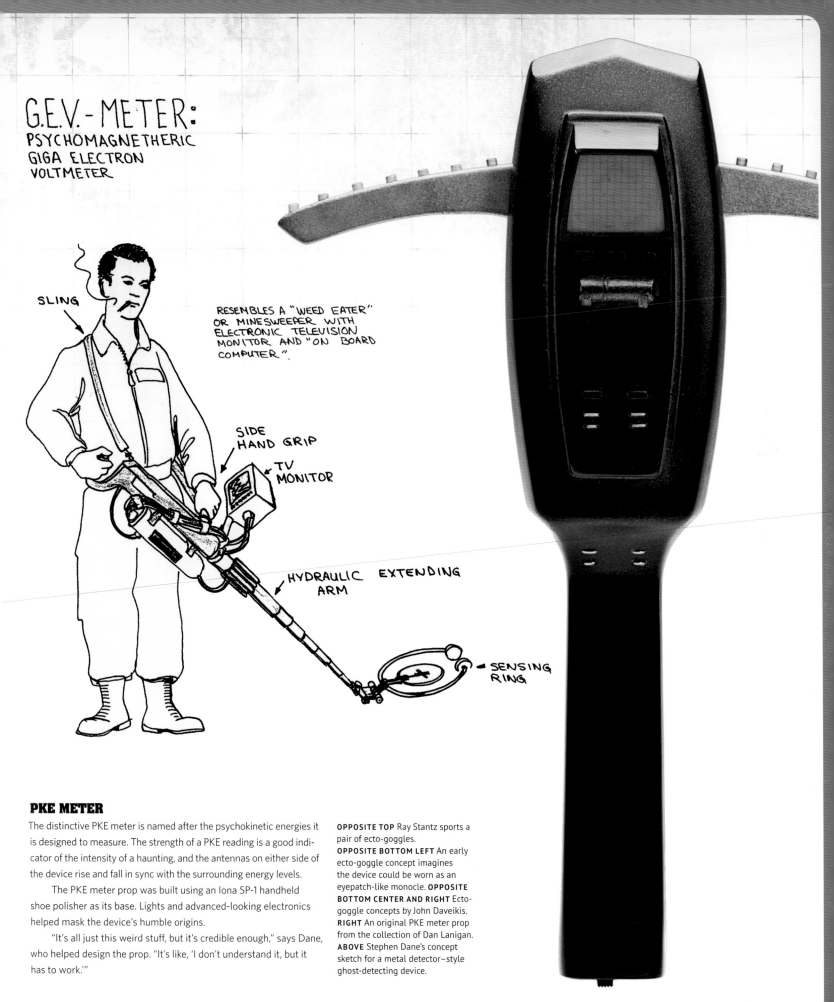

G.E.V.-METER:
PSYCHOMAGNETHERIC GIGA ELECTRON VOLTMETER

SLING

RESEMBLES A "WEED EATER" OR MINESWEEPER WITH ELECTRONIC TELEVISION MONITOR AND "ON BOARD COMPUTER".

SIDE HAND GRIP

TV MONITOR

HYDRAULIC EXTENDING ARM

SENSING RING

PKE METER

The distinctive PKE meter is named after the psychokinetic energies it is designed to measure. The strength of a PKE reading is a good indicator of the intensity of a haunting, and the antennas on either side of the device rise and fall in sync with the surrounding energy levels.

The PKE meter prop was built using an Iona SP-1 handheld shoe polisher as its base. Lights and advanced-looking electronics helped mask the device's humble origins.

"It's all just this weird stuff, but it's credible enough," says Dane, who helped design the prop. "It's like, 'I don't understand it, but it has to work.'"

OPPOSITE TOP Ray Stantz sports a pair of ecto-goggles.
OPPOSITE BOTTOM LEFT An early ecto-goggle concept imagines the device could be worn as an eyepatch-like monocle. **OPPOSITE BOTTOM CENTER AND RIGHT** Ecto-goggle concepts by John Daveikis.
RIGHT An original PKE meter prop from the collection of Dan Lanigan.
ABOVE Stephen Dane's concept sketch for a metal detector–style ghost-detecting device.

5. WHO BROUGHT THE DOG?

At 55 Central Park West, Dana Barrett and Louis Tully are twenty-second-floor neighbors, separated by a hallway and apartment doors, which often end up being closed in Louis's face. Dana's unit is 2206, Louis's is 2202.

The entire set took shape on Stage 12 in the Burbank Studios. In an unconventional move, both apartments and the hallway between them were constructed as a single continuous expanse, using no trickery to hide scene transitions.

"It is kind of unusual," says John DeCuir Jr. "Usually they would be separate, but we had the luxury of connecting them, and that hallway was the connective tissue between Louis's apartment and Dana's. It wasn't a huge stage by any means, and there was a lot of wrestling around to get Louis's apartment in conjunction with that hallway."

Because the effects crew needed to manipulate full-size Terror Dog puppets from below, the set needed to stand a full six feet above the ground. "They took a chainsaw to the floor," remembers John Bruno, of the holes carved for the Terror Dogs.

Dana first realizes something's rotten in her apartment when eggs fry themselves on her kitchen countertop. The effect involved weakening the eggshells with small scoring cuts and pumping air into the eggs from beneath. Hidden propane burners raised the countertop to cooking temperature. Rejected practical effects included a loaf of bread that toasted itself and a magnetic refrigerator door that attracted metallic kitchen utensils from across the room.

The weirdness in her apartment prompts Dana to seek out the ghostbusters, but Peter Venkman's scan turns up nothing. Later, however, Dana is alarmed by lights emanating from behind a bizarrely bulging door. The illumination peeking through the doorframe was Reitman's nod to a similar effect in Spielberg's *Close Encounters of the Third Kind*. To achieve the door transformation, crew members simply poked at a duplicate rubber door with foam shapes attached to sticks.

For the scene in which Dana is attacked by demonic arms erupting from her chair, effects designer Don Carner weakened the chair's fabric with acid and razor blades to allow it to rip easily. Each of the arms was essentially a long-sleeved glove, worn by off-camera operators Mike Hoover, Michael Jones, and sculptor Steve Neill.

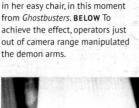

OPPOSITE Dana Barrett is attacked in her easy chair, in this moment from *Ghostbusters*. **BELOW** To achieve the effect, operators just out of camera range manipulated the demon arms.

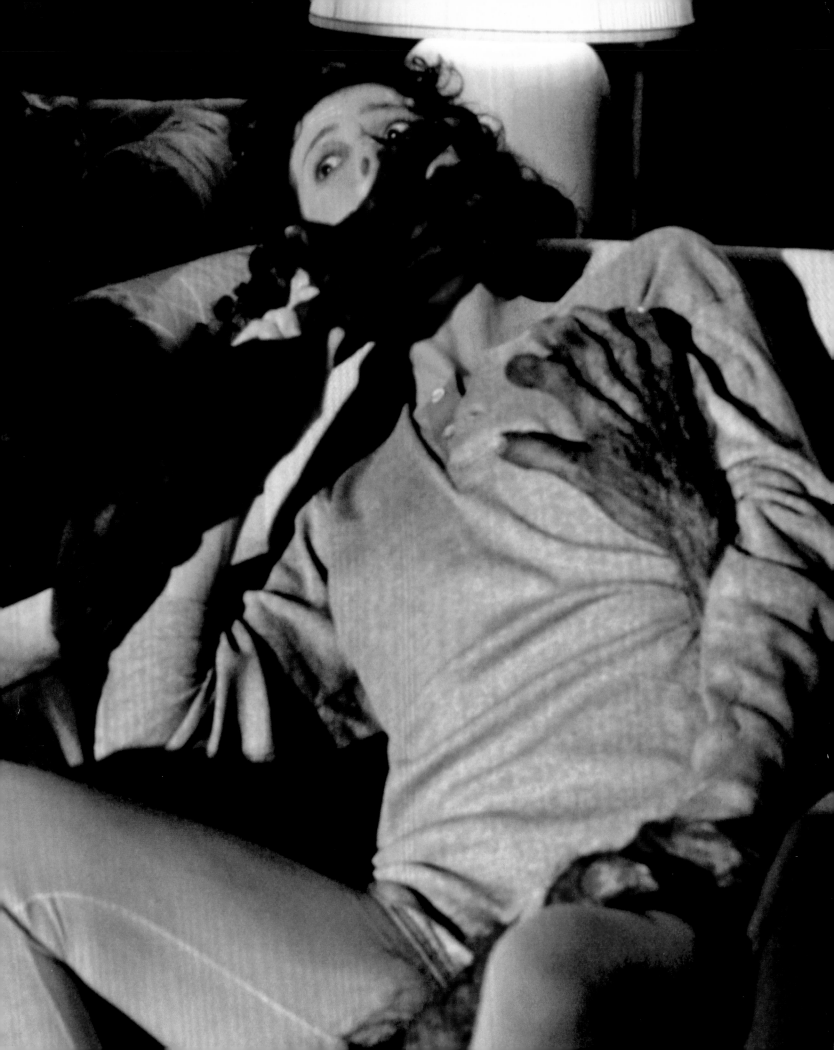

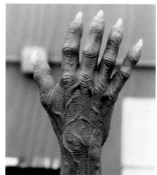

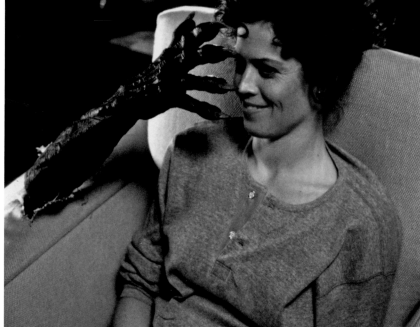

TOP LEFT A rejected "frog hand" for the chair attack sequence, created by Steve Neill. ABOVE Two more demonic hands, also sculpted by Neill. TOP RIGHT Ivan Reitman directs Sigourney Weaver and Rick Moranis on the apartment set. BOTTOM RIGHT Sigourney Weaver smiles as a demon hand closes in for the kill. OPPOSITE TOP Weaver is outfitted for her levitation scene by members of Chuck Gaspar's physical effects crew. OPPOSITE BELOW Sigourney Weaver, cinematographer László Kovács, and Ivan Reitman during the filming of the scene in which Venkman learns that Dana is possessed by Zuul.

"We made arm casts using my own arms, and we did three different hands," says Neill. "Ivan didn't like one that he said looked like a frog hand. He wanted something scarier, and I said we were short on time. So he said, 'Why don't you just take one of those other hands, paint it a different color, give it different nails, and put some hair on it?' So that's what we did."

During filming, Neill worried that the claw tips on his monster arm might scratch Weaver's face. "We had been doing the breakaway shot several times, and every time I would grab Sigourney, I was careful not to hit her hard," he says. "Finally Sigourney leans over and says, 'I can't *act* the scene of being hit in the face as well as if you actually *did* it.' I said that the nails would hurt, and she said, 'I'll deal with that, that's what makeup is for.'"

Adds John Bruno, "When the monster arms grabbed her, everybody was nervous about *where* they were going to grab. And Sigourney just grabbed somebody's arm, put it right on her breast, and said, 'Let's do it.'"

The armchair sequence was a relatively late addition to the script. "As we got into production I kept trying to add more scary moments," says Reitman. "We needed something more frightening, so that scene came at the last minute. I developed it just weeks before we started shooting and figured out how we could do it live, on the stage. I thought that if we could give the scary parts of the movie a true weight, the comedy would be heightened that much more."

Later, Venkman returns to the apartment to woo Dana, setting up a scene in which he laconically takes note of her

demonic possession by Zuul. "[Sigourney's] scenes with Bill Murray are sexy, they're funny, and they're unusual," says Reitman. "Suddenly, in the middle of this big science-fiction movie, he's going on a date, he's got flowers, he comes over to her house—and she's floating off the bed."

Sigourney Weaver relished the chance to inhabit an entirely new persona. "I wanted to have fun with it because—besides working with the guys—turning into this creature was the main reason I wanted to do the role. Ivan indulged me by letting me play Zuul as I wanted to.

"But, I was very disappointed that I was looped when I said, 'There is no Dana, only Zuul.' I thought I could do that voice!" Ultimately, Reitman provided the rough, raspy voice of the demon.

Dana's demonic possession is also evidenced through levitation—"four feet above her covers" as Venkman puts it. Reitman didn't wait for postproduction and instead executed the effect on set, using traditional stage magic tricks. "I had this magic background because I did *The Magic Show* and *Merlin* on Broadway," he says. "We did like, 80 percent of the movie practically, live on the set as we filmed. It grounded the film in reality."

6. AIM FOR THE FLAT TOP

The street-level entrance to Dana's apartment building had already been filmed during location shooting in New York, but to achieve a sufficiently spectacular earthquake effect, a matching site was constructed at Columbia Ranch, a studio back lot now owned by Warner Bros.

A stretch of pavement and three floors of the building façade were built to perfectly match the New York footage. Chuck Gaspar's crew now had free reign to destroy a piece of Big Apple real estate without worrying about zoning laws.

On cue, jagged slices of pavement collapsed into a thirty-foot pit, with a police car and four stunt actors tumbling into the depths. According to Reitman, the effect cost $250,000, drawing objections from the budget-minded studio—but Reitman felt the heroes needed to face genuine physical peril to properly set the stakes for the movie's climax.

Production designer John DeCuir prepped the set for the ghostbusters' confrontation with Gozer atop "Spook Central," the very top of his version of 55 Central Park West. DeCuir's Gozer temple, constructed inside the cavernous Stage 16 at the Burbank Studios, was one of the largest sets ever built for a film.

The rooftop shrine filled the entire expanse of the soundstage and stood sixty feet high.

When lit, the set drew so much power that Columbia had to shut down adjacent stages to provide the required 50,000 amps. The lights burned so hot that the crew switched off the automated sprinkler systems and kept firefighters on standby. Ultimately, the Gozer temple required an estimated three thousand construction hours at a budget of nearly $1 million.

"One big challenge from a design standpoint was that it was quite a baroque set," says John DeCuir Jr. "Not architecture-specific, but with a lot of ornamentation and detail, a lot of plaster casting and sculpting. The challenge on that job was getting all the pieces sculpted and cast in a timely fashion, brought in, and plastered up on stage."

A curved backdrop surrounded the set, providing a view of the New York City skyline from every vantage point within the temple. "We had probably one of the largest backings that anyone ever put up in Hollywood," says DeCuir Jr. "Seldom do you ever wrap a backing 360 degrees, which we did around the entire set. That in itself was a major endeavor."

OPPOSITE Actress Slavitza Jovan as Gozer. **BELOW** Jovan relaxes with Bill Murray, Harold Ramis, Ernie Hudson, and Dan Aykroyd on the Gozer temple set.

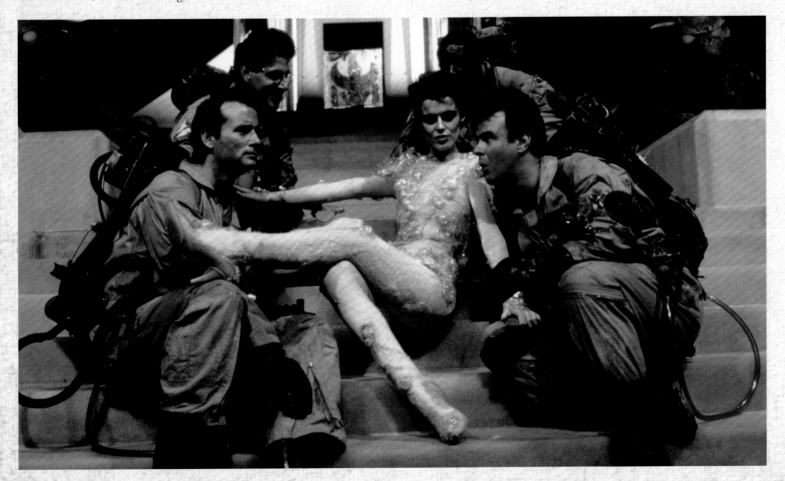

John Bruno agrees. "The background was forty feet tall, a gigantic cyclorama painting. Trees were layered on stands so they would have dimension when the camera was moving, and they cut holes for city lights. It was a very deep set." Ingenious lighting, made by rotating tubes wrapped in spirals of tape, caused car headlights to seemingly slide past in the far distance.

The Gozer temple resembles a sacrificial altar, and its mad mix of Gothic and Deco is both strange and architecturally familiar. Reitman and Aykroyd drew inspiration for the setting from similar examples in the photography book *Rooftops of New York*.

Yugoslavian model Slavitza Jovan joined the production for the Gozer temple shoot. Reitman wanted Gozer to look androgynous, after rejecting an early concept that described Gozer as a "thin, hollow-cheeked, distinguished-looking man in his early sixties," who resembled building architect Ivo Shandor. Before hiring Jovan, Reitman had considered Grace Jones (*Conan the Destroyer*) and Anne Carlisle (*Liquid Sky*) for the role.

"They wanted a certain look, a handsome face and good body," says Jovan. "The modeling agent thought that would be for me, because of my accent, and my whole look was kind of specialized. I met Ivan Reitman and the producer, and I was booked the same day."

Jovan developed a regal air for Gozer, knowing that the success of her portrayal would hinge on her body language. "I thought she would be a powerful goddess," she says. "Like

a ghost from pagan times, when the emperors and empresses would have people worship them. I just stepped forward as this powerful woman and tried to be somewhat seductive."

Jovan spent three weeks on the Gozer temple set—"The actors kept saying, 'Oh, this is Gozer's set,' so that was fun for me"—but she had little familiarity with the movie's comedy stars.

"I did not know them very well, and even though I was playing a strong character, in person I was shy," she says. "Bill Murray would make comments like, 'Dangerous woman!' and I did not know why he was saying that. I guess he was going according to the character? But at that time I did not know; I was thinking, 'Dangerous? What? I'm so shy.' I don't know what to say to that. They probably did not know, because they did not know me in person."

For the shoot Jovan spent most of her time wrapped in an exotic bubble costume, wearing colored contact lenses, and suspended on wires; her lines were later dubbed over by voice actress Paddi Edwards.

"They made only one version of that costume," she says. "It was not easy to get into it. They had to sew on the back part, so if I had to take it off, the wardrobe people would sew it up again. I could not wear my contact lenses too long because they would make my eyes sensitive, and I could not see anything with them. I was all the way up on those stairs, and I had to act in total darkness.

OPPOSITE Between takes on the Gozer temple set, filmed on Stage 16 at the Burbank Studios. **ABOVE** Detail of the Gozer temple's architecture, designed by John DeCuir. **BOTTOM LEFT** View of the cyclorama painting that surrounded the Gozer temple to provide the illusion that the set looked out onto New York's cityscape. **BOTTOM RIGHT** Slavitza Jovan's stunt double is suited up for filming.

"Underneath the costume I had belts and I was lifted high. I was a little bit afraid of that, but the stuntwoman, who was more of an athlete, did the dangerous part, the circling in the air."

Gozer's subsequent manifestation as the Stay Puft marshmallow man would be realized with extensive effects work in postproduction. But the actors on the temple set did get a physical encounter with Stay Puft in the form of his marshmallowy guts, simulated with gallons and gallons of shaving cream.

Those same vats of shaving cream were pressed into service on the Columbia Ranch back lot so EPA agent Walter Peck could get his karmic comeuppance.

"It was only one take, but I got nervous because it was *so much* shaving cream," says William Atherton. "It was a huge vat. They said it was about fifty pounds, and I remembered from eighth grade science class that fifty pounds of feathers and fifty pounds of lead are the same. So they tested it with a stunt guy and it knocked him flat! When they put me in, they only dropped about half that amount."

7. MAYBE IF WE START DANCING, OTHER PEOPLE WILL JOIN IN?

Principal photography concluded in early February 1984. Months of effects work remained, but at last the actors could breathe a sigh of relief.

Annie Potts started the shoot not quite sure about the loose, improvisational approach of her fellow actors, but learned to appreciate the atmosphere by the end. "I was a little stumped at first," she admits. "I was like, 'The words that are in the script are pretty good; could we just stick to that?' I came in and had my lines memorized—I'm not sure Bill even looked at the script. But we all have our methods."

Dan Aykroyd acknowledges the best performances relied on a healthy "winging it" philosophy: "We all came from the same school: Billy, Rick Moranis, myself, Ramis. Second City has a tradition of collaboration. It stresses teamwork in a way that other mediums don't. When you blend people together there's always going to be friction, there are always stovepipes separating the talents, but not with Second City, and not with improvisation. Everybody's thinking of their friends and wanting them to look good. And I think that's why it works so well."

Reitman likens it to music: "All performances are about editorial rhythms—how fast people are speaking, tempo, energy, and volume. They're musical ideas played out in film."

THEY CAUSED AN EXPLOSION!

When principal photography wrapped in February 1984, Richard Edlund and his crew at Boss Film Studios had just four months to complete the remaining postproduction work on nearly two hundred optical effects.

Edlund, out on his own after leaving ILM, needed to quickly staff up Boss Films to tackle *Ghostbusters*.

"I had the good fortune to have a really great group of people that were willing to leave ILM," he says. "But it took so much damn time to put the deal together [with Columbia]. By the time the lawyers got done, we basically had ten months to build the studio, design all the FX, and shoot all the FX. It was a few hundred shots but they were difficult, and it was the photochemical era, and that was a much more unwieldy process than the world we are in now."

BELOW The ghostbusters strike a relaxed pose following the defeat of Gozer. **OPPOSITE** Harold Ramis and Annie Potts take a break during filming.

Boss Films operated out of headquarters at Marina Del Rey in Los Angeles County, having acquired the facility through Edlund's buyout of Douglas Trumbull's Entertainment Effects Group. Within these walls the crew of Boss Films practiced arts including sculpture, puppetry, stop-motion animation, traditional cel animation, rotoscoping, and miniature construction. The first item of business? Delivering the ghosts promised by the movie's title.

"The feeling was that we would *not* be silly," says producer Michael C. Gross. "We were shooting all the spooks and all the creatures as real horror. So you get that payback where you're fighting for your life—and then you get a joke. The joke is funnier if you play the rest straight."

Visual effects director John Bruno had worked with Ivan Reitman on the animated feature *Heavy Metal* and had conjured up ghosts for 1982's Spielberg-produced horror hit *Poltergeist*. While working on another film project, Bruno received a call from Richard Edlund. "He said, 'Hey man, this movie *Ghostbusters* is happening. Can you do it?'" he recalls. "When I came back to LA they were already set up in Marina Del Rey. We just got to work."

With a tight schedule and a looming deadline, the crew couldn't afford to overthink the process. Furthermore, the movie had earned little notice from Hollywood professionals, meaning Boss Films was free to set its own expectations. "No one in the film industry was worried about *Ghostbusters*," says Bruno. "The big film was going to be *Indiana Jones and the Temple of Doom*. *Ghostbusters* was not on anyone's radar.

"And no one [at Boss Films] was talking about it being high art," he continues. "We had an idea—I would say about 85 percent—of how to do everything. The rest we didn't know but we knew we'd get there, because we were going to look for happy accidents."

Associate producer Joe Medjuck recalls one of his visits with Edlund in Marina Del Rey. "It was clean, it was neat, everything was organized," he says. "They served the best coffee in town. I remember thinking these guys were like mad geniuses. There seemed to be nothing improvisational about it—they knew what they were doing, and it was amazing to watch. It was a Silicon Valley kind of thing before there was Silicon Valley. They were all business, and they were very organized, but we kept adding shots."

Edlund prepared for the pressure by staffing Boss Films with names he trusted and building an environment that favored collaboration. "My management style was kind of like a hunting band," he says. "About a dozen people as department heads, who knew each other and who knew everybody's strengths and weaknesses so they knew exactly who they needed to go to for help. It was a really crack team, developed through the ILM period from *Star Wars* to *Empire Strikes Back* to *Raiders of the Lost Ark* to *Poltergeist*."

That experience came in handy. "On *Raiders* we did a lot of experimentation on ghosts," says Edlund. "We wound up using gauze in a tank with a stick—you'd swim this gauze around in the water, and if you ran it backwards, it looked like the figures were coming out from this gauze. It had a very peculiar and unearthly look to it, and we used that to some degree on *Ghostbusters* as well."

Pulling off the work required by Reitman's vision meant nailing down the true definition of the director's needs. "I spent

a lot of time with Harold and Ivan tearing down the script," says Edlund. "The photochemical process is kind of like photomasochism. It was so complicated and difficult to get all the elements into the shot, free of matte lines and to get everything balanced. Working with Ivan and Harold was figuring out how to get the most on the screen for the money that was available."

Edlund had implicit trust in his crew, but he knew the pressures of the project offered little room for error. "It's like going to battle—you have to have all your weapons right there," he says. "Each shooting day is very expensive, so you have to not only be prepared, but you have to be quick and deft so you can move in, set up your shot with whatever floor effects and physical effects need to be done, get the shot, and then get out of the way."

Stuart Ziff helped run the creature shop at Boss Films. "I can't sculpt creatures, and I really can't draw," says Ziff. "So I looked at myself more like a maître d', making sure everything went well. Ultimately I think we ended up [hiring] like fifty-four

people. Things kept growing. It was a balls-out operation."

Underneath Ziff, broad responsibilities for the movie's ghosts fell to Steve Johnson and Randy Cook. "We just split the work up," says Johnson. "Randy said, 'I'll do the Terror Dogs and we'll do them in stop motion, so that's a huge chunk. Which ones do you want?'" Johnson picked the librarian, the Onionhead (aka Slimer), and two spirits—an undead cabdriver and a subway ghost—needed for a montage sequence. In addition to the Terror Dogs, Cook agreed to work on the Stay Puft marshmallow man.

"Because I hired all these different people, and they had different responsibilities—Stay Puft, Slimer, Terror Dogs—each person gave it a different look," says Ziff. "That put the creatures of *Ghostbusters* apart from other films where you had one central master of effects, and his look permeated through all the creatures. With *Ghostbusters*, [each ghost] looked very different."

Mark Stetson ran the model shop, and his crew was tasked with constructing the miniature 55 Central Park West apartment building and a scaled-down version of Central Park West to be terrorized during Stay Puft's rampage. Thaine Morris performed the roles of stage manager, rigger, and pyrotechnician.

"We would all watch the dailies and discuss the fact that we were the only people who were going to think this was funny," recalls Bruno. "We were making this stuff for us. There was no time, there was no checking with anyone—even Ivan was still editing while we were trying to shoot. We sent over some of our test footage and said, 'What do you think of this?' and Ivan says, 'Done. It's in the movie.'"

Richard Edlund prized cross-pollination over hierarchy. "How did we figure out the shots? I had a very democratic approach. Everybody in the crew was invited to dailies, and it was fine for them to kick out an idea if they had something better. I think that was a really important aspect of why *Ghostbusters* was visually successful."

ABOVE The artists and technicians of the Boss Films creature shop amid their creations. Randy Cook can be seen holding the Terror Dog's horns, Steve Johnson (left) and Mark Siegel (right) pose with Slimer, while Stuart Ziff can be seen with arms extended in the foreground.

8. LIBRARY GHOST

The ghostbusters, whose previous experiences consisted of administering phony ESP tests and observing mass sponge migrations, make their first real connection with the supernatural amid the New York Public Library's book stacks.

Concept artist Bernie Wrightson produced multiple renditions of the library ghost, and actress Ruth Oliver portrayed the specter in live-action footage shot at Edlund's Marina Del Rey facility.

John Bruno storyboarded the sequence: "The ghost is described as floating in the air, so as a joke I thought she should look over and put her finger up to her lips and tell them '*shhh*.' She's a librarian; that's why she's still there.

"I learned on *Poltergeist*, on cloth simulation, to film it normally and then reverse print it," he continues. "Everything is moving slightly off. So I filmed her acting the shot out in reverse, then we printed it normally."

A life-cast of the actress became the basis for a terrifying animatronic figure that was employed when the ghostbusters foolishly rush the phantom.

"I spent weeks on the librarian ghost transformation figure," says puppeteer Mark Wilson. "Since I was a puppet maker, I knew how to rig things with string and eyelets and pulleys. The first thing I did was a mock-up using PVC pipe, duct tape, and clips to pull the foam latex likeness of the actress into an odd shape. Then Steve would say, 'I want the muzzle to come out farther,' or 'I want uglier teeth,' and so for several weeks I just cut and pieced her together as a mock-up.

"We sent that out to John Alberti who did the mechanics, which were mainly done out of wood: tiny wooden pulleys, little pistons so the arms could stretch out, and a set of drawer slides that allowed us to motivate the body to rise up."

OPPOSITE Actress Ruth Oliver, wearing the costume and makeup that turned her into the library ghost. **BELOW** Stuart Ziff and Steve Johnson work on the library ghost transformation, a puppet operated through pulleys and slides.

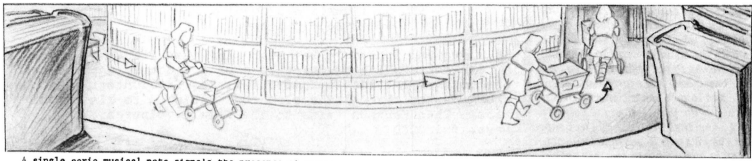

⑥

A single eerie musical note signals the presence of something strange looking down on the librarian from a vantage point high above the room. It follows the librarian as she pushes her cart around a counter.

⑦

ENTERS AN AISLE OF CARD FILE CABINETS...

⑦A

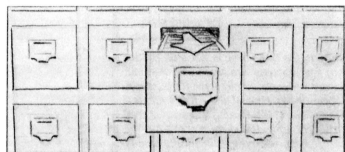

ONE FILE DRAWER SLOWLY SLIDES OUT –UNNOTICED.

⑦B

AS SHE MOVES FAST THE CABINETS, DRAWERS SLIDE OUT SILENTLY BEHIND HER.

⑦C

INDEX CARDS START POPPING OUT...

Steve Johnson praises the puppet's engineering: "One person could pull the levers and stretch the torso, shorten the neck, elongate the jaw, sink the eyes, elongate the arms, open the mouth—all of these things controlled with these two levers. So instead of having twelve, fourteen, or sixteen puppeteers, I made it so that one or two people could operate it."

As a finishing touch, Wilson attached the foam-rubber "hero skin" of the actress, along with four handles attached to clusters of cables that would activate the various mechanisms. "I had two, and Steve had two," recalls Wilson. On cue, the figure's clothes tore away, while an air hose and a fan blew her hair back from her face.

An even more terrifying incarnation of the librarian was sculpted but never used, though Johnson recycled the puppet for the 1985 horror feature *Fright Night*.

"I wanted to go even crazier," recalls Johnson. "The first stage puppet ended up being this incredible beast, nothing like the human form, but I wasn't satisfied with that. We actually created another which was more bestial, but everyone saw the test on the first stage and said, 'Why are you spending all this money doing a whole other puppet? This is fine, it works great.'"

According to Reitman, the audience at a test screening "screamed and laughed at the same time" upon seeing the library ghost's surprise shape shift. Adds John Bruno, "The woman who played the library ghost, she didn't look mean. And she turns into something *horrific*."

ABOVE Storyboards by Kurt Conner for the ghostly encounter that would open *Ghostbusters*. **OPPOSITE TOP** A close-up of the sculpted librarian puppet. **OPPOSITE BOTTOM** Library ghost transformation concepts by artist Bernie Wrightson.

9. SLIMER (AKA ONIONHEAD)

"There was something about this sort of spud-like quality of what became Slimer that I just thought looked different than anything I'd ever seen as a ghost," says Reitman. "After seeing an enormous amount of spiky-teeth, scary-eyed, traditional monster stuff, [I thought] this one looked cuter and funnier. We knew he had to have a large mouth, and it's pretty crude in the movie, but it's all extraordinarily effective and, I think, different."

Dan Aykroyd described the Onionhead ghost—so named for its supposed stench—as a confluence of stored-up psychic energy that wasn't prepared to vacate the hotel it was haunting. One of Aykroyd's early scripts cast the Onionhead as a misty yellow FRVP (free-repeating vaporous phantasm) lurking in the rooms of the rural Greenville Guest House. Though the ghost was known as the Onionhead behind the scenes, it later acquired the nickname Slimer thanks to Venkman's famous line, "He slimed me."

Steve Johnson refined Slimer's look, working from an initial maquette by Thom Enriquez. Johnson crafted multiple maquettes that ranged in size from four inches to full scale.

Johnson sought inspiration from the malleable cartooning of animator Tex Avery and from John Belushi's raised-eyebrow expressions. Ivan Reitman confirms the influence the late Belushi had on the meaty green ghost. "When Danny wanted to do this movie, originally it was for him and Belushi," he says. "We thought we should pay some hidden tribute to John. We always thought of Slimer as a spiritual embodiment of what John's character did in *Animal House*."

The full-sized, foam-rubber Slimer got its moves from puppeteer Mark Wilson. A second puppeteer manipulated the ghost's tongue by wearing it like a glove. Cables controlled Slimer's eyes and eyebrows. For big, stretchy expressions, Wilson

BELOW Slimer feeds his face in a final frame from *Ghostbusters*. **OPPOSITE** A team of operators gave Slimer a hefty amount of personality. Steve Johnson can be seen in the background.

simply manhandled the foam rubber skin from the inside. Ivan Reitman provided Slimer's gibbering and cackles, with a few of the character's more extreme roars coming from a stock sound effects track labeled "Mad Gorilla."

"The bottom of his pear shape only came down to my navel," says Wilson. "My arms went out his side—I slid on a shirt with the foam latex arms attached. I would stick my head into a fiberglass shell that allowed me to turn and rotate anything from the upper lip and up. I could see through the mouth to look at a video monitor or to get some air."

Backup performers aided Wilson when it came to some of Slimer's moving parts, including operating the mechanical controls around the eyes. "There was an aluminum bar attached to the inside of the lower lip, which Craig Caton operated to gyrate the mouth and make the jaw drop open and swing shut," says Wilson. "I would do the gross body movements, and Craig would do the mouth. Other puppeteers would do subtler stuff, like squinting, or a wide-eyed look. Slimer's tongue was a hand puppet that creature maker and puppeteer Mark Siegel helped sculpt—it was all jellied up, and it needed to slide in past my head to fit it through the mouth."

Recalls Siegel, "I was squeezed in behind the puppet, with my hands through the back of the head, to operate the tongue.

Mark Wilson had to bend down with his arms in the puppet, and my arm was resting on the back of his neck. Steve Johnson was squeezed in really tight with his arms around me and in the puppet's cheeks. I did the tongue movements, and Steve did the cheek operation to give him some chewing motion and to support the top of his head so it didn't collapse. Mark had to lift up this plate of food scraps—crumpled lettuce, Jell-O, mashed potatoes—and dump it into the mouth, which meant dumping it over the tongue and right onto the back of his neck. At the end of the shot I could hear Mark's voice inside the puppet going, 'Get me out of here!'"

Ziff praises the unique qualities of Wilson's performance. "We would film Mark in the Onionhead costume and one day he was sick, so I was inside of it for a day," he says. "And we had to throw all that film out, because I didn't move like Mark did. That's one thing I learned—the personality of the puppeteer comes through the rubber."

"We tried to have logic," says John Bruno. "If you're a ghost, it means you lived once, so what did you do while you were on the planet? For the Onionhead, the guy was a slob and always eating, but because he didn't exist as a creature anymore, he didn't have a stomach. So when he's eating and drinking at the hotel, it's just going right through him."

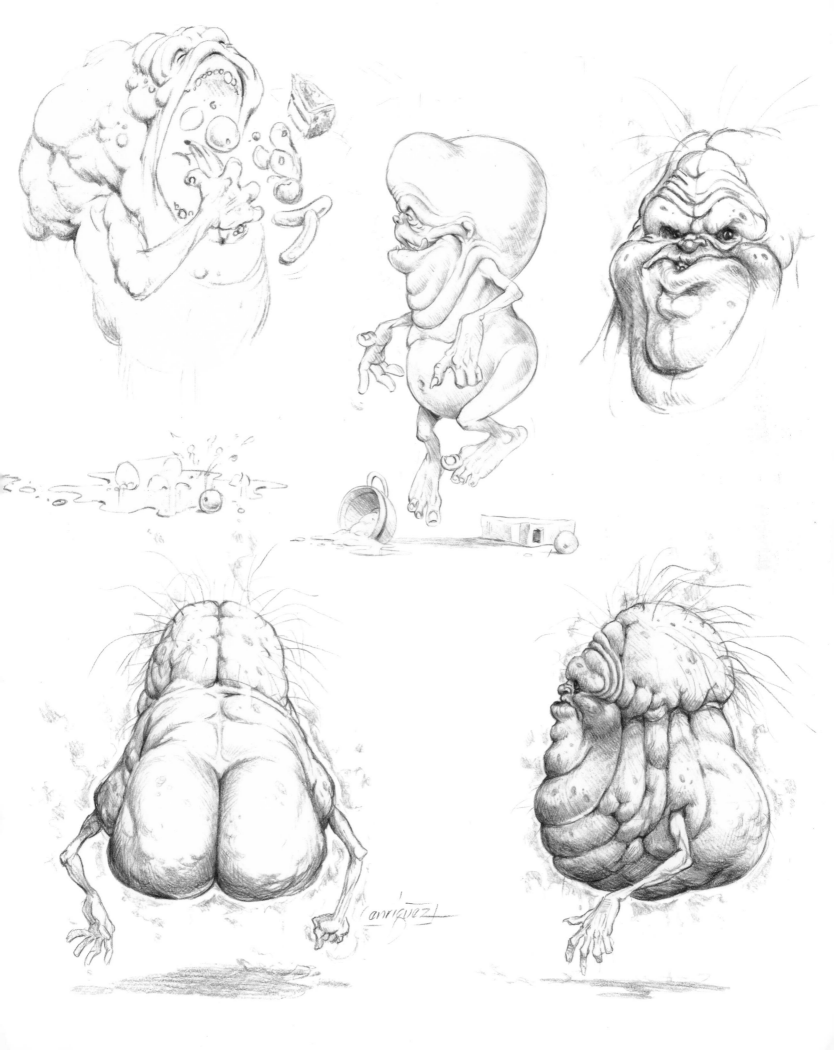

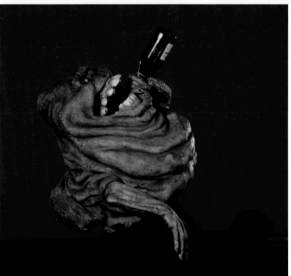

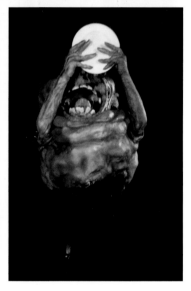

Puppeteer Wilson interacted with oversized props while playing Slimer so that, when the footage was composited into a live-action scene, it would make the ghost appear smaller than a human. "What they ended up doing is going to Pier 1 or someplace where you can find an oversized martini glass," he says. John Bruno recalls using a hefty magnum of champagne to achieve the drinking effect. "We had an oversized bottle for that, which looked like a regular bottle," he says.

Bruno reveals how the team solved shots that required interaction between the ghost and the camera: "The camera was locked and didn't move," he says. "So when the Onionhead had to come through a wall, then stop and react, we didn't move the camera—we moved *him*, as an object. And along with him all of the puppeteers, on a wheeled moving cart."

"I had an umbilical of about five to eight puppeteers attached to me by cables, so it was a lot easier to move a camera than to move the group," says Wilson. "If Slimer was rotating, then I was on this big lazy Susan, being rotated by the grips."

Slimer's terror-driven flight down the length of a hallway necessitated the creation of a small puppet—nicknamed the "speeding bullet"—sculpted by Mark Siegel. "It was about the size of an egg," recalls Wilson. "It was just an oval-shaped character with a screaming, gaping mouth."

Effects director Gary Platek handled the moment when Slimer vanishes through a solid wall. After positioning a camera directly above a flat pane of glass, he dropped a dollop of dry ice fog onto the surface and lit it up with a laser. The resulting shock wave glowed and dispersed in an appropriately ghostly manner.

One final version of Slimer rounded out the array required for all of the ghost's scenes. "It was a miniature, three or four inches tall, with its arms out to the side," says Wilson. "We used it for the scenes up in the chandelier, when he's spinning in a circle. The effects guys put that miniature on a turntable and shot it as a separate plate."

The ghostbusters finally nab Slimer by unleashing the full force of their proton packs and neutrona wands. The team's first capture is a triumphant moment, but as Reitman pointed out in a 1985 interview,[13] Slimer never really puts up a fight: "It's not really doing anything. It's minding its own business, which is a totally different approach to [other] movie ghosts. It's the ghostbusters who harass the ghost, not the other way around."

OPPOSITE TOP Steve Johnson sculpts the full-size Onionhead. **OPPOSITE BOTTOM LEFT** Sculpts show a range of potential facial expressions for Onionhead. **OPPOSITE BOTTOM RIGHT** A technician works on the interior mechanics of the ghost's mouth. **TOP LEFT** Dave Stewart takes a look inside the Onionhead's mouth. **TOP RIGHT AND ABOVE** The finished Onionhead design needed to interact with oversized bottles and plates in order to maintain the illusion of scale.

10. DREAM GHOST

The montage that conveys the ghostbusters' rise to success is told through quick cuts and magazine headlines, with little need for postproduction effects. The one exception is a dream sequence in which Ray Stantz is sexually serviced by a stunning female phantasm.

That moment is all that remains of what was to become the Fort Detmerring sequence. As scripted, Winston and Ray arrive at the Fort Detmerring guardhouse in the Ectomobile and split up to investigate the historical site. Ray, after donning a vintage military uniform, falls asleep in the officers' barracks and awakens to a surprisingly pleasant ghost encounter. The live-action Detmerring footage was in the can, with Dan Aykroyd and Ernie Hudson having put in their performances on the Columbia Ranch back lot and Stage 12 at the Burbank Studios.

"The idea behind the scene was to give Dan a love interest—a woman who's been dead for a hundred years," said Ramis.[14] "But the scene was too long, and it was in the wrong place in the film."

Playboy centerfold Kym Herrin played the ghost, allowing herself to be encased in a rigid plaster body mold and suspended by cables to simulate weightlessness.

"We had to make a body cast of her," says Stuart Ziff. "So there's Steve Johnson and Mark Wilson, and they're soaking these gauze bandages in water and gently draping them on her with this disposable paintbrush. Finally she looks at them and just goes, 'Go for it.' And in unison Steve and Mark fling this paintbrush in the air, look at each other, and just start patting these bandages on her with their hands."

The invisible unfastening of Ray's pants had a simple solution, involving a puppet of Aykroyd's crotch that employed a wire pull to draw down the zipper. "I hired this guy, Al Coulter, who worked it out," says Stuart Ziff. "Al made these pants, and when you pulled some levers underneath, the zipper would come down, and the pants would open." Says John Bruno, "That puppet was just a test, but when we sent the test over they cut it into the movie. So I was like, 'OK, I guess that's done!'"

Reitman felt that the Fort Detmerring scene didn't have a place in the final edit, but he salvaged the completed ghost effects for the montage. Dan Aykroyd, though enthusiastic about the scene's genesis, didn't object to its omission. "I don't miss anything that we didn't use," he says. "The ghost in the fort—the seduction ghost—in paranormal research that's a common thing, ghosts doing sexual things to people. I have a friend who had three women visit him in a haunted house in Louisiana, and it was one of the greatest nights of his life. But in under two hours, you obviously can't have everything."

BELOW Bill Neill, Richard Edlund, John Bruno, and others test the rigging and body cast they will use to suspend the dream ghost, played by model Kym Herrin. **OPPOSITE** Kym Herrin as the dream ghost.

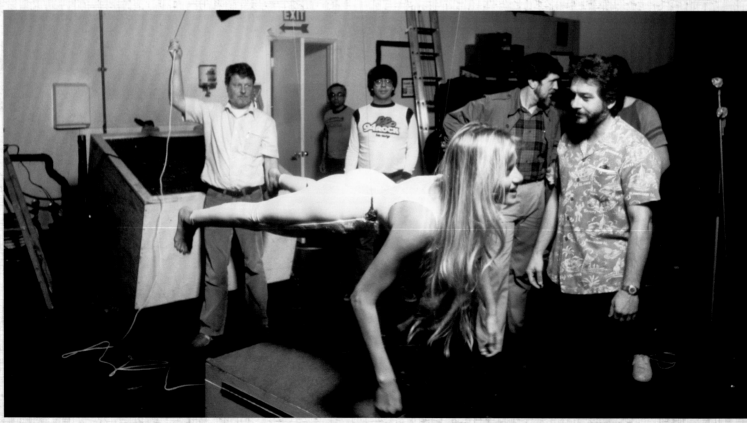

11. THE ESCAPEES

At the ghostbusters' firehouse headquarters, the containment unit in the basement serves as a poltergeist prison. Unfortunately, every new capture adds to the total volume of stored ectoplasmic energy. And according to Egon's Twinkie analogy ("let's say this Twinkie represents the normal amount of psychokinetic energy in the New York area . . .") continuing to stuff the containment grid will end in disaster.

As originally conceived, audiences would have gotten a look inside the containment unit thanks to a built-in monitor. Given the chance to see ghosts with his own eyes, EPA agent Walter Peck would have rejected the offer by sneering he had "no time for television." The shooting script described the nether realm thusly:

It is a bleak repository for souls of many species. Strange lights, mists, and spectral shapes waft about aimlessly. Human-like figures lean against the walls in despairing convict poses. Others flit and hang on the ceiling. It is a sad and frightening limbo and a most unholy makeshift asylum.

Multiple problems doomed the evocative shot: time, expense, difficulty (compositing multiple, semitransparent figures would have resulted in a hard-to-read image and story). At the end of the day, Reitman felt it was important that the audience's sympathies remain with the ghostbusters, not the ghosts.

Sculptor Steve Neill designed at least one "jail ghost" before Reitman pulled the plug. "They told me, 'Why don't you free-form some puppets and we'll shoot them?' It was this very strange, pot-bellied man with an elongated face and drooping arms. I worked on it until they finally said stop."

In the film, Walter Peck—after enlisting the municipal authority of ConEd—shuts off power to the containment unit. It bursts, blowing a hole through the roof in a geyser of supernatural power. Streaks of light fan out across Manhattan in a high-altitude panoramic image captured by Edlund's crew during their time in New York.

"That was shot from the roof of the Gulf Western building, looking toward the Empire State Building," says Edlund. "[Animation supervisor] Garry Waller did the pinkish and green streaks of the ghosts flying around New York."

A montage of memorable spooks follows, including the return of Slimer inside a hot-dog cart and the introduction of two new terrors: a subway ghost and a zombie cabdriver.

"It's my costume, but I'm not in it," says Mark Wilson, of Slimer's emergence from a food cart with his mouth stuffed with sausages. "Because we had to get all those hot dogs into his mouth, it was just easier for me to get out of the way, but I did perform the arms from underneath."

Just like with Slimer's scenes inside the Sedgewick Hotel, the food-cart scene required oversized foodstuffs to make the ghost look smaller than human scale. "The hot dogs were about twenty-four inches long and two inches across," says Wilson. "They were made by vacuuming foam latex into PVC pipes, taking the material out, and clipping the ends."

OPPOSITE A Bernie Wrightson concept illustration shows the trapped ghosts inside the containment unit. **BELOW** A high-altitude view of Manhattan, with the streaks of escaping ghosts added in postproduction.

Mark Siegel controlled the chain of hot dogs using a length of monofilament. "I was behind, pulling them in, as Slimer chewed on them," he says.

Steve Johnson brought the cackling subway ghost to life. Designer Brent Boates had originally proposed that the apparition be a three-headed monster played by an operator in a rubber suit.

The final design was a flying horror with pointy limbs and a tentacled face, sculpted by a friend of Stuart Ziff's who didn't work in the creature shop. "We were so desperate to get enough ghosts because everything kept growing," he says. "Melody Peña actually sculpted that ghost. We had all different types of people, all bringing their own sensibility, to make these ghosts look so different."

The flexible vinyl model built for on-camera use was filmed in a water tank to simulate a floating effect. "I always felt it was a wonderful way to create a creature," says Johnson. "When you place something in the water, the density of the vinyl comes to life all by itself. The model was probably about eighteen inches, but it appears to be eight or nine feet long in the film."

A live-action scene, shot at the New York subway station on Broadway west of City Hall, became the backdrop for the composited footage of the subway ghost.

Steve Johnson also handled the zombie cabdriver—a half-rotted corpse still wearing his jaunty cap. "I built it in my bedroom," he says. "I stayed up for twenty-four hours doing everything myself, the sculpture, the mold making, everything.

"I had been hired by Rick Baker on *An American Werewolf in London* to work with him in creating the Jack character, [a corpse] who keeps deteriorating until the point where we needed to create him as an animatronic puppet. So I already knew how to do it, but I thought, 'Let's take it a little bit further.' In *Werewolf* the puppeteer's hand went up into the character's neck, so I thought [I should also] make the cabdriver's neck thin, so the audience knew there was nobody wearing this thing."

After finishing construction, Johnson operated the zombie during pickup location shooting. "We had a crew that went back to New York, so the cabdriver was shot in real time in an actual cab," says Edlund.

For scenes where the taxi peels away from the curb, a stunt driver wore a zombie-like mask. "We couldn't have the puppet driving a cab through the streets of Manhattan, so for the wider shots we had a driver wearing the same look as the puppet," says Johnson.

Several ideas didn't make it into the montage, including a host of glowing orbs emerging from a 3-D movie screen and wowing a bored audience. A second sequence would have followed an invisible poltergeist around while it harassed female office workers.

"Ghost sex is a classic supernatural phenomenon, so we thought it would be funny and sort of naughty to have an invisible ghost molesting all these typists—tickling them and goosing them and ripping their blouses open," said Ramis.[15] "The more we thought about it, though, the more adolescent and tasteless it seemed."

TOP Walter Peck flees as the containment unit blows at Ghostbusters HQ. **OPPOSITE TOP LEFT** The cabdriver puppet with creator Steve Johnson. **OPPOSITE TOP RIGHT** The zombie cabdriver puppet constructed by Steve Johnson. **OPPOSITE CENTER LEFT** The subway ghost puppet. **OPPOSITE BOTTOM LEFT** The "jail ghost" created by Steve Neill for the abandoned scene that would show the inside of the containment unit. **OPPOSITE BOTTOM RIGHT** An early subway ghost design by artist Brent Boates.

12. TERROR DOGS

Zuul and Vinz Clortho, also known respectively as the Gatekeeper and the Keymaster, are the demonic harbingers of the apocalyptic god Gozer. When not inhabiting the forms of their human hosts, Dana Barrett and Louis Tully, they appear as horned, reptilian canines known during production as Terror Dogs.

In one draft of the script, the Terror Dogs hailed from an alternate dimension and sought out the help of the ghostbusters to protect them from Gozer. Concepts for the Terror Dogs included skeletal bodies and creatures with drooling, canine behavior.

"The word was 'dog,' so my first design was a couple of skinless dogs—little hideous things running around in an alley," says Thom Enriquez. "I did probably thirty-six designs trying to find them."

In the final film, Terror Dogs appeared in two forms: as full-sized figures and as small stop-motion armatures. Randy Cook did the sculpting for both versions and performed the stop-motion animation.

"We started with very detailed clay sculpting," recalls John Bruno. "Then we had to figure out how big each one of these would be, to be photographed. And then how we would give them animation, as physical motion."

The life-sized Terror Dogs were built as a pair for early filming on the Gozer temple set; a third version with detailed facial articulation was completed later in the schedule and featured in inset shots. Each measured nearly eight feet in length. Multiple operators controlled the Terror Dogs through wires, poles, and cable mechanisms.

"We had the Terror Dog set up on a platform at our ghost shop," says Stuart Ziff. "There would be the puppeteer from the waist up inside it, and all the cables going to half a dozen other

OPPOSITE A Thom Enriquez Terror Dog concept illustration from 1983. **BELOW** One of the Terror Dogs shot on the Dana/Louis conjoined apartment set. The creature was puppeteered from beneath the floor. **FOLLOWING PAGES** Working with producer Michael C. Gross, artist Thom Enriquez went through multiple Terror Dog concepts to find elements that could be incorporated into a usable design.

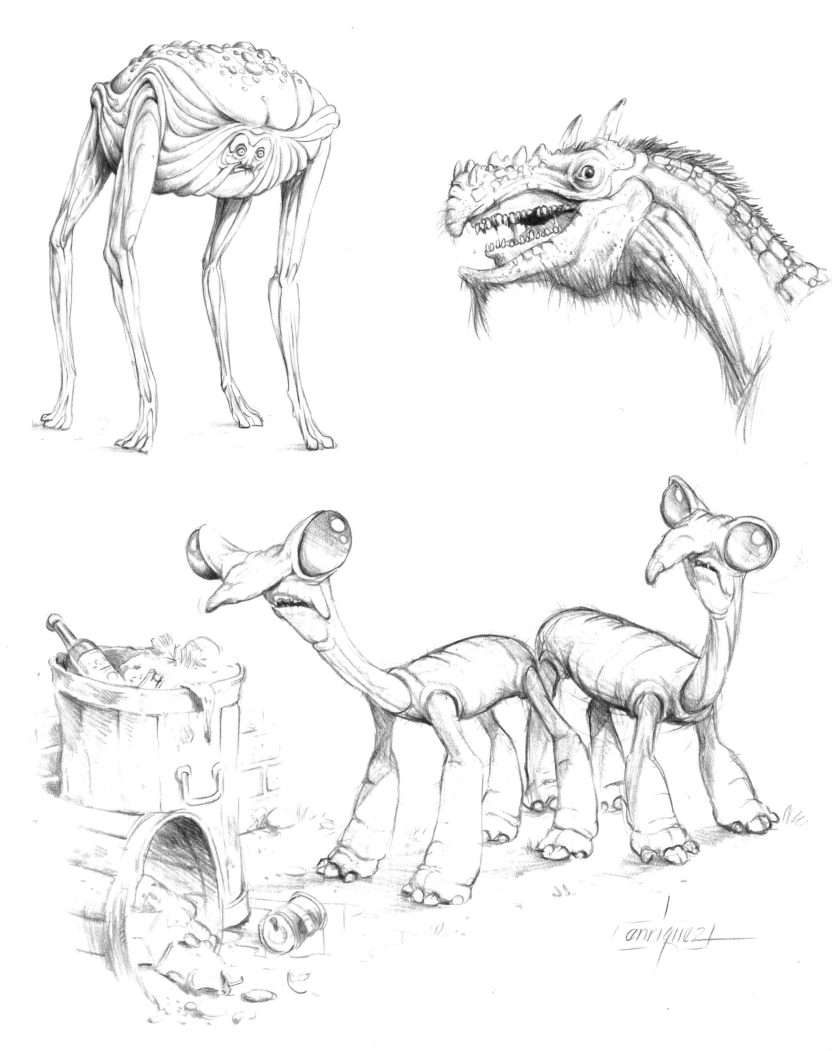

TERROR DOG

THESE PAGES Thom Enriquez got closer to the final design with these Terror Dog concepts. Eventually a handful of illustrations was handed over to Randy Cook at Boss Films who would amalgamate them into a final design and sculpt the initial Terror Dog maquette.

TERROR DOG

- GHOSTBUSTERS -
. TERROR DOGS .

enriquez

puppeteers pulling levers. And for the first few hours you're going, 'Oh my god, we're in trouble. This looks horrible.' And then they pull it together and all the motions work in unison. It's like an orchestra coming together."

Mark Wilson worked as one of the Terror Dog operators during the Gozer temple scene. "We cut a hole where the dog's belly touches the ground and stood under the floor," he says. "I would grab the back of his skull, like a handle, on either side. If I forced my right hand forward, that would turn the head. And by having a pole running down the back, we were able to lean into that. By leaning all the way down, the legs would spread out so it would look like the dog was resting on his haunches.

"We had a little black-and-white Sony Watchman inside so we could see what the camera was seeing, but of course it was only a two-inch screen so it wasn't a lot of information. But I could at least see when Gozer was walking over to my dog, and that was when I would look over toward her."

Wilson points to the timeline pressures that led to the Terror Dogs appearing in the film as both closed-mouth and fully fanged variants. "The production deadline was so tight to get the first Terror Dogs on set that we didn't have time to finish the mechanical heads," he says. "Those are simple rudimentary heads for the long shots. And when they cut close you can see

TOP John Bruno throws a jacket at the Terror Dog puppet, hoping to land it perfectly on the creature's head, while Bill Murray looks on.
RIGHT Steve Johnson and another artist sculpt the full-sized and stop-motion Terror Dogs at the same time. For consistency, any changes in one sculpt would be reflected in the other. **OPPOSITE TOP** Rick Moranis interacts with the puppeteered Terror Dog on the apartment set. **OPPOSITE CENTER** A lighting test for a Terror Dog head, which features illuminated eyes (and missing horns).
OPPOSITE CENTER RIGHT A piece of concept art details the final design for the Terror Dogs.

that this dog has had dental work all of a sudden. The two cuts were shot months apart.

"We finished one of them with a full head—teeth, mechanical jaw, eyes lighting up, and all that stuff," he continues. "Then we just had to switch the horns back and forth. The girl had smaller horns, and the guy had a slightly longer set."

"Based on our schedule, we tried to get as much in camera as possible," says John Bruno. "The fewer shots we had to mess with [in postproduction], the better. What helped Ivan and the camera crews and the actors was that we had these physical characters. They could react to them. Those practical effects helped."

The full-sized Terror Dogs worked perfectly for scenes atop temple ledges, in apartment hallways, and above the covers on Louis Tully's bed. For more active shots, the crew needed to employ a different method.

"The stop-motion techniques were for running, jumping—doing something that we can't do with a full-fledged creature," explains Bruno.

Randy Cook built a poseable foam-rubber Terror Dog around a metal armature approximately fourteen inches long. During stop-motion animation, a computer added motion blur into each frame, providing a more natural cast to the Terror Dog's rapid leaps.

13. MR. STAY PUFT

An ancient god of destruction manifesting as a jolly advertising mascot? It's the perfect example of *Ghostbusters*' approach to blending the disturbing with the hilarious, and Mr. Stay Puft had been a story cornerstone since Dan Aykroyd's earliest scripts.

The look of Stay Puft came from Aykroyd's friend John Daveikis who provided artistic accompaniment for Aykroyd's concepts during the pitch stage. "I said, 'John, I want a brand symbol—kind of like the Michelin Man and the Pillsbury Doughboy, but he's the Stay Puft marshmallow man,'" recalls Aykroyd. "John said, 'Yep, I got it,' went away, and drew it. I couldn't believe it when he sent me the drawings and he'd made Mr. Stay Puff a sailor with a sailor hat. I called John and said, 'You are a genius!' It was so funny and so cute and so innocent, and yet he's a villain."

Artist Thom Enriquez came up with many derivations of the design that ultimately proved superfluous. "One idea was that there wasn't going to be a Stay Puft, just something horrific, a big Godzilla-like monster," he says. "I also did a lot of variations of Stay Puft after Ivan said, 'I don't think we ever got it right the first time, so let's keep trying.' I was kind of frustrated.

I said, 'I can't make it better than this, this is as good as it gets!'"

Stay Puft's sailor look completes his authenticity as a corporate mascot. In fact, Reitman briefly considered making a stop-motion Stay Puft advertisement, and giving audiences a glimpse of it in the movie right before the ghostbusters' own sales pitch plays on Dana Barrett's television. But Stay Puft's marketing-friendly appearance also presented a challenge: how to ensure the movie's apocalyptic climax didn't look ridiculous in all the wrong ways.

"My very first attempt was to carve marshmallow shapes out of blocks of soft urethane foam," says Stay Puft sculptor and operator Bill Bryan, "but since they were solid there was no apparent movement within each piece. The next version was hollow, with plenty of empty space inside. When I moved with this suit on, it squished and expanded, giving it an elastic feel." The team put this version—fitted with two left hands because the right-hand mold wasn't yet finished—in front of the cameras to see how it looked.

"We basically had a yellow foam-rubber suit for the film test," says John Bruno. "It wasn't finished, it wasn't painted—it

OPPOSITE Dressed in the Stay Puft costume, Bill Bryan positions himself on the miniaturized street, while John Bruno oversees.
BELOW Bill Bryan sculpts an early version of Stay Puft's head.
FOLLOWING PAGES A number of Thom Enriquez designs for the Stay Puft marshmallow man that experiment with differing approaches to height, mass, and shape.

Pops Marshmellows into his mouth, swallowing them whole

Bowls Marshmellow into a stack of Marshmellows and then breaks into a laugh.

Bouncy marshmellow man

• unconnected joints
• animated

looked a lot like the Michelin Man. I used the storyboards as a blueprint, and we put the camera where we thought the shot would work."

The crew chose to shoot Stay Puft at an overcranked rate of seventy-two frames per second, which would make his human-performed motions look slow and gargantuan when played back at normal speed.

"I was looking at the motion and the weight, but the marshmallow man was doing an animated, double-bounce walk, like in the old Mickey Mouse era of animation," says Bruno. Adds Bryan, "I gave a gentle genuflection with each step. To time it out I would say, *boom, boom, boom* to myself at the proper rhythm."

The character's peppy gait looked silly when performed at full speed but was effective when slowed down. "It broke up his rhythm so there was always something moving. It wasn't left foot, right foot, left foot, right foot, there was a double bounce in between, but looking at it while it was being filmed, you would have thought we were crazy."

Reitman apparently was among those questioning the effect team's sanity. "We showed Ivan and he was shocked," says Bruno. "He was like, 'I can't believe that the end of my movie is based on this piece of crap' or something worse. He actually got depressed. So I said, 'No, no, it's going to be funny, it's going to be OK. This is just a test.'"

Another problem, according to Bryan, was an uncomfortable wrinkling effect occurring between Stay Puft's legs. "When we viewed it in the screening room, the soft foam was compressing in the crotch area," he says. "[Effects advisor] John Berg demanded we make a fiberglass shell to hold everything rigid. I suggested a layer of semi-rigid foam, and they gave me a day to demonstrate my solution, but the second test was a home run."

Some moments proved superfluous to the story of Stay Puft's rampage, including his transformation into a third form—envisioned in concept art as a colossal skeleton and a dinosaur-like horned demon—and his emergence from the waters of the East River. For the latter, Edlund emphasized the overall cost savings to the production if the monster simply conjured itself into existence at Columbus Circle.

Bill Bryan sculpted Stay Puft and performed the marshmallow man's movements from inside, but the demands of the effects required a rapid ramp-up in staffing. "Bill used foam material and would carve it with an electric knife," says Stuart Ziff. "He made the whole costume. But the thing just grew and grew, and I think eventually we had fourteen or fifteen people [working on it]. We rented a different space just for his crew, because it took so much room to make the Stay Puft costumes. Because the latex rubber head could only be moved so much, you had to make one with the mouth wide open, and another for when it was happy. And a whole other set of costumes had to be made for the stuntman, when he was on fire."

BRILLSTEIN CO/ RHINOCORP 1983

At first the monster is glimpsed only in part, as a pale, bobbing head visible in the gaps as it passes behind rooftops. Model shop supervisor Mark Stetson helped set up the shot. "For the peek-a-boo scene, that row of buildings in the foreground was actually recycled from *Blade Runner*," he reveals. Barely visible are tiny bits of detritus on each rooftop—wine bottles, old mattresses, tar buckets—plus a miniature pigeon coop, sculpted as a joke in response to an unworkable request to work an animated flock of startled pigeons into the scene.

In the next shot, Stay Puft is revealed in full next to buildings that reflect his enormous scale. "There was a discussion of how big the marshmallow man should be," says Bruno. "Some people said Godzilla, but Ivan didn't want that." Faced with two camps arguing for both 100 and 125 feet, Reitman chose to split the difference. "Finally, Ivan said, 'He's 112½ feet tall.' So we scaled everything to that."

That meant a stretch of Central Park West needed to be built to match the scale of Bryan's Stay Puft costume, including miniature buildings, trees, taxi cabs, and fire hydrants. These shots would be captured from a high angle, simulating what the ghostbusters would see from their vantage point on the build-

ing's rooftop. "We didn't add anything [optically] to the shot; it's just a marshmallow man stepping on cars," says Bruno.

Stay Puft's 112½-foot height meant that the doomed cars would need to appear at ⅛18 scale. Model shop supervisor Mark Stetson scoured local toy stores in vain to find vehicles that would fit the bill. "We finally found one police car at Toys "R" Us that was the right size," he says. "Our purchaser in the model shop basically called every Toys "R" Us in Southern California and bought them all. We ended up with about fifty or sixty, and we turned them into fire chief cars and taxis. Because we were planning to shoot at speed, the police cars had to be refit so the blinking lights on top would flash really fast."

Miniature vehicles got into gear by means of a simple wire pull. "We'd go 3-2-1 and try to get everyone to pull at the same time, so the cars were all moving for three seconds," says Bruno. Other cars motored down the street using an even more primitive method. "We'd just gravity roll them down the slope, like in the pinewood derby," says Stetson.

In one sequence, Stetson maneuvered a moving car into a tiny hydrant, which sprayed a jet of sand that, on camera, looked like water. "We used a little spray gun rigged underneath

TOP Fiberglass Stay Puft heads prior to foam "skin" application. Mechanism designer Lance Anderson can be seen behind. **ABOVE** Two Stay Puft maquettes, the left one showing his badly burned look. **RIGHT** An unused, melty-mouth Stay Puft head. **OPPOSITE TOP** The full-size Stay Puft suit is prepped for filming as VFX director of photography Bill Neill takes a light meter reading. **OPPOSITE BOTTOM** Stay Puft concept art by Ron Croci.

the tabletop and pumped through a pipe," he says. "It was silica, like sand-blasting sand."

Bill Bryan, inside the Stay Puft suit, took care of the marshmallow man's footsteps and body language. "I had a radio headset, so I could get instructions from the FX director Bill Neal," recalls Bryan. "He would tell me when to pull in my arm so I wouldn't knock over a streetlight. When I had to look up at the guys, the head wasn't made to look up, so I had to lean way back. To keep from falling over I sat on [sculptor] Linda Frobos's back."

Frobos handled the final design of Stay Puft's face, and Ziff reveals that the marshmallow man wears the subtle influence of its crafter. "If you look at the head of Stay Puft, and you look at a picture of her, you can see her eyes and the bridge of her nose."

Stay Puft's precise facial expressions fell to a team of off-screen operators. "The cables that operated the face went from the back of his leg into a slot in the floor to four puppeteers on a cart, who were pulled along on a rope like a mine car," says Bruno. "They had monitors so they could see what the camera saw. When he looked up, the puppeteers would move his eyebrows and mouth and eyes."

After putting his foot through the roof of the Holy Trinity Lutheran Church, Stay Puft begins to scale the side of the building to execute the four mortals who dared challenge a god. The ghostbusters make their counterattack, fire roasting Stay

Study for the Stay Puff Giant and street scene: "ghostbusters"

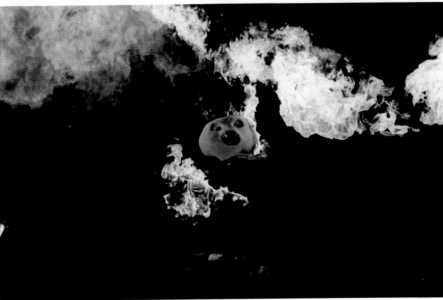

Puft's marshmallowy bulk with their proton streams. Bryan notes that, in the first quick shot of the blast, Stay Puft isn't wearing his tie. "[Effects artist] Joe Viskocil was adding flash bulbs and spark generators to the bib when I tried to attach the tie," he recalls, "and didn't want to lean on it and mess it up. Later, I awoke at 2:00 a.m. sweating, 'He wasn't wearing his tie!' I told Michael Gross, but he said, 'There's so much going on in that shot nobody will notice.'"

To film the flames, the crew deployed a fire-retardant version of the Stay Puft costume incorporating an outer layer of flammable Scott foam and an inner layer of fireproof Pyrothane, all to shield a stuntman wearing a protective Nomex suit and breathing his own air supply.

"The first few takes were with the stunt coordinator's son in the suit," says Bryan. "Joe Viskocil had made a hedgehog-like array of tiny mortars on the front of the suit, and each one held a morsel of strontium, which burns red. When the pyrotechnics were activated he just stood, waiting for his cue, and finally started moving on 'Cut!'"

Later shots occurred with Tony Cesar, a stunt artist described by Bryan as "the fire-gag king."

"Tony was brought in and we knocked out the rest of the shots," he says. "Joe Viskocil would slather rubber cement on part of the suit and ignite it. Tony would climb or wave, signal to be extinguished, and treat it all as a regular day at work. We built eight suits, and we burned seven of them. Once he was burning, each take was a suit."

Not even the mighty marshmallow man can survive the shockwave when the ghostbusters make the decision to cross their proton streams. The shot of Stay Puft incinerated by fire was achieved by pointing the face of a marshmallow head at

the ceiling and hitting it with a flamethrower blast from above. As bits of the face loosened, gravity pulled them off and away.

"When he comes up over the top and gets blasted by fire, I think we shot it one frame every two seconds and we wound up skip-framing it to make it happen even faster," says Edlund. "That was a one-take thing—we only had time to do it once. And it worked."

The sequence could have been far more gruesome had the team followed the shooting script, in which the peeling pieces of Stay Puft expose "horrid musculature and a skeletal rib cage."

For Bruno, the Stay Puft shoot exemplified the loose, exploratory tone of the entire production. "We would just shoot stuff and turn it in," he says. "It was, 'This is the way we're going to do the marshmallow man sequence and we're proceeding,' so there was no second guessing. Short and sweet. We didn't want to make a shot that was one second long last for eight seconds.

"We didn't even know it would work until we saw the dailies, because it looked stupid in real life. The whole thing was just really crazy."

OPPOSITE Inside a fireproof Stay Puft costume, a stunt performer prepares to be ignited by Joe Viskocil. **TOP LEFT** Flames overtake the Stay Puft costume. **TOP RIGHT** The crew preps Stay Puft's head for incineration. **ABOVE** Jets of flame melt the specially created Stay Puft head.

14. TOTAL PROTONIC REVERSAL

Dana's apartment building—crowned by the otherworldly Gozer temple—bears the brunt of the marshmallow man's assault and suffers the explosive result of crossing four proton streams at once. Boss Films needed to construct a building replica that could absorb the damage and remain standing.

Mark Stetson supervised the construction of the miniature tower, beginning at the eighth floor. "It was 1/17 or 1/18 scale, and it was about twenty feet high including all the bottom floors," he says. "We didn't build it all the way down to the street level and the entry façade, only the upper floors.

"Usually we drew up buildings ourselves, but we got construction drawings from the production art department. John DeCuir actually did our construction drawings for us. It was fantastic, and I've never seen anything like it since."

Nearly as soon as it was completed, the top of the building had to go. Mechanical effects supervisor Thaine Morris worked with Stetson to plan an explosion of sufficient force to obliterate the upper stories.

"Thaine did the pyro work, but we did the prep work of building a blast cage and the breakaway pieces that blew out of it," says Stetson. "I spoke with Thaine about how to build the cage inside the temple to withstand the blast. We wanted a cruciform shape, as if it was blasting out each of the doors. Thaine specified that we build it out of welded quarter-inch steel, and we put a blast diverter inside the ceiling of the temple area to push the blast out like an inverted pyramid."

The detonation proved so strong that a tiny bench, launched airborne by the burst, ricocheted off the safety Plexiglas and grazed photographer Virgil Mirano's head.

"He was crouched behind a parapet on a rooftop next to it, on a warehouse building that was probably twenty feet tall and sixty or eighty feet from the model as it was blowing up," recalls Stetson. "He was very proudly wearing a bandage the next day."

A high-speed camera captured the explosion at more than 250 frames per second. "It blew so quickly we had to look at the footage to see what we had," says John Bruno, who adds that Ivan Reitman worried that the blast might be *too* spectacular. "Ivan freaked out and said 'They'd be killed!' But that's the joke!"

A final effect for the apartment involved the ominous rings of roiling vapor that form in the skies above it. Boss Films built a 1,500-gallon cloud tank and used paint injections and layered densities of saltwater and fresh water to conjure up the atmospheric phenomena.

"We built a huge cloud tank so we could shoot the clouds above Gozer temple," says Edlund. "You fill it up with water and you fill half the tank with salt brine, then you put a piece of plastic on top of that and fill the rest with fresh water. You carefully roll the plastic up and take it out, and basically what you have is fresh water floating on salt water. Then you squirt

tempera paint onto that surface, and it's like an inversion layer, and when the paint hits the salt water, it floats on that surface."

Some of the effects handed to Edlund and Boss Films couldn't be completed by deadline. A scene in which the possessed Louis Tully scares off a group of muggers by spewing ectoplasmic energy from his mouth numbered among the casualties. As the end of postproduction neared, Richard Edlund took a hard line with Reitman to bring his expectations in line with reality.

"He wanted to add like, a hundred shots," Edlund says. "I thought, that's going to kill everybody—we don't have enough adrenaline to do that many shots. So I met him in the parking lot with my samurai sword saying, 'You've got to make a cut, Ivan!'"

With the final shots in the can, Boss Films completed its work on *Ghostbusters*. Stuart Ziff recalls the crew's last day at the ghost shop. "As we were shutting down, my assistant gets on the PA and goes, 'OK, everyone can take anything they want!' It was a mad grab. The big creatures were taken back to Columbia, but with any little bits it was, 'I get a claw, you get this, another person gets that.' It was a mistake. Feeding frenzy at the fat farm, that's what it was."

All told, the visual effects for *Ghostbusters* provided a phenomenal view of the film's paranormal world and cost an estimated $5.6 million. "You learn by doing," says Edlund. "You basically get painted into a corner and have to figure out how to invent your way out of it. You come up with a means to the end."

"There were some rough edges, but at the same time that kind of funkiness kind of works for the movie."

OPPOSITE The upper floors of the miniature apartment building explode with a controlled, shaped detonation. **ABOVE** The miniature's upper stories incorporated a blast cage welded from quarter-inch steel. Mark Stetson (right) prepares the structure for the coming pyrotechnics.

FOR YOUR CONSIDERATION.

BEST ORIGINAL SCORE
ELMER BERNSTEIN

GH😮STBUSTERS

15. HOW ABOUT A LITTLE MUSIC?

Elmer Bernstein had composed sweeping, epic scores for films such as Cecil B. DeMille's *The Ten Commandments* and the Western classic *The Magnificent Seven*. Yet Bernstein was no stranger to comedies. After meeting Ivan Reitman during the production of John Landis's *Animal House*, the composer entered into a fruitful partnership with the young director, collaborating on *Stripes*, *Heavy Metal*, and *Spacehunter*. After signing on for *Ghostbusters*, Bernstein began reviewing raw footage in December 1983. The new movie required a score both lighthearted and petrifying, and Bernstein didn't have much time.

"It was a complex relationship," says Michael C. Gross. "It started with Ivan's approach to doing comedy, which is to ground it in reality. By using Elmer Bernstein to do the score, there was not a lot of *mwack, mwack* . . . that will tell you that a joke just happened. When [Bernstein's] music played, it underplayed the comedy."

"I think one of the reasons that the scores I've written for [comedies] work, is that I do not denigrate the film," Elmer Bernstein told the magazine *Cinefantastique* in 1985. "I don't try to do anything hokey or make the music funny. My theory is that if the comedy is working in the film, let the film do the comedy, and let the music get behind the emotion or action. You have to

believe, along with these guys, that the ghosts really do exist. The score had to walk a very fine line. What I did was to create a kind of an 'antic' theme for them—it's kind of cute, without being really way out. The last part of the film, with the possession and the climax on top of the building, was much easier to do conceptually."

The animated, playful tune that backs the core cast members when they appear on screen was dubbed the "Ghostbusters Theme." Other highlights of the score include the delicate notes of "Dana's Theme," while a rare French instrument, the ondes Martenot, produced theremin-like oscillations that contributed to the otherworldly atmosphere of pieces like "Zuul."

Peter Bernstein had worked with his father for ten years by the time of *Ghostbusters*, and, with David Spear, served as one of the film's two orchestrators. He and Spear created fleshed-out versions of Elmer Bernstein's compressed-score "sketches," allowing the full pieces to be performed by musicians.

"I'd be sitting next to Ivan in the recording booth, and my father would be out in the recording room conducting the orchestra with the picture projected in front of him," he recalls. "The epic music had to sell that the ghosts were real and terrifying. For the bouncy theme, he was playing with the light-

OPPOSITE A trade industry advertisement aimed at securing an Oscar nomination for Elmer Bernstein. **BELOW LEFT** The album cover for Elmer Bernstein's *Ghostbusters* score. **BELOW RIGHT** Composer Elmer Bernstein.

heartedness of the film itself. He said that it was one of the more difficult jobs he'd ever had, because he was walking the fine line between comedy and drama. He and Ivan spoke constantly about how to toe that line."

The Jazz-Age ondes Martenot generated appropriately ethereal, ghostly noises, but the *Ghostbusters* score also benefitted from a more modern invention. "There was a new synthesizer on the market, the Yamaha DX-7," says Peter Bernstein. "The first commercially available, relatively inexpensive synth. They were imported into the United States from Japan in horrifyingly small numbers and were horrifyingly popular.

"My father just happened to be friends with the main Yamaha instrument importer in Los Angeles, so I showed up at the back door and carted one of these things out of there. The very first note of the *Ghostbusters* score—when the torch on the Columbia figure blazes forth—that's a factory-programmed DX-7 sound. It might be the first use of a DX-7 in a film score."

Despite this opportunity to add innovative touches, *Ghostbusters* was operating on a compressed schedule, with unfinished visual-effects shots of undetermined length that presented a major challenge for Bernstein. "The way my father and Ivan normally worked is that they would have recording sessions spaced by several days, where they could discuss and make changes because Ivan didn't like to put him on the spot in front of an orchestra," says Peter Bernstein. "But this time he didn't have any choice. The film was being mixed down the hall; as soon as a piece of music was recorded, it was rushed down there. The second-to-last day, not all the special effects were ready, and the film had a piece of blank film in it, called a slug. An associate producer came up to the podium and said to my father, 'There's a slug in this cue where the special effect would be.' Then my father asked him, very routinely, 'Well, is the slug the right length?' And he answered, 'I don't know.'

"That resulted in a major temper tantrum—a bit terrifying, and a bit hilarious. And after half an hour everyone got over it."

Like everything else on *Ghostbusters*, the composition and recording of the musical score went right down to the wire. "After

that particular session ended, the next day was the final day of recording," says Peter Bernstein. "There was probably fifteen minutes of the movie to score, and none of the music was written. None. After everybody left at five in the afternoon, my father sat down at the piano and put together 'roadmaps' for his orchestrators, myself, and David Spear. He would say, 'Take Q3M7 and copy bars 1 to 40 but transpose them up a whole step.' And he would write eight or ten bars of connecting music, and then say, 'Now go to Q6M2 and use bars 30 to 40 in their original key.' Two hours later, David and I took these roadmaps, went back to my house, and worked from nine at night until five in the morning to have the music ready to play in the studio by 10 o'clock."

Musically, *Ghostbusters* attracted a large amount of attention for Ray Parker Jr.'s iconic hit single. During several key sequences, Ivan Reitman included additional pop songs in the film in lieu of orchestral accompaniment.

"It was a transitional stage," says Peter Bernstein. "My father was a champion of the art of film scoring, so he was very ambivalent about what Ivan was going to do, even though he loved Ivan." Reitman has nothing but praise for Bernstein's role. "Ray Parker Jr.'s ['Ghostbusters'] turned out to be the number one song in 1984, but really it's Elmer Bernstein's score that makes the movie work," he says. "His music gives the film its weight and grandeur."

One nighttime scene, featuring Winston Zeddemore behind the wheel of the Ectomobile engaging Ray Stantz in a chat about Jesus, was originally intended to be backed by a pop song. Peter Bernstein composed an orchestral accompaniment just in case, which ultimately remained intact in the final film (labeled "Judgment Day" in the full soundtrack release).

Looking back, Peter Bernstein is satisfied with Reitman's balance of musical styles: "I have no problem with it artistically. They were taking song submissions at the same time the score was being written, and I think it works great."

BUSTIN' MAKES ME FEEL GOOD

"I've had a great career," says Ray Parker Jr. "I've personally written twenty-nine hit records. But nothing comes close to 'Ghostbusters.'"

Everyone knows the song, from its upbeat bass line to its call-and-response chorus. Released as a single for radio airplay, "Ghostbusters" spawned multiple catchphrases ("Who you gonna call?" and "I ain't afraid of no ghost.") and spent three weeks in the top spot on the Billboard Hot 100. Yet it nearly didn't happen at all.

Ivan Reitman didn't need a single, only a short snippet of music to accompany the movie's intro. Early versions of the script had included a promotional jingle during the *Ghostbusters'* TV commercial (sample lyric: "If you have a ghost, but you don't want to play host, you can't sleep at all, so who do you call? They can be bad houseguests, and all-night pests, you can't sleep at all, so who do you call? Ghostbusters, Ghostbusters!"), and Reitman wanted this short piece to be just as effective at delivering the movie's name and tagline. Efforts by other musicians—including Hughes/Thrall, featuring former Deep Purple bassist Glenn Hughes—didn't pass muster. Then Ray Parker Jr. came on board to record a demo.

"They had hired people for a year trying to write the same song," he says. "A buddy of mine who worked at Columbia Pictures said, 'I think you're the right man to do this. You'll make this, the humor, the whole thing.' And I said, 'Yeah, I don't know.'

"I had retired, because my mom and dad were sick. I was young, I was twenty-eight years old, and I was trying to figure out what else I wanted to do with my life. When I got to California I got a call to go see this movie, and I said, 'You guys don't understand, I'm not working.' I remember the offer was to stay two more days, see this film, and see what I could come up with."

Parker Jr. immediately ran into a logjam over how to work the mandated term *ghostbusters* into the lyrics of a hit song. "Nobody could figure out how to say 'ghostbusters' to music," he explains. "It's unfair now because you've already heard the song, but if you just heard *ghoooostbustersss* and tried to put that to music, that's a very unfriendly word to sing. So the biggest thing for me was to decide *not* to sing. I don't sing 'ghostbusters,' I let the crowd scream 'ghostbusters.'

"It was an eighteen-year-old girl and her friends, and before they went to high school they did it for me. It was early in the morning, and they were just screaming at the top of their lungs, having the greatest time. And somehow that transferred into the song."

The music production seemed similarly charmed with an infusion of positive magic. "There was just nothing, absolutely nothing I could do wrong to screw this record up," says Parker Jr. "I think of it as if God took the electric current and went through me like a ghost. When I went into the studio, the drums sounded right. The guitars sounded right. The bass sounded right. Anything I hooked up that day just sounded great.

"I stayed up all night, came up with the lyrics, and came up with the idea," he continues. "The director heard it and said, 'That's wonderful—maybe we should make a record.' I was scared to death, because I'd only done a verse and a half—one verse, one chorus. My vocal was supposed to be a demo vocal for the background singers. I kept saying, 'We're gonna have the girls here,' but he said, 'No, no, I like the way you're singing.' And he was a Jewish guy from Montreal, so his lingo was a little different from mine. When I was singing 'I ain't afraid of no ghosts' he was asking, 'What are you saying?'"

Ivan Reitman directed the "Ghostbusters" music video, which featured celebrity cameos from Chevy Chase, John Candy, Carly Simon, Al Franken, Melissa Gilbert, Danny DeVito, and more. The video ends with the ghostbusters—Bill Murray, Harold Ramis, Ernie Hudson, and Dan Aykroyd—dancing in formation through Times Square with Ray Parker Jr. in the lead.

"For them, it didn't happen until the end," says Parker Jr. "They were done with the film, and then they're thrown out into New York and are like 'Who the hell is this guy?' Then all of a sudden they're hearing the song. They're my first audience." The five quickly forged on-camera camaraderie; when Bill Murray humorously fails to execute a break-dance spin, Parker Jr. gives him a push. "That's me spinning Bill around in a circle," he says. "We were all friendly. We all got along."

The 1984 Academy Award nominations included a nod for Ray Parker Jr.'s "Ghostbusters" in the category of Best Song, though it lost out to Stevie Wonder's "I Just Called to Say I Love You."

A best-selling soundtrack album, anchored by "Ghostbusters," featured other songs from the film including Alessi's "Savin' the Day," "Cleanin' Up the Town" by The BusBoys, Mick Smiley's "Magic," and two selections from Elmer Bernstein's orchestral score. Among the rarities released in conjunction with the single was a twelve-inch vinyl picture disc emblazoned with the red-and-white No-Ghost logo. It featured an instrumental version of "Ghostbusters" and a remix entitled "Searchin' for the Spirit."

The song spread around the world at lightning speed. "A friend of mine was in Africa, and a guy was carrying a boom box playing 'Ghostbusters,'" recalls Joe Medjuck. "The Olympics were that summer, and when Ivan went to some event, the band started playing 'Ghostbusters.' It was everywhere."

It also served as a wake-up call to studios that music could be an effective cross-promoter for movies. "That really changed things," says Parker Jr. "People didn't know that the song could be that advantageous to the film. And it's so cheap to promote the record. We're already buying all these posters, TV time, Super Bowl time—if you could get a song to do that, all you gotta do is spend a few hundred grand to promote the song. We spend a few hundred grand on a billboard."

Ray Parker Jr. still can't quite believe the song's impact on global pop culture.

"I can't even call it American folklore, because it's international. It's like saying 'hello' or 'happy birthday.' It's a universal thing."

OPPOSITE TOP Ray Parker Jr. joins Harold Ramis, Bill Murray, Dan Aykroyd, and Ernie Hudson during filming of the "Ghostbusters" music video. **BELOW** Cover for the extended-version UK single for "Ghostbusters."

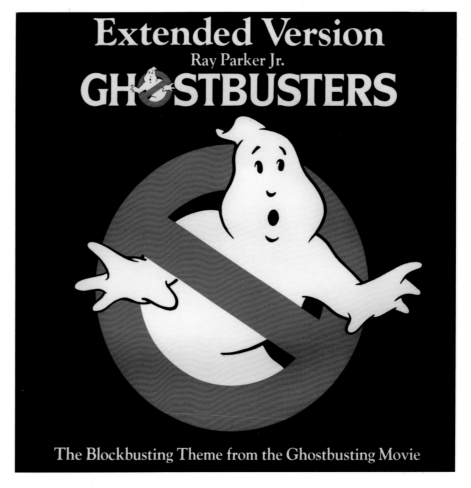

Extended Version
Ray Parker Jr.
GHOSTBUSTERS

The Blockbusting Theme from the Ghostbusting Movie

16. SUPERNATURAL SUCCESS STORY

The early teaser poster hanging in theaters to advertise *Ghostbusters* didn't list the names of the movie's A-list stars, or offer up headshots of their likeable, bankable faces. It didn't even list the movie's *name*. The stark black poster bore only a No-Ghost logo and the words, "Coming to Save the World This Summer."

As the June 8, 1984, release date neared, an official one-sheet poster replaced the teaser and fulfilled the promise of its mysterious tagline. "They're Here to Save the World," it announced, above an action shot of the costumed trio of Murray, Aykroyd, and Ramis and large type promoting costars Sigourney Weaver and Rick Moranis.

The June 8 date meant that *Ghostbusters* would be swimming in the wake of the juggernaut sequel *Indiana Jones and the Temple of Doom*—released two weeks prior—and fighting for air with another scare-based comedy debuting on the same day, Joe Dante's *Gremlins*.

"We were worried about the opening," admits Joe Medjuck. "We were opening opposite *Gremlins*, which had Spielberg's name on it, and the sequel to Indiana Jones opened that summer. But I remember Bill turning to Ivan at one point and saying, 'Don't worry, [*Ghostbusters*] is a freight train. Just get out of the way.'"

Ghostbusters won the opening weekend box office title, the first of seven straight number one performances. Critics loved the film. "Rarely has a movie this expensive provided so many quotable lines," wrote Roger Ebert in the *Chicago Sun-Times*.

"I think one of the nicest reviews we got for this movie said the whole film was like a perfectly told joke," remembered Harold Ramis in 1999.[16]

The movie broke Columbia's own record for best opening week, but it needed to keep growing to become popular. Fortunately, word of mouth helped *Ghostbusters* maintain its lead with box office grosses increasing week over week. By August the film had steamrolled its way past *Tootsie* to become the top movie comedy of all time.

In a canny promotional move by Ivan Reitman, the Ghostbusters TV commercial seen in the movie began unexpectedly popping up throughout the summer in late-night advertising breaks across the United States. At the end of the spot, a toll-free telephone number allowed fans who dialed it to hear a prerecorded bit featuring Venkman and Stantz (in new lines laid down by Bill Murray and Dan Aykroyd), as if callers had reached the answering machine at the ghostbusters' HQ.

Eddie Murphy's *Beverly Hills Cop*, released in December, took *Ghostbusters*' crown as the biggest movie of 1984, but a *Ghostbusters* re-release in August 1985 pushed the movie back on top. When the dust settled, *Ghostbusters* had made more than $225 million, Columbia had a new crown jewel, and the film's cast had become international celebrities.

"I was world famous for being dickless," remembers William Atherton. "It was kind of hard because I had a very large opinion of myself, and I may not have been as gracious at conveying that as I could have been."

"We knew we had a hit," says Michael C. Gross. "We just knew it. What we didn't know was that it would be a phenomenon. We did the box office, we thought it was good, but we certainly had no idea that it would take on a life of its own."

The movie's winning mix of chills and wry wit hung on the appeal of its core characters, whose brainpower underscored their raw courage when they stood united to prevent the earth's destruction. "They're the smartest guys in the room," says Reitman. "Even when they're acting silly, or they're making mistakes."

No longer just a movie, *Ghostbusters* had become a marvel. "About a year later I was having a conversation with Ivan," remembers Gross. "I said, 'You know, the way this is going, twenty or thirty years from now this is going to be a generation's *Wizard of Oz*.

"You don't plan that. You can't make an icon happen."

PART 2

THE SEQUEL

17. WILL THERE BE ANY MORE OF THEM?

"It's not going to be called *Ghostbusters II*," promised Bill Murray in March 1989.[17] "We'll burn in hell if we call it *Ghostbusters II*. I've suggested *The Last of the Ghostbusters*, to make sure there won't be anything like a *Ghostbusters III*. But the script is nowhere near ready, and we start shooting soon."

Getting *Ghostbusters II* to the big screen turned out to be an enormous challenge for all involved, and as a result, the project spent half a decade in gestation.

"[The studio] wanted to do it immediately, but everybody had other things going on in their lives," says Dan Aykroyd. "The five-year gap happened not because anyone was delaying it. It was just the evolution of how it got made, because we were all doing other things."

The ghostbusters hadn't been entirely absent from the public's consciousness in that stretch, at least not among the youngest fans. An animated series, *The Real Ghostbusters*, and a top-selling toy line gave the franchise momentum, but ironically hampered the sequel's success according to Michael C. Gross.

"[The animated series] turned out to have a life of its own," says Gross, who co-produced the cartoon. "We had toys for the kids who had seen the movie before, and then we had their younger brothers playing with the toys too. In a way, it was their product now—kids were playing the [video] games, et cetera. They were so familiar with that, so how the hell do

we do the sequel? To some degree—through the fact there was a toy line and a cartoon show for so long—people thought they'd seen [the sequel] in all those configurations. And it weakened our position."

It was a tall order: how to follow up one of the biggest films of all time. The original had a lightning-in-a-bottle quality, and no one knew if they could capture the same sparks.

Other factors that led to a lack of focus included British film producer David Puttnam, who took control of Columbia Pictures in 1986. Puttnam had no interest in green-lighting a sequel to *Ghostbusters*.

"That was a blip on the radar," says Reitman. "Really, it was that we didn't want to do it. For the longest period we just found no reason. We felt very happy with the first film, and we all had other things we wanted to do."

When Dawn Steel, former vice president of production at Paramount, replaced Puttnam as head of Columbia in 1987, she made *Ghostbusters II* a priority. At a lunch she chaired at Jimmy's restaurant in Beverly Hills, Murray, Ramis, Aykroyd, Reitman, and Murray's agent Michael Ovitz reunited around a single table. By the time the principals said their goodbyes, a *Ghostbusters* sequel had momentum.

"I think walking into the meeting no one really felt we'd make the movie," said Murray.[18] "But in the course of lunch we

PREVIOUS PAGES At center, Ivan Reitman joins his cast in this publicity still for *Ghostbusters II*: (clockwise from upper left) Harold Ramis, Sigourney Weaver, Bill Murray, Ernie Hudson, and Dan Aykroyd. **BELOW** The four original ghostbusters suited up again for the sequel. **OPPOSITE** Aykroyd and Murray pose for a *Ghostbusters II* publicity shot.

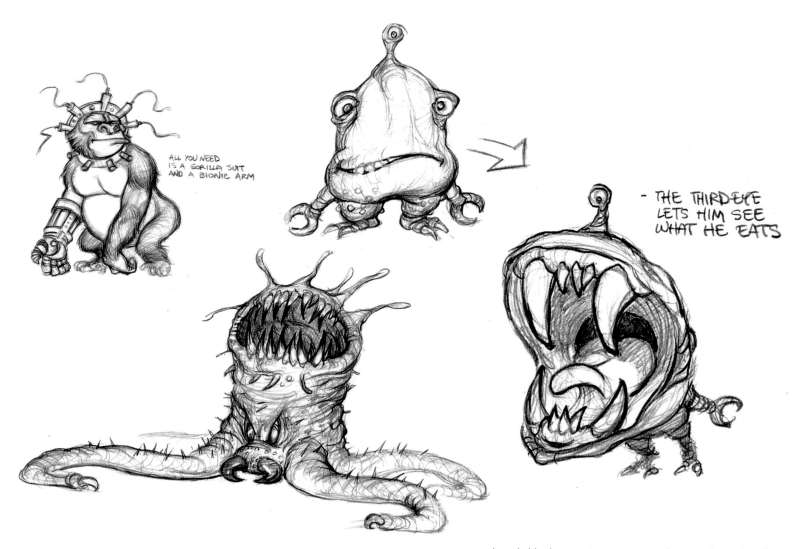

ALL YOU NEED IS A GORILLA SUIT AND A BIONIC ARM

- THE THIRD EYE LETS HIM SEE WHAT HE EATS

had so many laughs and so much fun that it became clear we'd really enjoy working together again."

The emotional and professional bonds uniting the core *Ghostbusters* team went a long way toward clinching Murray's participation. "There's a certain amount of enjoyment you get just from seeing the people," said Murray.[19] "I really enjoy [...] unconsciously is funnier than [...] making Harold laugh because [...] is an easy laugh, but in the [...] become a businessman. He [...] really has the weight of the [...] you make someone like that [...] doing everyone he sees that [...] would want to come back," [...] ration of Independence 2!' No, [...] we probably should have left [...] Harold and Dan were convinced that they could make something a little worthwhile, so we said, 'Oh, what the heck? Let's go out there on the edge.' You know, they'll crucify us if it's no good, so let's try it."

Months of deal making followed. The movie ultimately received a budget similar to that of the first film—approximately $30 million—thanks to its stars accepting lower salaries in exchange for a back-end percentage of the profits. Dawn Steel staked the success of *Ghostbusters II* on the studio's financial health.[21] "In the dollars and cents point of view,

it's probably the most important, eagerly awaited sequel in the history of Columbia Pictures."

I HAVE ALL NEW CHEAP MOVES

In a first-draft screenplay for *Ghostbusters II*, Dan Aykroyd returned to the more outlandish universe he had invented for his original *Ghostbusters* script treatment. Believing that the sequel should leave New York City behind, Aykroyd wrote a story in which a kidnapped Dana Barrett is taken to Scotland where she encounters fairies and an underground civilization.

As co-writer, Harold Ramis contributed concepts including the idea that the bustin' business had expanded to become the worldwide conglomerate "Ghostbusters Inc." Another idea involved a baby—possibly the child of Dana Barrett and Peter Venkman—who received preternatural reflexes through ghostly possession.

"[It was] an effect I once thought about, of an infant not yet able to walk who suddenly wakes up one day with adult agility and focus," said Ramis.[22] "I had originally thought of it as a horror story, but then I decided it was just too horrible for a movie."

The duo of Aykroyd and Ramis soon hit on an ethical element that could power the theme and drive the plot of the movie. Their notion—that negative emotions could manifest as physical consequences—meant that the ectoplasmic slime popularized in *Ghostbusters* would be back in a big way.

"The whole key was Harold and [me] talking about psychic energy and ectoplasm and how negative energy can affect a

DR. PETER VENKMAN

Business:
110 North Moore Street
New York, NY 10012
(212) 555-6311

Residence:
14 Beecher Street
New York, NY 10019
(212) 555-8027

ABOVE Potential ghost ideas for *Ghostbusters II* by concept artist Henry Mayo.

whole city," says Aykroyd. "And maybe there was so much of it in New York City that there might be some tangible example of it. That's how we came up with the river of slime. Once we had that and the abduction of the baby we combined them and were able to come up with the second movie."

Ramis shared similar thoughts:[23] "The moral issue was important to us. The source of the slime would come from negative human behavior. Comedically, it suggested, what if everyone in New York City had to be nice for forty-eight hours?"

For Ramis, this was an opportunity to approach the comedy in a way that had some underlying substance:[24] "We try to do comedy that's usually thought of as dumb and broad, but in the most intelligent way we can and with some deeply buried theme somewhere. We try to keep the morality straight."

Emotional slime seemed too abstract to be the actual villain, so Ramis and Aykroyd introduced Vigo the Carpathian as the puppet master behind the latest supernatural crisis. "Vigo came out of the idea of the Carpathians, the Dracu, Vlad the Impaler—that part of the world where there was a lot of demonology and possession and magic," says Aykroyd. "We drew on Sumerian mythology for the first movie, and we drew on Carpathian mythology for the second movie. Vigo was an invention of Harold and myself, almost like a Dracula figure."

Through it all, Aykroyd and Ramis fixed their attention on the three characters they had created years ago as the archetypes of brains, heart, and mouth. Audiences had connected with the comedic interplay between Egon Spengler, Ray Stantz, and Peter Venkman, and the writers knew that element would prove far more important than story mechanics.

As the story took shape, returning concept artist Thom Enriquez helped provide visual definition. "Michael Gross, Ivan, and Harold Ramis would be pitching a sequence to me, and I would doodle my first impressions of the staging or what the ghosts might do," he says. Working closely with the core team had its benefits, especially for an artist with a young child.

"I came into work one day and I had my son with me," says Enriquez. "He was about five, and he had seen the first *Ghostbusters* so he was totally into it. Dan Aykroyd and Harold Ramis were in the next office, and I told my son to knock on the door. I had told them he was coming, so he knocked, and they opened it and went into character. My son turned to me and goes, 'Dad, they're real!'"

WELL, BETTER LATE THAN NEVER

Ivan Reitman was set to return as director of *Ghostbusters II*, but the film's projected summer 1989 release date required him to juggle competing schedules. Reitman still needed to deliver his Danny DeVito/Arnold Schwarzenegger comedy *Twins* in time for a 1988 holiday debut.

BELOW Thom Enriquez contributed this ghost concept as a possible design for the kidnapper ghoul in the apartment ledge sequence (which would ultimately become the ghost nanny).

"We were in postproduction on *Twins* and Ivan was in the editing room a lot, but that just made it easier to find him," recalls Joe Medjuck. "Basically we never let the editors leave the editing room. One day the name on the door was *Twins*, and when we were starting to shoot we just put up a sign saying *Ghostbusters*."

Michael C. Gross joined Joe Medjuck in the ranks of the re-enlistees, with both men promoted to executive producer. Physical effects supervisor Chuck Gaspar agreed to oversee the creation of in-camera physical effects, applying the lessons he had learned on *Ghostbusters* to achieve new hauntings in the sequel.

"All the pieces were in the right place at the right time," says Gross. "The actors, the writers, Ivan, all said OK, let's do a sequel. And I guess it was no surprise—when you go to number two you're seeing the car, the outfit, the firehouse, but you know what all of that is. The first movie, it was all a great surprise. The second movie, it's just something where you go, *ho hum*. We had a good story but it just didn't have the same feel as the first time."

Many new faces joined the behind-the-camera ranks. Michael Chapman (*Taxi Driver, Raging Bull*) replaced László Kovács as cinematographer, and production designer Bo Welch (*The Lost Boys, Beetlejuice*) signed on to perform the job previously handled by John DeCuir.

Most significantly, the visual effects for *Ghostbusters II* would not go to Richard Edlund's Boss Films, instead landing with visual effects supervisor Dennis Muren at Industrial Light & Magic.

All players had assembled, but Joe Medjuck knew that movie magic couldn't be conjured by following a recipe. "You want to make it as good as the first one, which is really hard to do," he says. "It can never be that first love, 'I've never seen anything like this before.' But the studio wanted it out there. They understood the power of a sequel.

"The pressure was on us to try to make it good."

WE'RE BACK!

Ernie Hudson re-upped for a second tour as ghostbuster Winston Zeddemore. "I think the difference between [Winston in] the first film and the second film is he really considers them friends, which kind of parallels my own life," Hudson told MTV in 1989.[25] "When I first joined the group, they were just a bunch of crazy strange people. And I guess I've become a little crazy and strange because they all make sense to me."

Annie Potts—then a small-screen star thanks to the CBS sitcom *Designing Women*—returned as office secretary Janine Melnitz. Rick Moranis's nebbishy Louis Tully received an expanded role as the team's lawyer and accountant. While pursuing his dream of becoming the fifth ghostbuster, Louis strikes romantic sparks with Janine.

"We thought it was more effective with those two," says Reitman, of the decision to shift Janine's attention away from Egon. "I felt there was enough for Harold to do as a ghostbuster, and it was clear that both these secondary characters in the first movie deserved more space in the second one. It seemed a good way to break them out, that they would have some kind of romance together."

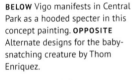

BELOW Vigo manifests in Central Park as a hooded specter in this concept painting. **OPPOSITE** Alternate designs for the baby-snatching creature by Thom Enriquez.

Sigourney Weaver's Dana Barrett once again served as the conduit for the netherworldly weirdness that threatens the Big Apple. A single mom who has sidelined her career as a cellist to work as a restorer at the Manhattan Museum of Art, Dana gets pulled into the action when her baby boy, Oscar, takes a terrifying, supernaturally fuelled buggy ride through 77th Street traffic.

Weaver felt that the sequel benefitted from the five-year filmmaking gap: "I think the bar was so high after the first one that I'm glad it took so long. I think we really needed to think about, was it possible to do it? And how would you create something that could stand on its own?

"The better a movie is, the more difficult and complicated it becomes to do a decent sequel," she continues. "It was a hard act to follow. But we all thought that it would be fun to continue the story, and to do a sort of older, soberer *Ghostbusters*."

"I think the story between Sigourney Weaver and Bill Murray and whose baby it is we never really explained," says Reitman. "It's apparently her ex-husband's, but we left it purposefully vague so it could actually be Bill's. There's a way that he deals with that child that is extraordinarily fatherly and lovely."

Casting director Michael Chinich hired a number of actors for all-new roles. Kurt Fuller became Jack Hardemeyer, the loathsome assistant to the mayor of New York (played again by David Margulies). Brian Doyle-Murray—Bill Murray's older brother—agreed to a small role as a skeptical psychiatrist. Wilhelm von Homburg lent Vigo the Carpathian his imposing physical presence. "We picked him because of his size and his look," says Joe Medjuck. "But his English wasn't that good." Vigo's menacing tones came courtesy of Max von Sydow.

YOU ARE LIKE THE BUZZING OF FLIES TO HIM!

Vigo the Carpathian may have been the script's "big bad," but the true antagonist of *Ghostbusters II* would be an odd, fastidious eccentric. Peter MacNicol, known for his roles in *Sophie's Choice* and *Dragonslayer*, signed on to portray Janosz Poha, Dana's colleague at the Manhattan Museum of Art, whose reverence for a painting of Vigo puts him under the Carpathian's spell. In the film, Janosz's romantic overtures to Dana are both menacing and pathetic.

"When I first read the script my character was named Jason, and he amounted to no more than a nondescript mind slave to Vigo," says MacNicol. "There was nothing the least bit foreign about Jason; he could have been played by most of the Screen Actors Guild.

"I happened to be in Los Angeles trying to get some film work. I had placed an ultimatum on myself that I couldn't return to New York until I got a job. Happily, I got the *Ghostbusters II* call within two days. I greedily read the script but couldn't find myself in it at all."

MacNicol instructed his agent to turn down the job, but after a night of contemplation he resolved to give it one last look. "At some point in that second reading it occurred to me that Jason, as an art curator, might be a little fussy," he says. "As for Jason's attachment to the painting of Vigo, my imagination began to provide him a missing connection. What if Jason was a middle European, and what if he and Vigo were fellow countrymen? In the space of minutes, I became a fussy Carpathian."

Once MacNicol had committed to the concept, he began adding layers on top of the bare-bones character sketch he saw in the script. "I began to supply Jason with Euro malapropisms, and I laid on an accent [that] got thicker as the character took hold," he says. "I went in and met Ivan Reitman, Dan Aykroyd, and Harold Ramis. They were affable when we shook hands, and only slightly worried when I asked them if they would mind my taking some liberties with the part. I let loose with this character that Ivan would later denominate as 'Janosz Poha.'"

Even after winning the role, MacNicol never stopped finding new ways to freshen up Janosz's screen presence. "I bore down on the accent," he admits. "I stopped by the Romanian tourist agency and pretended I was planning to holiday in Bucharest. I carefully studied the agent's voice, but his accent was too good, too refined—too unfunny. Instead I simply let Janosz have his way with me, and the result is all there on camera."

Many of MacNicol's wittiest embellishments never made it into the movie. "During my alone time in the trailer I filled in the world of Mr. Poha by designing the national flag of Carpathia," he reveals. "I had a different take on the 'Don't Tread on Me' motif— my Carpathian flag featured a snake stepping on a man.

"Our national motto was all consonants, since we were too poor a nation to afford vowels. And our economy was entirely based on the sale of firewood."

OPPOSITE An early concept for Vigo the Carpathian by Thom Enriquez showing the villain's face disappear behind a fanged maw. ABOVE Peter MacNicol as Janosz Poha. LEFT Dan Aykroyd, Bill Murray, and Peter MacNicol share a laugh between takes.

18. WHAT A TOWN

At the start of the sequel, the city of New York has revoked the ghostbusters' license to snare spooks. Peter Venkman now hosts a cheap-looking TV show about psychic phenomena. Egon Spengler is performing questionable research into human emotions at Columbia University ("let's see what happens when we take away the puppy," he observes, regarding a test subject played by Reitman's young daughter Catherine). Ray Stantz owns an occult bookstore and sometimes teams up with Winston Zeddemore as an entertainer at children's parties, dancing to a boom box playing Ray Parker Jr.'s "Ghostbusters."

"We needed to knock them down and build them back up again," says Reitman, regarding the heroes' fall from grace.

"I loved the first twenty minutes of it," says Joe Medjuck, "especially the way you're faked out into thinking the ghostbusters are rushing to save the day—and it's Danny and Ernie going to a birthday party."

Bill Murray likened it to a seasonal slump.[26] "It's like exterminators—they go through good periods and bad periods," he said. "The gypsy moths may not be here this year, but they'll come back—or the rats . . . somebody will come back. And the ghosts are back."

Ghostbusters II started filming on November 28, 1988, in New York City with a planned sixty-seven days of location shooting. With a few exceptions—including a baby carriage chase and a brutally cold underground emergence—most sites required only exterior shots and short character entrances and exits.

"Shooting in New York is not an easy thing," says Reitman. "You have the right to shoot on the street, but everyone has their own right to occupy and cross on the street as well. It can become chaotic unless you know how to handle it. Both Bill and Dan were very effective on the street. People love them, and they were not thrown by the energy and the thousands of people that would show up every day. It was a big party that needed to be controlled."

The harrowing trip of Dana's out-of-control baby buggy occurred early in the New York schedule. The driverless carriage started its journey on the sidewalk outside 325 East 77th Street and came to a halt at the intersection of First Avenue, half a block away. Physical effects supervisor Chuck Gaspar constructed five separate buggies, each tricked out with a driveshaft, a steering system, multiple redundant braking systems, and a radio-controlled steering mechanism. Jay Halsey, a champion

BELOW Ivan Reitman keeps pace with a speeding baby carriage during filming on the sidewalk of Manhattan's 77th Street.
OPPOSITE Candid shots captured between takes during filming of *Ghostbusters II.*

ABOVE The new Ectomobile, complete with new roof-mounted LED advertising sign, is shot in New York City.
OPPOSITE TOP Ivan Reitman looks on as Bill Murray entertains a crowd of onlookers through a megaphone during filming outside the U.S. Customs House.
OPPOSITE BOTTOM On Liberty Island, the ghostbusters receive the key to the city in a sequence largely cut from the film.

driver of miniature cars, steered the carriages through a moving gauntlet of cars, cabs, and buses.

"We took our time with that shot, and Chuck was just a know-it-all veteran—he knew what he was doing," says Medjuck. "Ivan liked to do as much practical effects work as he could, because it gave it a certain kind of feel."

Ray and Winston make their exit from a child's birthday party at a brownstone on the corner of 78th and First, while Egon's experiments were shot at Columbia University. When the ghostbusters are hauled before a judge for triggering a citywide blackout, the imposing Thurgood Marshall U.S. Courthouse in lower Manhattan conveys the seriousness of their situation.

The fictional Manhattan Museum of Art—the place of employment for Dana and Janosz Poha, and repository of the malevolent portrait of Vigo—required a grand exterior. Reitman selected the historic United States Customs House near the southernmost tip of Manhattan. Though most of the museum's interiors would be shot on an LA soundstage, some filming occurred inside the Customs House lobby to capture Peter Venkman's encounter with a security guard (whose praise for Venkman's TV show is soured when he compares it to *Bassmasters*).

In the script, Ray, Egon, and Winston—having suffered a long dunk in mood slime—emerge from a manhole directly in front of the Museum of Art. This narrative link between the slime and the painting proved especially difficult to shoot, thanks to equipment breakdowns, below-freezing temperatures, and a vicious wind ripping through Manhattan's Battery Park.

"We were supposed to be emerging from a sewer, but there was no active sewer line or manhole in front of the museum where we were supposed to be doing this," said Ramis.[27] "But they found a little junction box for the phone company, which was a hole in the ground filled with big cables. Danny and Ernie and I had to squeeze in there, then they poured buckets of slime over our heads."

The gooey mix of watery Methocel quickly hardened into frozen chunks in the teeth-chattering wind chill. To make matters worse, the script required the players to strip off their rain coats, rubber waders, and jumpsuits and perform the rest of the scene wearing only long underwear.

"We did it maybe fifteen to twenty times that night, from every camera angle," said Ramis. "The next morning we were in makeup, and Ivan Reitman came in and said, 'That scene

last night was great, but the camera jammed. We have to do it again.' We thought Ivan was kidding, but he wasn't—the camera had stuck. We had to do the scene over."

Jokes Joe Medjuck, "When we were out shooting in the cold, we used to say that we should have made it *Ghostbusters II: Ghostbusters Go to Hawaii*."

Bill Murray stayed far away from the misery. In contrast with the first film, the *Ghostbusters II* script didn't mix slime with Peter Venkman. "I convinced these fellas that I am a member of a religious cult that never gets dirty," said Murray,[28] "and that for me to cover myself in slime and stand outside when it's eight degrees in New York City in December would be a violation of my religious principles."

The final shoot in New York City took place on Fifth Avenue at 2:00 a.m. More than four hundred extras huddled together, singing and cheering for a nonexistent mobile, mood-slime-possessed Statue of Liberty (to be added during postproduction).

Recalls Dennis Muren, "At like three in the morning, I looked up and there was a guy sticking his head out the thirtieth-floor window of the Trump Tower saying, 'Shut up, we're trying to sleep up here!'"

For a movie practically costarring the statue, almost no shots of the New York icon were actually filmed in New York—with one big exception. In a scene nearly erased from the final cut of *Ghostbusters II*—making only a fleeting appearance during the end credits—the Statue of Liberty is restored to her podium and the mayor of New York honors the ghostbusters for saving the city once more. "We took the boat out to Liberty Island—Bedloe's Island—and shot a lot of outdoor stuff at the

Statue of Liberty," remembers David Margulies, who played the Mayor. "There was a lot of fun between everyone."

The missing Liberty Island scene is also notable for dialogue in which the characters, inspired by the site's "huddled masses" symbolism, reflect on their ancestry. Egon reveals that his family hails from Ostrov in Eastern Poland, and Ray mentions that his great-grandparents were Swiss. Dana's roots go all the way back to the *Mayflower*'s landing at Plymouth Rock, while Peter explains away his mixed Irish, German, French, and Dutch heritage by joking that the women in his family liked to sleep around. It is Winston who gives the lighthearted banter a reality check, when he points out that his ancestors came to the New World in the hold of a slave ship.

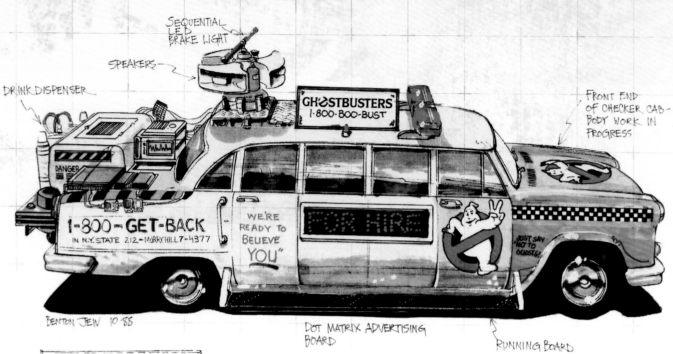

SEQUENTIAL LED BRAKE LIGHT

SPEAKERS

DRINK DISPENSER

DANGER

GHOSTBUSTERS
1·800·BOO·BUST

FRONT END OF CHECKER CAB-BODY WORK IN PROGRESS

1·800·GET·BACK
IN N.Y. STATE 212~MURRAY HILL 7·4377

WE'RE READY TO BELIEVE YOU"

FOR HIRE

JUST SAY NO TO GOOSTS!

BENTON JEW 10·88

DOT MATRIX ADVERTISING BOARD

RUNNING BOARD

VERSION CHK ③

RETRO FITTED CANOPY

1·800~9 BE·GONE

10·88

MIDSECTION GUTTED NOW CONTAINS G.B. EQUIPMENT AND BACKPACKS

BLUE LIGHTS IN WHEEL WELLS

VERSION ⑥ J17

ECTOMOBILE-MARK II

THE ECTOMOBILE RETURNS in *Ghostbusters II,* bearing minor cosmetic upgrades and new "ECTO-1A" license plates. (In some scenes the plates read "ECTO-2.")

"It was five years later, so I basically took my old drawings off the heap and added more detail to them," says Dane. "The look had been established for the first one, so it was just kind of pointing people in the right direction." Ideas incorporated into Dane's sketches but not in the vehicle's final design included NASCAR-style sponsor logos and a hood ornament resembling a streamlined Slimer.

Concept artist Thom Enriquez remembers the buzz when the Ectomobile showed up at the studio. "I had my office right at the entrance of Columbia in Burbank, and as I looked out the window a trailer truck was bringing in the Ectomobile," he says. "You wouldn't believe the reaction. I mean these were people who work in film all the time, but they started applauding and cheering."

The most notable changes to the vehicle were the sequel-friendly iterations of the No-Ghost logo on the Ectomobile's doors,

a prominent dish antenna on the roof, and two scrolling LED signs announcing "FOR HIRE" and "GHOSTBUSTERS: WE'RE BACK." With the ghostbusters firm believers in the power of advertising, the nose of the redesigned car bore the painted message: "We Believe You: Call JL5-2020."

"With the second vehicle you could see how much more complex it was, but it has that off-the-shelf hardware look which is what we were going for," says Dane.

The Ectomobile had a larger role in the shooting script, via a scene where a hypnotized Ray recklessly steers through the New York streets. When Winston warns him that if he doesn't slow down he's going to kill somebody, Ray snarls, "No, I'm going to kill everybody!" Quick shots from the sequence resurfaced in the film's montage sequence and—during the summer of 1989—in a Coca-Cola commercial.

OPPOSITE Concept illustrations for the revised Ectomobile by Benton Jew (top) and John Bell (bottom). **BELOW** Stephen Dane's illustration of the *Ghostbusters II's* Ectomobile, featuring a roof rack even more stuffed with gadgets than before.

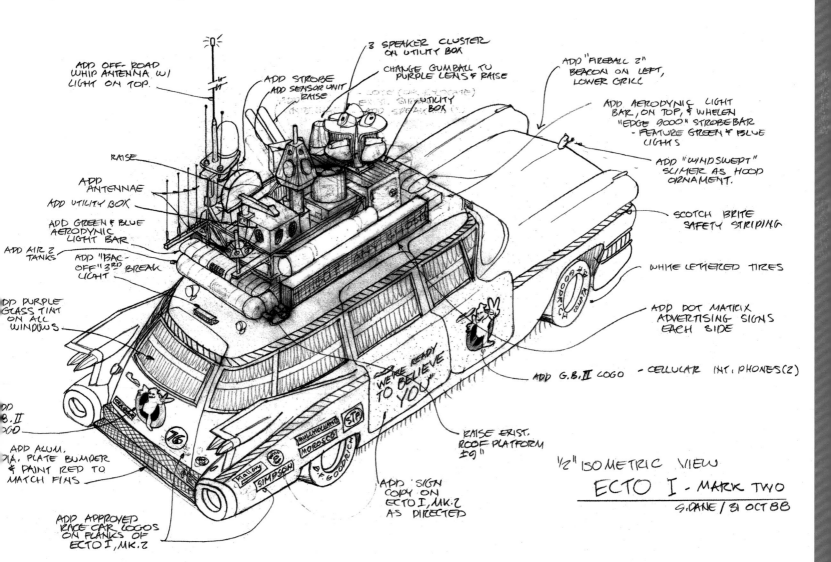

19. WE'RE GOING TO MAKE SOME HEADLINES WITH THIS ONE

The thirteen-week LA shoot allowed the crew to replicate environments too expensive to film in New York. To make the already-tight schedule more efficient, Los Angeles production ramped up while a second unit continued working in New York—an overlapping system not used on the first movie.

Much of the interior shooting took place at the Burbank Studios. "[We built] Venkman's loft, Dana's apartment, the art restoration room at the museum, the courtroom, and a few other things, plus the head of the Statue of Liberty," says production designer Bo Welch. "There was a lot of construction because most of the movie was done on stage." Art director Tom Duffield brought Welch's ideas to life through hammer-and-nails construction.

Welch had three films under his belt—*The Lost Boys, Beetlejuice,* and *The Accidental Tourist*—when he agreed to do *Ghostbusters II.* "It was my fourth movie, but it was my first *big* movie," he says. "I was the young, up-and-coming production designer who people traditionally want to hire."

John DeCuir had been a big part of the first film's visual appeal, a legacy that presented a challenge for Welch. "John DeCuir was a legendary production designer in Hollywood," he says. "That was one of the attractions for the job, but it was also intimidating. When you're starting out it's, *'Should I do a sequel?'* It always seemed better to do something original unless you had done the first one. But with how great the first *Ghostbusters* was—it's often referred to the most perfect script ever written—I thought, *'Yeah, I'll do it.'*

"Because it was a sequel, there's a certain amount of, "What are we preserving from the first one? Are we improving it? Are we altering it? Is their headquarters the same? You want carryover, but at the same time you want to try to outdo it."

Once soundstage filming ramped up, the film's stars found opportunities to pop in on other movie sets and visit former colleagues. Aykroyd and Ramis caught up with Eddie Murphy on the set of *Harlem Nights,* and also Chevy Chase during breaks in the filming of *National Lampoon's Christmas Vacation.*

OPPOSITE Bill Murray apes the grim-looking pose of Vigo the Carpathian. **BELOW** Eugene Levy, playing Louis Tully's cousin Sherm, helped free the ghostbusters from the psychiatric hospital but ended up on the cutting-room floor.

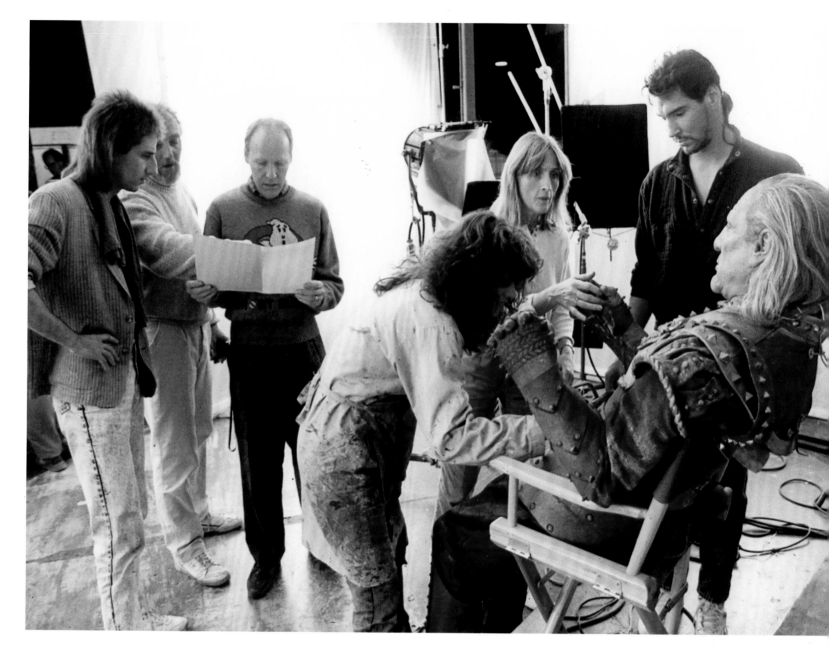

THE SORROW OF MOLDAVIA

In the real world there was no Manhattan Museum of Art, so production designer Bo Welch had creative leeway in depicting the space in which Vigo the Carpathian plots his escape from a 2-D canvas. At the same time, the U.S. Customs House that served as the museum's exterior suggested a place both elegant and imposing.

"We wanted that old Beaux Arts architecture," says Welch. "It was not a modern museum by any means."

Most of the action would take place in a high-ceilinged chamber capped by skylights and dominated by a life-sized painting of Vigo. "It was supposedly a room you restore art in, so in truth that would be a much smaller room," says Welch. "But because it's the climactic sequence of the movie, we made it a large, two-story, neoclassical piece of architecture."

Duffield agrees. "A real art restorer's space is kind of nasty in comparison, while ours is almost in the exhibition space. It was like a little church in there. We called it the cathedral of art.

"We made some faux brass grilles that were only finished on one side, because we figured they would only be seen from inside the set. But if you watch the movie when they're outside of the main room looking in, you can see that the grills are painted, but there's no detail on them."

None of the museum scenes would work if the Vigo painting didn't look convincing. It took a surprisingly long time to get there. "At one point it was going to be a small handheld Russian triptych, like a religious icon painting," says Ned Gorman, ILM's chief visual effects coordinator on *Ghostbusters II*. "But somebody decided a painting you could hold in your hands wasn't as scary as a giant ten-foot portrait. And they needed a physical painting, because Ivan wanted a painting on set for the actors to work with."

Early renditions of the Vigo painting earned Reitman's scorn as "too Conan the Barbarian." With time running out, producer Michael C. Gross reached out to the organizers of the "Pageant of the Masters" art festival in Laguna Beach.

OPPOSITE The final painting of Vigo the Carpathian, photographed at Sony's archive. **ABOVE** Actor Wilhelm von Homburg is outfitted for a day of filming as Vigo the Carpathian. On the left, painting supervisor Glen Eytchison, visual effects camera operator Terry Chostner, and associate producer Michael C. Gross discuss the upcoming scene.

VIGO STORMS THROUGH MUSEUM ON HIS WAY TO THE ICON. THE STATUES MAGICALLY TURN TOWARD HIM AS HE PASSES.

9/23 - HENRY MAYO
TIM LAWRENCE

ILM 1988 N8

VIGO DISCARDS JUSTIN   9/23 - HENRY MAYO
TIM LAWRENCE

D7

VIGO THE CARPATHIAN

OPPOSITE TOP A storyboard for an early *Ghostbusters II* concept by Henry Mayo in which Vigo's spectral essence is sufficient to animate the art museum's exhibits.
OPPOSITE BOTTOM LEFT An early concept by Henry Mayo shows Vigo in midtransformation.
OPPOSITE BOTTOM RIGHT A Vigo painting rejected as too "Conan the Barbarian." **THIS PAGE** Multiple Vigo design variants by Thom Enriquez.

TOP LEFT AND ABOVE Reitman and Sigourney Weaver pose with Vigo. Weaver holds twins William T. and Henry J. Deutschendorf, who played her onscreen son, Oscar. **TOP RIGHT** Wilhelm von Homburg as the three-dimensional personification of Vigo. **OPPOSITE TOP** On a soundstage, Ivan Reitman directs a special effects shot featuring von Homburg. **OPPOSITE BOTTOM LEFT** The museum set for *Ghostbusters II*. **OPPOSITE BOTTOM RIGHT** Storyboards depict Vigo's emergence from the painting.

Their artists regularly re-created classic paintings at life-sized scale, getting costumed actors to stand in for the paintings' central figures.

"We delivered a large negative of the actor in costume, which was then taken to LA to shoot in a huge photo enlargement on the canvas," says Gorman. The Pageant of the Masters artists overpainted the image, producing a suitably glowering rendition of a costumed Wilhelm von Homburg.

The set also offered opportunities for Peter MacNicol to indulge his love for physical comedy. "We filmed a bit where I tumble off a museum stepladder," says MacNicol. "I play comedy as honestly as I play tragedy, and I rehearse right up to the point where I'm risking injury. When my stand-in rehearsed the scene he took the sane approach of doing it safely. The problem is, safe isn't always funny. I asked if I could do the fall and that's the take they took. After that shot, our stunt coordinator presented me with a stuntman's union patch."

For Harold Ramis, the multistory set really shone when crews rigged it with rappelling lines for the moment where the ghostbusters arrive to stop Vigo. "I had a great time," he said.[29] "I kept sliding down from the top of the stage—about seventy feet. Of course, they had us on safety rigs. So it was foolproof—there was no way we could get hurt. So I got a lot of confidence and I went back to do it over several times."

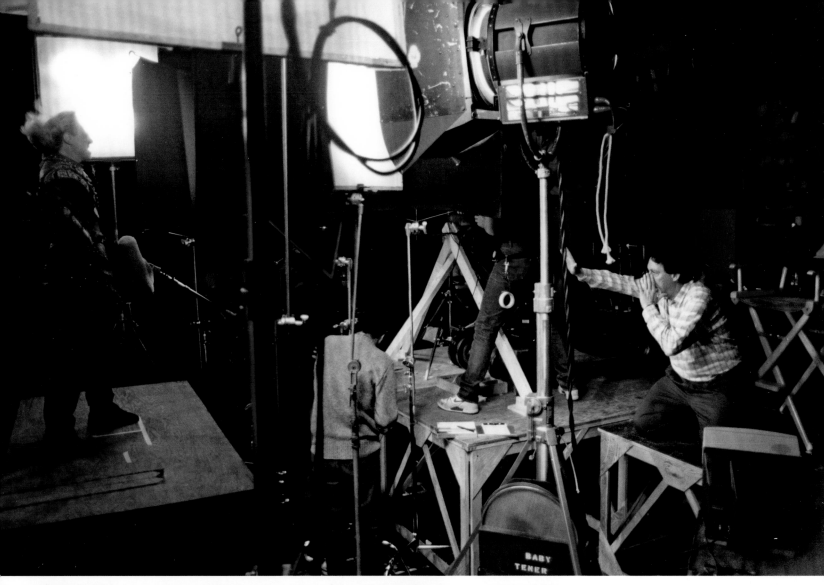

AND A BATHTUB TRIED TO EAT HIS FRIEND'S BABY

In *Ghostbusters II*, Dana Barrett has a brand new apartment—understandable, considering her previous one exploded. Inside Dana's roomy digs, Duffield and crew built a bathroom for a scene involving a killer bathtub brought to life by mood slime.

"Her place is more like a standard New York apartment, a brick building in the West Village or Chelsea," says Duffield. "Much nicer, much more refined."

The set also brought Sigourney Weaver and Peter MacNicol together for their first filmed dialogue scene.

"It was the doorway bit with Sigourney where I'm snooping on the sleeping child: 'How is the *ba-hay-bee?*'" recalls MacNicol. "Janosz was a bold characterization to be sure, and both the filmmakers and myself were taking a chance. But I got a round of applause from the crew at the end of that scene. And with that, Ivan relaxed with me. Most importantly, he trusted me."

Peter Venkman's apartment had a street address of 644 Broadway, but took shape on the same LA soundstage that housed the Gozer temple in the first film. "Bill's loft and the art restoration room both coexisted on Stage 16," says Bo Welch.

Designing the set meant getting into character—determining how Peter Venkman would approach the layout and décor of his own space. "Having the advantage of seeing the first film and being a huge Bill Murray fan, [I put] a lot of Bill Murray in the character," says Welch. "How we arrived at the loft and the details that followed was [by] asking, 'What would Bill do in this case?'"

Tom Duffield worked to age the set and give it a lived-in look. "We wanted to make it look like it was an old warehouse. You always want to inject a little humor in the sets."

Dana and baby Oscar move in with Peter after their run-in with the angry bathtub, leading to a rekindled passion between the two romantic leads. "The strongest thing to me is how effective their relationship is throughout the film and how strong Sigourney is," says Reitman, "how she deals with the sort of chaos around her in a lovely, funny way."

Welch completed Peter's loft both inside and out, preparing for a scene in which Dana's baby Oscar crawls out the window and balances at the edge of an apparent multistory plunge.

"The loft had an exterior finish so that we could shoot the ledge scene," Welch says. "We had to have it connected. It's an interior, but with a fully realized exterior finish. The ledge was eight or ten feet off the ground so we could get decent 'up angles' on it."

Even ten feet would be a disastrous drop for a baby. During filming, a Chuck Gaspar–designed harness secured the infant—portrayed by twins William T. Deutschendorf and Henry J. Deutschendorf, nephews of singer John Denver—inside a leather diaper affixed to a bolted-down metal pole.

As originally conceived, the ledge sequence relied much more heavily on effects. "I storyboarded the kidnapping of the baby with Louis and Janine," says Thom Enriquez. "In the

OPPOSITE Peter Venkman fights off a phantom clown in this Thom Enriquez concept illustration.
TOP Actor Peter MacNicol as the ghost nanny.

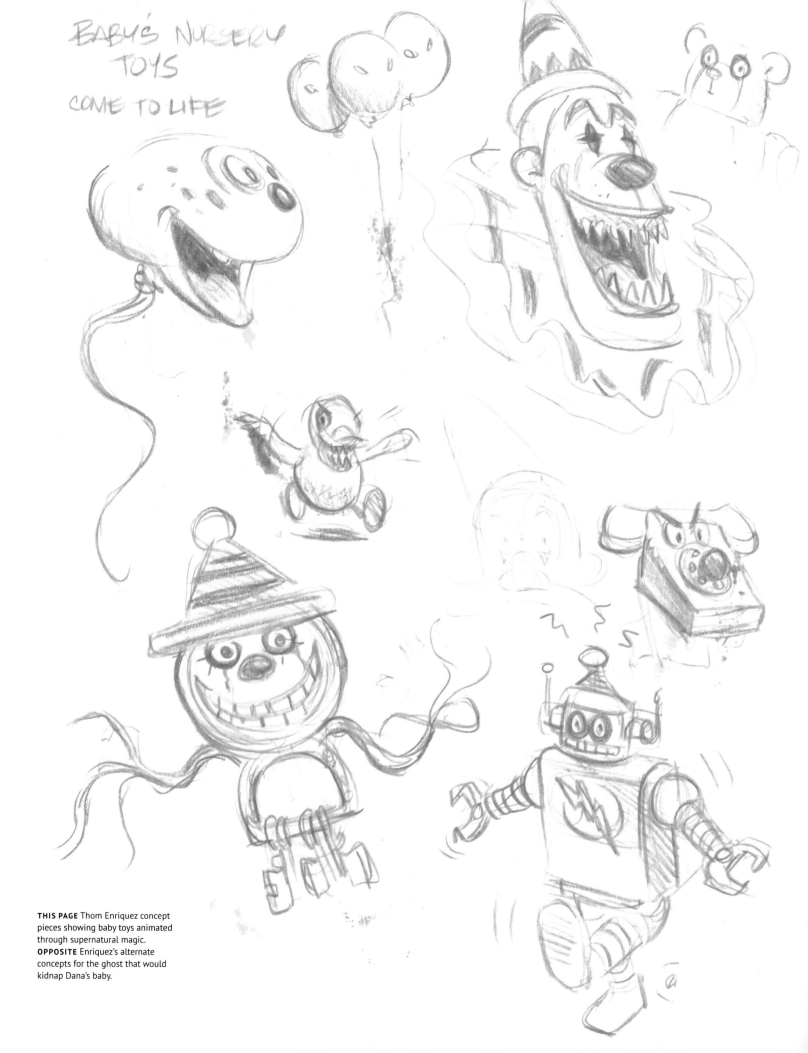

BABY'S NURSERY TOYS COME TO LIFE

THIS PAGE Thom Enriquez concept pieces showing baby toys animated through supernatural magic.
OPPOSITE Enriquez's alternate concepts for the ghost that would kidnap Dana's baby.

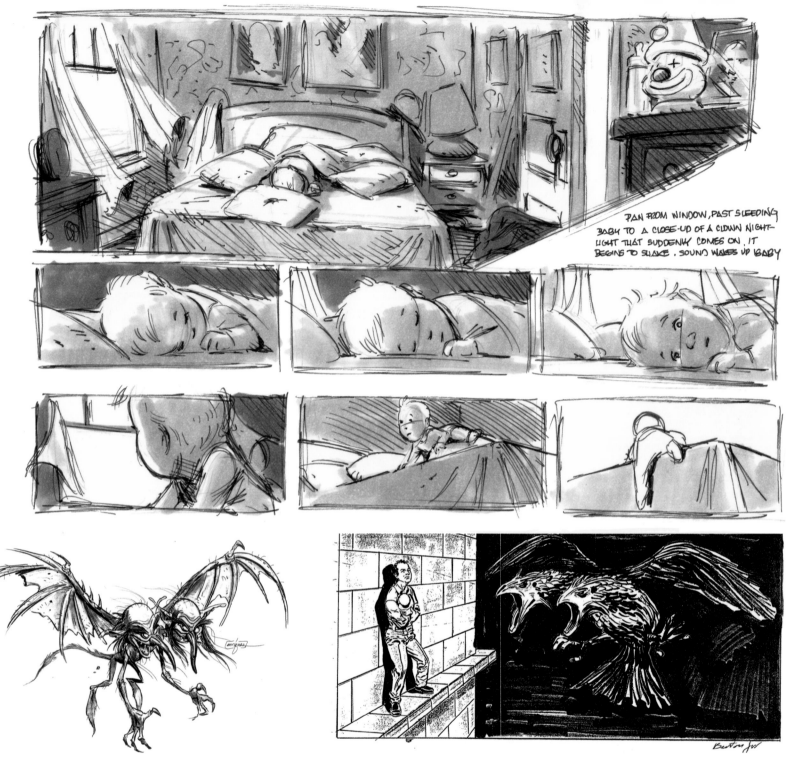

PAN FROM WINDOW, PAST SLEEPING BABY TO A CLOSE-UP OF A CLOWN NIGHT-LIGHT THAT SUDDENLY COMES ON, IT BEGINS TO SHAKE. SOUND WAKES UP BABY

TOP A storyboard sequence depicting baby Oscar's ghostly entrapment. **ABOVE LEFT** Thom Enriquez's discarded bat-winged concept for the ghost kidnapper. **ABOVE RIGHT** Another ghostly kidnapper design, this one depicting a two-headed demon bird.

version I storyboarded, Slimer was involved a lot more, so I had Slimer warn Louis that the baby was out on the ledge. Louis is trying to make out with Janine and he looks over her shoulder, and you see Slimer using all these gestures.

"The sequence was also longer. When Bill Murray shows up with Dana and they find out the baby is missing, they look out the window and see the baby on the ledge with a monster, and there's a physical struggle. Bill goes out there, Dana hands him a baseball bat, and he's swinging at this creature."

The creature responsible for Oscar's kidnapping—originally conceived as fanciful and frightening—eventually became a "ghost nanny" played by Peter MacNicol in a dress.

"When it came to the kidnapping Michael Gross was talking about a ghost nanny," says Enriquez, "and I said,

'What kid wants to play with a nanny?' I came up with designs for this two-headed creature that kidnaps the baby, and I thought the sequence might be fun if Vigo had the power to take over inanimate objects. I thought teddy bears could come to life and have a weird expression on their faces, and they could lift the baby up and help him walk to the window. I thought telephone poles could peer into the room at the baby, but Michael said, 'I think it needs to serve the script, we need to have the nanny thing.'"

Adds ILM's Ned Gorman, "The whole idea in the script was that she was a 'demon Mary Poppins.' There was talk about doing it as a grotesque caricature, but at some point it needed to be clear that this was actually the Janosz Poha character. We were like, 'Let's not gild a lily. Let's just have Peter do it.'"

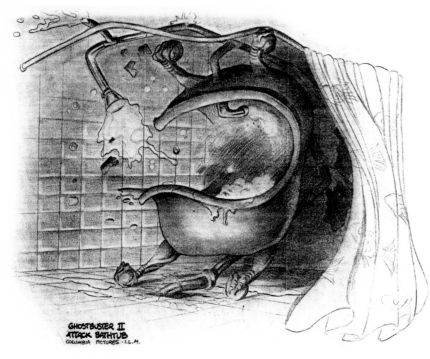

GHOSTBUSTER II
ATTACK BATHTUB
COLUMBIA PICTURES · I.L.M.

TOP Production painting of the apartment ledge sequence.
ABOVE External view of Venkman's apartment set. **LEFT** Concept art for the possessed bathtub by Henry Mayo.

CASE DISMISSED

After drilling a hole in a busy street and causing a citywide blackout, Venkman, Stantz, and Spengler seem bound for prison unless there is some kind of courtroom miracle. Luckily the villainous Scoleri brothers return from the dead to convert a sneering judge into the ghostbusters' biggest fan. One destroyed courtroom later, it's all over. "Two in the box, ready to go—we be fast, and they be slow," the heroes gloat above the smoking trap containing their captures.

For the sequel, Reitman wanted the ghostbusters to fight their way back to legitimacy. The courtroom becomes their arena, but due to the nature of the set, their ferocity had practical limits. Gaspar's crew had the freedom to destroy up to fourteen chairs during the scene—the rest were rentals. The room's pillars, defense table, and judge's box looked solid, but consisted of lightweight balsa wood that would explode and splinter with ease.

"In conversations with Ivan and with Michael Chapman—who shot it—we would say, 'How many times will we do this?'" says Bo Welch. "They want to know, 'How long is the reset time?' And sometimes if it's really elaborate, you say, 'We're going to do it once. It's going to work because the reset is too

huge.' When we had break-away stuff and exploding things we had multiple cameras. We'd do it once and then we're down for the rest of the day."

Tom Duffield snapped up the courtroom set from 1986's *Legal Eagles*, a Universal comedy starring Robert Redford, which Ivan Reitman had directed in between the two *Ghostbusters* films. "They said, 'We want a courtroom and we don't want to spend any money,'" says Duffield. "We pulled it out of stock and added stuff like the glass partition, because the director wanted glass to blow up.

"We put the stage on a platform because we had to get under the floor to drill holes for the chairs, which were on air mortars. If you look at the chairs as they're blown up off the ground, you'll notice there's a six-inch extension on one side of each chair leg. That's the part that was loaded into the air mortar tube.

"We also spent a fortune on the ceiling," continues Duffield. "We wanted a grand feeling, and we thought we'd see it when we were looking up at all the damage. We put in a really heavy cornice ceiling, and I got notices complaining about how much we spent."

TOP LEFT The ghostbusters, their lawyer, and the judge all take cover from the Scoleri brothers.
TOP RIGHT A concept illustration of the Scoleris complete with electric chairs. **ABOVE RIGHT** Storyboard illustration of the bubbling-over mood slime container sitting on the courtroom's evidence table.
OPPOSITE TOP Henry Mayo concept art depicting Tony Scoleri wreathed by electrical fire. **OPPOSITE CENTER** A Thom Enriquez storyboard shows a terrified prosecutor running from the Scoleris. **OPPOSITE BOTTOM** Another storyboard panel, this time depicting the Scoleri brothers movement through the scene.

GHOSTBUSTERS II · COURTROOM SEQUENCE

Duffield also needed to prep the set for the destructive trails inflicted by the proton streams. "We laid in primer cord to make burn marks in the walls," he says. "We routed lines in the walls, they'd rig them, and we would cover them with plaster. When the actors point their rifles in that direction, the crew lights it off to pretend they're streaking the walls—they add the sparks and color in post."

Thom Enriquez storyboarded the courtroom sequence. "It's really fun to see your drawings affect not only the sets but the angles," he says. "They had the storyboards on the set and were looking at them, and Bill Murray got under the table and was trying to pose the same way that I drew it. It's like directing without being a director."

VENKMAN CATCHES THE SCOLERI BETWEEN TWO PILLARS WITH HIS STREAM AND HOLDS HIM.

SUCK IN THE GUTS, GUYS, WE'RE THE GHOSTBUSTERS

COSTUME DESIGNER GLORIA GRESHAM had just finished up with Ivan Reitman on his movie *Twins* when the director offered her the opportunity to work on *Ghostbusters II*. Unfortunately, Gresham had already committed to Rob Reiner's *When Harry Met Sally*. "I said, 'I can't do it,' and he was not a happy camper," Gresham recalls. "So I went off to do *Harry*, and he hired another designer."

When that fix didn't pan out, Reitman came calling again. "This was only three weeks before they rolled camera," says Gresham, who ultimately proposed a solution to Reiner that would allow her to work on both films during a brief but intense stretch of schedule overlap. "I told [Rob Reiner] the whole story about how Ivan was really in a bind. He looked at me and said, 'If you want to ruin your health and have no personal life, it's up to you.' So I came to it very late in the production schedule, after everybody else had been working on it for weeks and weeks."

Gresham views the role of a costume designer as an integral part of the storytelling process, equally as important as that of a production designer. She began her work on *Ghostbusters II* by considering Theoni Aldredge's designs from the first film. "What was helpful was the broad brushstrokes already in place for the main characters," she says. "Ivan liked it that I was very hands on. We were on the same page in that it was a sequel, but there would be a lot of novelty that wasn't there on the first one."

Nowhere is that novelty more apparent than with Janine Melnitz, the ghostbusters' secretary, who seems to have undergone a head-to-toe makeover during the intervening years. "To do Annie Potts was so much fun," says Gresham. "It was fun to find quirky things that were not what the average person was wearing that year. Annie was responsible for some of that, because she wanted to look different. The hair was totally different, the makeup was different. We had five years of styles from which to choose, and she came at the project very single-minded about the hair and makeup."

The ghostbusters themselves had more subtle updates to their civilian attire, speaking to the half-decade shift away from their team successes and into a hodgepodge of replacement roles. "We know that Bill's character is a TV-show host psychic," says Gresham. "So what does that tell you? It tells you that he's a TV personality and that maybe he's a little flashier than, say, Harold, who's a professor and lives in a lab. And Dan runs an occult bookstore. They each had their little niche, and you take that ball and run with it."

Each of the main characters received a "closet" of complementary wardrobe items, described by Gresham as their "uniform for everyday life."

"Consider the closet you need for Bill Murray," she explains. "Does he get a flashier sports jacket? Yes, he does. Harold needs a lab coat. Ray needs a sweater vest and a conservative sports jacket. When they're all in court together, that's the only time when they're dressed vaguely out of the same silhouette. But it's different fabric, it's different colors, and it still makes a statement about who they are."

When the ghostbusters finally suit up in their coveralls, it's a comforting return to form—but Gresham recalls her efforts to rework the iconic uniform were trimmed from the final film for the most part: "When Ivan first called, he was already saying to me that he would like to see a new design, a different ghostbuster costume. I did different shapes, different colors, different fabric. Then we'd go to dailies and we'd look at it on film, and Ivan would say 'No, that's not it.'" In the film, dark-fabric variants of the ghostbusters jumpsuits can be seen in montage shots.

Newcomer Peter MacNicol played Janosz Poha as a high-strung bundle of quirks, and Gresham carried the qualities into his clothing. "As an actor he was working very hard to create this character, and he needed something eccentric," she says. "His shirts and sweaters have a lot of high contrast in them: black and white, or checks. None of that is an accident; it's done because in that scene he's the star. So I don't have to worry about him competing with another actor."

This collaboration with cast and crew to shape the visual impact of a film is what attracted Gresham to *Ghostbusters II*, and it's the aspect she's most satisfied with. "That's what costume designers do—you take into account the character as its given in the script, you take into account the actor playing the part, you talk to the director to say, 'Are there any special things that you want to see done?' and you sift it out as you go along.

"It was a great project for a costume designer."

OPPOSITE The ghostbusters strike poses around Sigourney Weaver. Note the darker costumes designed by Gloria Gresham but only worn during brief scenes in *Ghostbusters II*. **TOP** Bill Murray and Sigourney Weaver during the same publicity shoot for the sequel.

STANZ PASSES PIPE & CABLES ON WAY DOWN...

DERAILED IN 1920

In one memorable sequence, Ray Stantz is lowered on a rope through a jackhammered hole, breaking through into the cavernous and long-abandoned Van Horne subway station. Patterned after actual turn-of-the-century New York transit architecture, Van Horne became one of *Ghostbusters II*'s most distinctive environments. Bo Welch constructed a partial set of the station and extended its borders using strategically placed matte paintings.

"We built Van Horne station on stage," he says. "Obviously you're not going to be able to fill a real subway with slime. It was a chance to show the archeology of New York by creating an old, tile, vaulted subway station."

Van Horne bore influences from Alfred Ely Beach's prototype pneumatic transit system from the 1870s. Its tiled, vaulted arches and gaslight sconces are relics of a long-vanished era of everyday grandeur.

"We built the subway as though it was from the turn of the century," says Duffield. "The roof, the deck, the tunnels—we built everything. We had brass handrails. The tricky thing about the ceiling was the two-toned tile—we cut Masonite and shaped it like ceramic tile, and our painters two-toned it and placed it in a checkerboard.

"We did everything grand, like it would have been done back in those days. It was like you were in a portion of Grand Central."

MY BEST TO THE COVEN!

Miscellaneous scenes filled the crew's remaining studio time. Venkman's introduction to the audience occurs in the context of *World of the Psychic with Dr. Peter Venkman*, a low-budget talk show aired on New York's WKRR Channel 12. The set's décor is appropriately pitiful, with swivel chairs, random orbs glued to the walls, and the program's title printed in gold glitter lettering.

"That's my favorite stuff to do in a movie, because it has a sense of wit to it," says Bo Welch. "The idea is to show how far he has fallen from the first *Ghostbusters*. That it's come to this."

Adds Duffield, "We wanted it to be kind of cheesy, like a teacher's low-budget TV show. It was basically a one-wall set, and we put the goofy planet things and the sparkly letters on it."

The interior of Ray's Occult Books came to life on Stage 15, right next to the *World of the Psychic* set. "In New York, real estate is expensive, so we built it with tight little passageways," says Duffield. "We filled it up with a lot of old used books that our LA set decorator, Cheryl Carasik, put in there."

The Statue of Liberty's effects-heavy scenes could mostly be saved for postproduction, except for shots of the actors spraying slime on her innards and peering out from the windows of her crown.

Duffield built a small cross section of the statue's interior for the slime-coating scene. "We got pictures of the inside, with all the copper and the bracing, and it was really fun to build all that," he says. "We built it so that they could spray that stuff maybe eight or ten feet vertically."

For the crown, a replica took shape on a soundstage—scaled 30 percent larger than the actual headpiece for better visibility of the actors inside.

"Bo said, 'OK, we want to build the head of this thing,' and it was up to me to figure out how to do that," says Duffield. "We got drawings of everything we could from the Statue of Liberty and worked it out, and we put it on a gimbal so it would tilt and move."

The rented gimbal mechanism, built in the 1940s, simulated Lady Liberty's heavy steps, but broke down on the first day of shooting. "You put all that weight on it and sometimes it breaks," shrugs Duffield. The crew soon got things working again, with enough success that Bill Murray complained of nausea and seasickness.

IS THAT FOR PERSONAL OR PROFESSIONAL REASONS?

Filming spilled out into the streets of Los Angeles for several scenes, including downtown LA stand-ins for First Avenue, where Peter, Ray, and Egon dig a very big hole.

"We needed to get a permit, jackhammer a hole in the pavement, stack the dirt around it, and put up the barricades," recalls Duffield. "I went to the unit manager and asked, 'You want to give me a price on that?' And he said, 'It costs what it costs.' It was the first and only time I ever heard that in all my years in the business."

Interiors of the ghostbusters' firehouse would be shot in the same location as the first film: LA's Fire Station No. 23. "It's not like the place was sealed off for five years," says Bo Welch, who made only slight updates to the location. "Basically you looked at the first movie and regenerated it with some added value."

One notable change in how the ghostbusters handled themselves during firehouse down time? The total absence of cigarettes.

"If you watch the first *Ghostbusters*, the guys are smoking all the time," points out Joe Medjuck. "They're handing off cigarettes to each other. They light each other's cigarettes. It wasn't that we were making it for kids the second time, but times had changed. In the five years between [the movies], smoking pretty well disappeared from movies." Though the crew has apparently sworn off cigarettes, Ray chomps on an unlit cigar while busting the ghost jogger and again during the group's slime-coating of Lady Liberty.

One scene shot in the firehouse's interior involved a small-scale demonstration of mood slime's ability to motivate inanimate objects. Let loose in the center of a pool table, a slime-primed toaster hops in time to the music. Chuck Gaspar mounted tiny air cylinders triggered by microswitches inside the toaster. The toaster's power cord acted as the air supply line.

In a subtle bit of location trickery, the previously unseen third floor of the LA firehouse doubled as the site of the birthday party where Ray and Winston perform for an ungrateful audience of fifth graders.

"Upstairs was the old captain's quarters, and we knew we could use it as the party scene," says Duffield. "Studios always want to lump as many sets together as they can, so they don't have to move from set to set." Ivan Reitman's son Jason—who would later direct *Juno* and *Up in the Air*—is the party kid who tells Ray, "My dad says you guys are full of crap."

Elsewhere, Val's on Riverside Drive (identified in dialogue as Armand's) served as the site of Peter and Dana's dinner date. "It was two blocks from the studio," recalls Duffield. "It was the closest restaurant that still had an upscale feeling to it."

The ghostbusters' conversation with the mayor occurs at his home, Gracie Mansion, though filming actually took place at Greystone Mansion in Beverly Hills—a site previously visited by Reitman, Ramis, and Murray during the filming of *Stripes*, where it doubled for a German resort.

"It's a big mansion that was donated to the city of Beverly Hills, and a lot of people film there," says Duffield. "It has a certain look. We wanted a big, paneled office for the mayor, and rather than spend the money to build one, it was just easier to shoot it there."

One additional scene occurred at the Veteran's Administration Medical Center. This would serve as New York's fictional Parkview Psychiatric Hospital, where straitjacketed ghostbusters are incarcerated thanks to the meddling of the mayor's aide.

"The interiors were set at the VA Medical Center in Brentwood," says Duffield. "When they're coming out of the mental hospital in their ghostbusters uniforms, that was shot at a side door service entrance of the Biltmore Hotel."

OPPOSITE TOP Concept art shows Ray's emergence into the splendor of Van Horne station. **OPPOSITE CENTER LEFT** Filming takes place on the partial Van Horne set. **OPPOSITE CENTER RIGHT** A storyboard panel outlines Ray's descent into Van Horne station. **BELOW** A hardhat from the set of *Ghostbusters II* that now resides in the Sony archive.

TWO IN THE BOX. READY TO GO.
WE BE FAST AND THEY BE SLOW.

THE PROTON PACKS FROM *Ghostbusters* returned, sporting a near-identical appearance but redesigned to make hauling them easier on the actors. While the original packs weighed as much as fifty pounds when loaded with batteries, the models used in *Ghostbusters II* came in at a relatively light twenty-eight pounds.

"Ivan said, 'Guys, look at the proton guns and the ghost traps in the first movie, and don't reinvent the wheel,'" says Ned Gorman. "There was discussion of, if we have Harold or Dan lasso the fat Scoleri brother with the beam, are people going to say, 'That didn't happen last time,' or are they going to think it's cool? And we were like, 'We just never saw them do it before, but the proton guns were always able to do that.' If you jog the thing with your arm and do a little tennis move, you can make a loop out of it."

SLIME BLOWER

A new piece of gear, the "slime blower," was both heavier and bulkier than the original proton pack and required a small crew to mount each onto a cast member's back.

"One of my military magazines showed guys with big flamethrower backpacks, so I went with that idea," says Stephen Dane, who lent his skills as hardware consultant on *Ghostbusters II*, expanding on the designs he had contributed to the first film. "You have a fat tank in the middle, which is pressurized into two smaller tanks on each side. Things like the custom grip for the left hand I designed according to stuff I got out of magazines, all off the shelf. My imagination was in putting the pieces together."

Consisting of a large metal tank and a handheld nozzle, the blower released an air-blown stream of positive-energy mood slime. Prior to their confrontation with Vigo, the ghostbusters spray the Statue of Liberty's metallic innards with a dripping coat, which allows the statue to move to the musical backing of "Higher and Higher," as performed by R&B singer Howard Huntsberry.

In reality, the amount of goo released from the slime blowers in the scene is an order of magnitude greater than the volume of slime that could actually fit inside the prop tanks. During filming, off-screen vats—each nearly five feet tall—were fitted with hoses to feed the blowers with a steady slime supply.

OPPOSITE Close-up view of a slime blower tank prop. **TOP** The ghostbusters douse Janosz Poha with concentrated mood slime. **ABOVE** A slime blower sprayer nozzle prop used in the filming of *Ghostbusters II*.

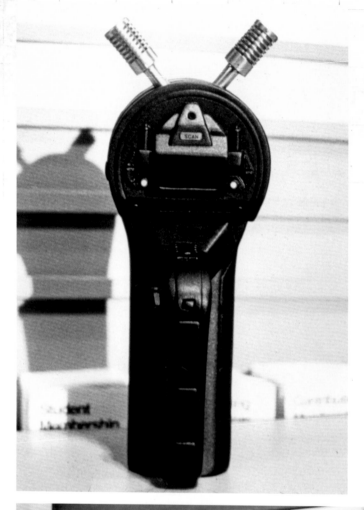

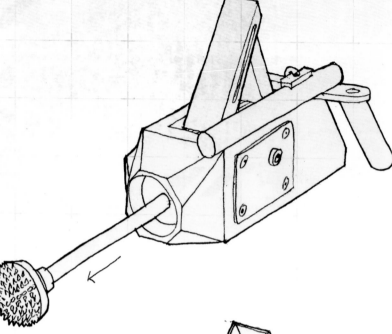

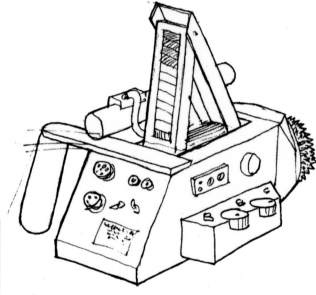

GIGA METER

Joining Egon Spengler's high-tech arsenal in *Ghostbusters II* is the Giga Meter: a spectral sniffer designed to measure psychomagnotheric energy in gigaelectron volts. It is deployed by Dr. Spengler during his investigations of the out-of-control baby carriage and an ominous painting inside the Manhattan Museum of Art.

"I would draw this stuff up," says Dane. "I configured the whole thing in detail, to make it something you'd really build in order to detect certain frequencies or whatever the presence of the ghost would be."

The Giga Meter prop was built around an off-the-shelf, hand-held cleaning device, the Redman Corporation Power Scrubber 'N' Buffer. The finished prop had a plastic dome equipped with spinning lights added, plus a pair of motorized condenser microphones.

SLIME SCOOPER

Ray Stantz carries a slime scooper as he's lowered through a hole in a New York street, and uses it to secure a testing sample from a raging slime river. "I designed one with a compacted view, and the prop department made one with an extended handle," says Dane.

"In my design there's a sliding switch near the handle and an air attachment used to extend the rod. But they're not going to spend the money to make all of [the mechanics] work on camera."

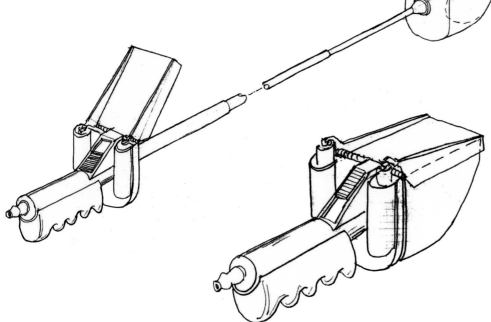

OPPOSITE TOP LEFT The final Giga Meter prop. **OPPOSITE TOP RIGHT AND CENTER** Stephen Dane's early sketches for the Giga Meter. **OPPOSITE BOTTOM LEFT** Egon uses the Giga Meter. **TOP AND ABOVE** Ray deploys the slime scooper. **LEFT** Stephen Dane's concepts for the slime scooper sample collector.

20. NOW IS THE SEASON OF EVIL

Industrial Light & Magic had nearly 180 shots to complete for *Ghostbusters II*, and the film's ferociously tight shooting schedule gave the company pause, despite its status as the world's number one visual effects house.

"At ILM we were a bigger facility than Boss Films was [for the first film], but even for us, it was a stretch," says Dennis Muren. "They started shooting at Thanksgiving, and they were still shooting into March or April.

"It was just impossible, and it was pretty darn crazy to even try to do it because at the same time we had these other super big shows going through the joint [at ILM]. But we pulled it off."

Ned Gorman served as ILM's visual effects coordinator. "We had absolutely no time," he says. "Ivan and company had decided to follow the same pattern that they had on the first one, and they had very little preproduction time given the scope of what they were trying to do. We needed to amp it up and bring in a lot of LA people."

Ghostbusters II also marked the end of an era in the visual effects industry. "It was an interesting time because we were at a fulcrum point," says Gorman. "It's the last show I did at ILM that had absolutely no digital production whatsoever. At the same time we were doing *Ghostbusters*, Dennis was doing the pseudopod sequence for *The Abyss*, which is now seen as one of the major waypoints in digital effects. We were right in the vortex of the change away from traditional photochemical techniques."

One of the traditional effects called for by the script was ectoplasm—gallons and gallons of it. The *Ghostbusters II* script practically oozed with slime. Slime flowed beneath the city in subway tunnels, covered a museum in an impenetrable shell, and fed new weapons in the team's arsenal.

"There was a lot of discussion as to what color the slime should be," says Ned Gorman. "We needed to know the color and what kind of radiance it would give off, because the director of photography was going to have to shoot outside the museum. The reflected light on the crowd's faces had to have some cohesion to what color the slime was going to be. We wound up with this pinkish stuff. The one thing that was ruled out immediately was green, because it was too much like Slimer."

All told, *Ghostbusters II* required 100,000 gallons of slime. Eventually, physical effects supervisor Chuck Gaspar and his crew locked down a recipe: 8 cups of Methocel, 4½ cups Separan, 32 gallons of water, and 50cc of red food coloring. Each batch made 32 gallons.

One of the repositories for this slime would be the Van Horne station—this time, cast in miniature. Where the subway tracks used to run, a slime river flowed down a channel a foot wide and ten feet long.

"We built a trough at a slight angle, so the thing would flow downriver," says ILM model maker Lorne Peterson. "And we had a drop tank that could flow in more Methocel slime. It was delivered to us in three-foot-by-three-foot polyethylene tanks. That's quite a few gallons, and we would sometimes have dozens out back."

For added effect, this slime came laced with mica dust and topped by a layer of mineral oil to create the illusion of currents at varying depths. At the mouth of the river, pumps recirculated the slime back to the source. Despite this, the supply needed to be thrown out and replaced every time its color grew too uniform.

In the script, the river posed a physical threat to the dangling Ray Stantz. "The slime had to act like it was alive," says Ned Gorman. "We talked about, 'OK, when Dan is hanging over the slime river, what's grabbing his feet? How are we doing that? Are they little hands, or are they claws? Or are they tentacle-like blobs?'"

In the finished shot, the slime manifests as gooey blobs and hooked tendrils. "We wound up splitting the difference," says Gorman. "Ivan wanted it to stay amorphous."

OPPOSITE One of the photographs taken by Venkman at the museum that reveal the evil lurking in Vigo's portrait. BELOW Special effects supervisor Dennis Muren (foreground) and chief model maker Jeff Olson observe the subterranean river of slime in miniature.

21. THE SCOLERI BROTHERS

They may not have meant to, but Tony and Nunzio Scoleri provide some postmortem assistance that sets the ghostbusters back on the track to success. In *Ghostbusters II*'s first big action sequence, the two career criminals return from the netherworld to terrorize the judge who sentenced them to the electric chair.

The Scoleris got their exaggerated appearances from the designs of storyboard artist Thom Enriquez. Inspired by the Blues Brothers, Enriquez and ILM creature-designer Tim Lawrence created the visual contrast of a rail-thin Tony and an impossibly overstuffed Nunzio. The script's description of the Scoleris as "big in life, even bigger in death" led Lawrence to push the designs toward caricature, under the rationale that the evil hearts of the brothers had twisted their exterior shells.

"There was a question of, 'OK, are we going to try to one-up Slimer?'" says Ned Gorman. "Are the Scoleri brothers going to follow the fanciful look, or are they going to be more human? Is it gonna be guys in suits? Is it gonna be stop motion? Are we going to cast actors, or is it going to be some grotesque Big-Daddy-Roth caricature types?"

Howie Weed helped finalize the design of the brothers. "We never worried about realism, it was more of a cartoony approach," he says. "We decided on one extremely skinny and one rotund, and I sculpted character studies in goofy poses to get a feel for the characters and to help sculpt and fabricate the final costumes."

The original concept for the courtroom battle required the Scoleris to insult their attackers using colorful Italian epithets. ILM equipped each head with a SNARK (synthetic neuro-animation repeating kinetics) module, permitting the recording and playback of facial servos and pneumatics that simulated lip-synching. Ultimately the hardware went unused, a casualty of time and expense. "It was pretty much all sculpted expression—there wasn't much facial articulation," says Weed.

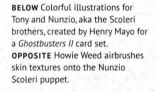

BELOW Colorful illustrations for Tony and Nunzio, aka the Scoleri brothers, created by Henry Mayo for a *Ghostbusters II* card set.
OPPOSITE Howie Weed airbrushes skin textures onto the Nunzio Scoleri puppet.

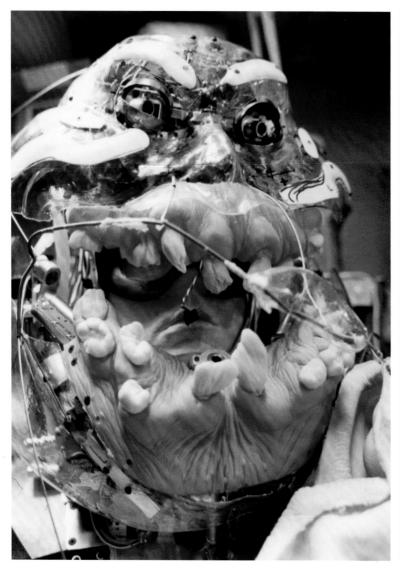

Specialty costumer Camilla Henneman—who had inflated Weird Al Yankovic for "Fat," his music video parody of Michael Jackson's "Bad"—built Nunzio Scoleri's blubbery latex suit, incorporating sacks of lentil beans to provide a bouncy motion, for Tim Lawrence to wear. The head came in two sections, an upper cranium and a lower jaw that could move grotesquely in opposite directions. The full suit, packed with gelatinous spandex pouches, weighed nearly eighty pounds.

For maximum skeletal effect, Tony Scoleri was to be an articulated puppet, but became a costume due to concerns over the additional hours required for the puppetry. Jim Fye, a lanky actor hired to portray the Statue of Liberty, stepped in to portray Tony.

"The Tony costume was a pretty easy fitting," says Fye. "It was mostly the shirt and the jeans and the boots, plus the chest piece, the arms and hands—which were like big rubber gloves—and of course the head, which sat on top of my own head. My favorite part of the costume was the moleskin undergarment, which the wires attached to. It was my favorite because if it hadn't been for that, being suspended in the air for hours would have been very uncomfortable."

The Scoleri brothers took turns in front of the camera, with each actor forced to hang by wires for a very technical bluescreen shoot that was filmed over the course of several days.

"There were animatronics in the face controlled by someone on the ground with a joystick, so all I could do was body movement," says Fye. "I was mostly stationery about ten feet off the ground. When I needed to fly, two guys controlled that movement with wires. On cue, I made specific motions with my body."

The process left almost everything to the performer's imagination. "In the scene when Tony and Nunzio throw the table," says Fye, "I was up in the air—without Nunzio, without the guys under the table, and without the table!"

ILM added cold blue sparks to the brothers in postproduction. "These guys were electric because they were sent to the electric chair," says Ned Gorman. "So we got the old classic lightning boxes. It was all pretty straightforward."

The brothers also exhibited a stretchy shape-changing effect. "We projected them onto a screen and reflected it in a sheet of Mylar," says Muren. "If you grabbed the sheet from behind, you could change of the shape of it. The result was interesting, like a funhouse mirror. The Scoleris come in as little tiny things and then expand, and that wouldn't have happened if we had just shot them straight."

SCOLERI BROS.
"TONY"
(DARKER THAN "HARRY")

22. SLIMER–MARK II

Thanks to his comic-relief role on the animated show *The Real Ghostbusters*, Slimer had oozed his way to star status among the school-going set. In *Ghostbusters II*, Reitman initially included a running subplot in which Louis Tully would try to trap Slimer, only to befriend the stubby spud by the end of the movie.

"Kids love Slimer," said Harold Ramis.[30] "In fact, kids love anything associated with slime. Whenever kids would visit the set, one of the first things they would ask was, 'Where's Slimer?' The second was, 'Is there any slime around?' One kid said, 'I want to come in on a slime day.' I guess they love repulsive substances in general."

Thom Enriquez, who had designed Onionhead for his debut in the first *Ghostbusters*, returned to the drawing board and reworked Slimer with a wider grin and a more comical appearance. Sculptor/puppeteer Mark Siegel also reenlisted for a second tour with Slimer.

"By that time Slimer had become a popular character and even had a cartoon show," says Siegel. "And so the concept design started to go toward the cartoony look that people had gotten to know. In the original, he's not cute at all—he's really grotesque and horrible looking, and what makes him cute is that he's somehow charming and funny. Personally, that worked better for me than the cute version we did for *Ghostbusters II*."

Adds Ned Gorman, "We decided to do a lot more facial animation. There was a huge amount of work that went into the facial animatronics that doesn't actually show up in the film because a lot of it hit the cutting-room floor."

A gelatinous fat suit would be worn by operator Bobby Porter, featuring the same divided-head construction that had split Nunzio Scoleri's skull and lower jaw into two separate pieces. Servos and pneumatics would control Slimer's facial expressions—a technological step up from the first film, in which the ghost's movements were largely the result of hand puppetry.

"Technology had advanced quite a bit, so the mechanics of the puppet were all radio controlled with servo motors and even pneumatic cylinders to drive the mouth opening and closing," says Siegel. "Technically it was pretty cool, but it made for a different kind of performance, and I think he was much more limited in his expressions. The limitations of the mechanisms made him a lot less flexible and stretchy than the original."

Then the word came down from the production team: Slimer had been cut from the script. ILM turned their attention to other challenges, and operator Bobby Porter was let go. Two weeks later, a directorial change of heart restored Slimer's scenes, but at this point Porter could no longer spare the time commitment. ILM effects coordinator Ned Gorman recalled a colleague he'd worked with on Ron Howard's *Willow* who shared Porter's body type. Shortly thereafter, Robin Shelby (then Robin Navlyt) joined the crew.

OPPOSITE A Slimer character concept for *Ghostbusters II*.
BELOW Louis Tully confronts a hungry Slimer at the firehouse in a scene cut from *Ghostbusters II*.

controlled the subtle mechanics behind Slimer's facial expressions. "It was an effort of probably seven to eight people," says Shelby.

Reitman shot two additional scenes with Rick Moranis in the firehouse, detailing Louis's disastrous attempts to operate a proton pack and successfully nab Slimer.

A third deleted scene had a more positive vibe. After Louis stepped off the bus to face the soul-swallowing evil of Vigo's mood slime, Slimer rushed in to volunteer his services and give his new friend a wordless pep talk.

Unfortunately for fans of the toothy green ghost, preview audiences didn't respond well to any of those scenes. In the film's final cut, Reitman excised Slimer from all but two shots (plus a cameo in the end credits).

"The whole relationship between Moranis and Slimer was told in a series of funny vignettes," says Reitman. "When I was looking at it back then, it just didn't seem to work. Now I wish I had finished that material and put it in the film. Unfortunately, we had bigger issues to deal with trying to figure out how to make the last act work."

Most of Shelby's performances fell victim to the cut. "The scene I was most bummed about was the 'getting off the bus' scene. That was probably the best stuff that we shot. Slimer wants to go too and Rick says, 'No, you can't go, but maybe we can go bowling sometime.' They gave me the tape of what Rick was doing, and I would listen to it over and over to get the timing down on what Rick did previously. Then they would crank the sound—because it was really loud in the costume— and I would react off against essentially nothing, just knowing what the scene was."

22. SLIMER—MARK II

Thanks to his comic-relief role on the animated show *The Real Ghostbusters*, Slimer had oozed his way to star status among the school-going set. In *Ghostbusters II*, Reitman initially included a running subplot in which Louis Tully would try to trap Slimer, only to befriend the stubby spud by the end of the movie.

"Kids love Slimer," said Harold Ramis.[30] "In fact, kids love anything associated with slime. Whenever kids would visit the set, one of the first things they would ask was, 'Where's Slimer?' The second was, 'Is there any slime around?' One kid said, 'I want to come in on a slime day.' I guess they love repulsive substances in general."

Thom Enriquez, who had designed Onionhead for his debut in the first *Ghostbusters*, returned to the drawing board and reworked Slimer with a wider grin and a more comical appearance. Sculptor/puppeteer Mark Siegel also reenlisted for a second tour with Slimer.

"By that time Slimer had become a popular character and even had a cartoon show," says Siegel. "And so the concept design started to go toward the cartoony look that people had gotten to know. In the original, he's not cute at all—he's really grotesque and horrible looking, and what makes him cute is that he's somehow charming and funny. Personally, that worked better for me than the cute version we did for *Ghostbusters II*."

Adds Ned Gorman, "We decided to do a lot more facial animation. There was a huge amount of work that went into the facial animatronics that doesn't actually show up in the film because a lot of it hit the cutting-room floor."

A gelatinous fat suit would be worn by operator Bobby Porter, featuring the same divided-head construction that had split Nunzio Scoleri's skull and lower jaw into two separate pieces. Servos and pneumatics would control Slimer's facial expressions—a technological step up from the first film, in which the ghost's movements were largely the result of hand puppetry.

"Technology had advanced quite a bit, so the mechanics of the puppet were all radio controlled with servo motors and even pneumatic cylinders to drive the mouth opening and closing," says Siegel. "Technically it was pretty cool, but it made for a different kind of performance, and I think he was much more limited in his expressions. The limitations of the mechanisms made him a lot less flexible and stretchy than the original."

Then the word came down from the production team: Slimer had been cut from the script. ILM turned their attention to other challenges, and operator Bobby Porter was let go. Two weeks later, a directorial change of heart restored Slimer's scenes, but at this point Porter could no longer spare the time commitment. ILM effects coordinator Ned Gorman recalled a colleague he'd worked with on Ron Howard's *Willow* who shared Porter's body type. Shortly thereafter, Robin Shelby (then Robin Navlyt) joined the crew.

OPPOSITE A Slimer character concept for *Ghostbusters II*.
BELOW Louis Tully confronts a hungry Slimer at the firehouse in a scene cut from *Ghostbusters II*.

controlled the subtle mechanics behind Slimer's facial expressions. "It was an effort of probably seven to eight people," says Shelby.

Reitman shot two additional scenes with Rick Moranis in the firehouse, detailing Louis's disastrous attempts to operate a proton pack and successfully nab Slimer.

A third deleted scene had a more positive vibe. After Louis stepped off the bus to face the soul-swallowing evil of Vigo's mood slime, Slimer rushed in to volunteer his services and give his new friend a wordless pep talk.

Unfortunately for fans of the toothy green ghost, preview audiences didn't respond well to any of those scenes. In the film's final cut, Reitman excised Slimer from all but two shots (plus a cameo in the end credits).

"The whole relationship between Moranis and Slimer was told in a series of funny vignettes," says Reitman. "When I was looking at it back then, it just didn't seem to work. Now I wish I had finished that material and put it in the film. Unfortunately, we had bigger issues to deal with trying to figure out how to make the last act work."

Most of Shelby's performances fell victim to the cut. "The scene I was most bummed about was the 'getting off the bus' scene. That was probably the best stuff that we shot. Slimer wants to go too and Rick says, 'No, you can't go, but maybe we can go bowling sometime.' They gave me the tape of what Rick was doing, and I would listen to it over and over to get the timing down on what Rick did previously. Then they would crank the sound—because it was really loud in the costume— and I would react off against essentially nothing, just knowing what the scene was."

"They had started building the costume based on some-body between four foot ten and four foot eleven, so they were looking at people that could fit the same physical mold," says Shelby. "And they wanted somebody who had experience with special effects, and who had enough energy and stamina."

Three interlocking Slimer segments encased Shelby's head and torso during filming. "There was a shell of a body," she says. "There were gloves, so my arms were covered by Slimer arms that were green latex. And there was the head. It had a lot of motors and wires and servos. You could move every single piece of Slimer's face: the nose, the eyebrows, the cheeks, the chin. And all that was heavy because it took motors to run. We were using a blue screen, so I wore a black leotard to help them take out the legs when they were putting it all together [in postproduction]."

Creature-designer Tim Lawrence—who understood the challenges of emoting in costume after his portrayal of Nunzio Scoleri—gave direction to Shelby during shooting. Puppeteers

TOP Robin Shelby wears the Slimer costume during blue-screen filming at ILM. Creature and makeup designer Tim Lawrence (center) and associate producer Michael Gross (right) can be seen observing. **ABOVE** Thom Enriquez Slimer illustrations produced for *Ghostbusters II* marketing. **OPPOSITE** Slimer expression studies by Henry Mayo.

23. SPOOKS, SPECTERS, AND GHOSTS GALORE

In *Ghostbusters II*, a couple of montage sequences convey the scope of the dangers facing the city. The "We're back" montage follows the re-legitimized ghostbusters as they answer calls that include a ghost jogger and a levitating force inside a glassware shop.

"In the first movie, the montage capsulized the ghostbusters becoming famous," says Reitman. "In the second one, we found the montage was a useful way to demonstrate that ghosts were attacking New York and becoming a real menace again."

The ghostbusters use sneakier-than-usual tactics in their encounter with a spectral jogger, filmed near the Jackie Onassis Reservoir in Central Park. As the ghost sprints past, Venkman triggers a half-buried trap from his position on a park bench. In a deleted line, Venkman observes that the phantom completed his last lap in less than six minutes. Stantz responds, "If he wasn't dead, he'd be an Olympic prospect."

Having originally been hired by ILM to portray the Statue of Liberty, Jim Fye went on to not only play Tony Scoleri but also the ghost jogger. Covered from head to toe in white makeup, he performed in front of a blue screen with the footage later composited into live-action plates.

"His whole body had to be ghostly white," says ILM's Howie Weed. "I took this theatrical 'streaks and tips' hair spray

that you find at Halloween and sprayed his entire body. It was so early in the morning and it was so cold, but he was so good about never moving as I was spraying it up and down his back."

Adds Fye, "The jogger was the first thing I shot, in January of 1989. It was pretty chilly in that costume, and the spray makeup was like a cold shower, but the result was very cool looking. It was mostly running down an elevated platform, checking my pulse, and doing a little dance at the end to look like I was being captured in the trap."

The ghostbusters also visit Orrefors glassware shop where they are presented with an unusual supernatural phenomenon: a dozen pieces of costly crystal hanging motionless in the air. No ghosts are visible, and that was precisely the intent.

"We did not want to repeat any of the imagery in the first film," said Ramis.[31] "We wanted a scene with something other than an apparition or a materialized being of some kind. Another reason we did it was for the budget. Ivan said, 'Gee, can we come up with something that's mechanical and doesn't involve elaborate opticals?' So we thought, yes, the ghostbusters can encounter other things besides just spirits, and we came up with a straight polarity reversal."

The ghostbusters crack the case with a high-tech laser cage, which jams the field but sends the glass artifacts crashing to the

BELOW LEFT ILM's Howie Weed applies white hair spray to turn actor Jim Fye into the ghost jogger. **BELOW RIGHT** Ghost jogger Jim Fye puts in his paces in front of a blue screen. **OPPOSITE** Concept art shows a more skeletal Central Park jogger than the version that ended up on screen.

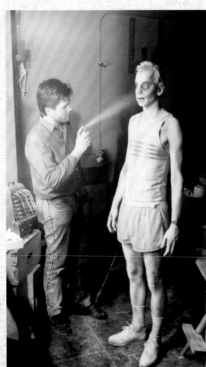

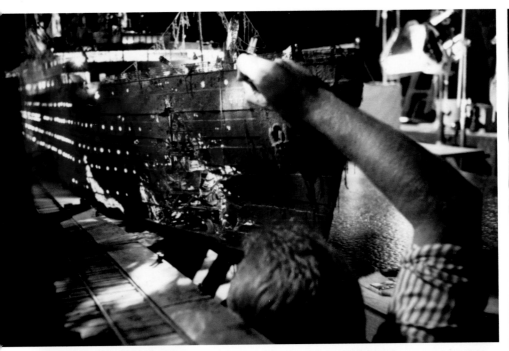

TOP LEFT Finishing touches are applied to the *Titanic* miniature. **TOP RIGHT** A woman's fur coat comes alive after being possessed, an illusion achieved through practical effects. **ABOVE LEFT** Paint and makeup study for the *Titanic* undead. About twenty heads were produced in all, in various colors and in various stages of decay. **ABOVE RIGHT** An extra is made up by Howie Weed for the Titanic scene.

floor. On camera, the effect involved cutting all the mono-filament wires suspending the crystals at the same time. In a deleted line, Ray caps the scene with, "Will that be cash or check?"

A later sequence demonstrates the growing influence of Vigo's mood slime by showing ghosts exiting movie theaters, haunting Washington Square, animating a woman's fur coat, and disembarking from the *Titanic*.

The Washington Square ghost allowed the crew to visit a location originally considered for the first *Ghostbusters*. Ultimately the Stay Puft marshmallow man started his rampage in Columbus Circle, not Washington Square as considered at one point, but a new spook occupied the space for *Ghostbusters II*.

The scene required the ghost to manifest inside Washington Square's iconic marble arch and scatter a mob of panicked New Yorkers. Live-action shooting took place at 5:00 a.m., attracting 750 extras—more than twice the number originally expected. By the third take, more than 2,000 had shown up.

Creating the ghost fell to legendary stop-motion animator Phil Tippett (*Star Wars*, *RoboCop*). "Ivan wanted more in that montage," says Ned Gorman. "There was some concern about us hitting our deadline, so Phil did that shot." Tippett accepted the assignment provided the work could be confined to 160 frames and built on top of an existing stop-motion armature.

The sequence also sees a ghost burst angrily out of a movie theater, the marquee above its doors advertising Reitman's 1973 horror flick *Cannibal Girls*. The monster's bizarre

biology came from an illustration by Henry Mayo. Effects designer Rick Lazzarini—enlisted to help whittle down ILM's monumental workload—had a mere three weeks to build and shoot the finished creature.

"They gave me the script pages and we got started," says Lazzarini. "It ended up being maybe seven feet long, with a human-sized head. It had six eyes, four arms, and a long scorpion-like tail. So how do you split up all these things? We needed to have the jaw open and close, the eyes and brows move, all four arms articulating independently, and to have the tail and these diaphanous black wings move."

After ensuring that only lightweight, easily manipulated materials went into the theater ghost's construction, Lazzarini used a variety of puppetry techniques to create the illusion. Prominent among these was the "facial Waldo"—a cap-and-vest system that could detect changes in the eyebrows, cheeks, lips, and jaws of its wearer and transfer those movements to puppet via wired-up servos.

The woman who suddenly finds herself wrapped up in a growling, snapping fur coat didn't require any postproduction optical enhancement. Four different coats, all outfitted with a variety of practical effects, were used in a late-night location shoot on an LA street outside the Biltmore Hotel, which doubled as the Sedgewick Hotel in the original film.

"There was a master coat that the lady was wearing, which had all the heads react and do stuff," says Gorman. "And there were close-up heads which were shot as inserts, where they were being [manipulated] from behind. We built the coats and did it all on camera—there was no post work." Creature-designer Tim Lawrence pulled off the runaway coat illusion through a mix of cable pulls and radio-controlled mechanics.

When the HMS *Titanic* pulls up to Pier 34 in New York City, audiences know the ghostbusters are facing a supernatural disturbance of historic proportions. The ILM model shop built a replica *Titanic* from plywood and urethane. Costumed extras, carrying seaweed-draped bags and dripping with water, silently file past as they disembark. "Better late than never," shrugs a dockworker, played by comedian Cheech Marin, in a scene shot on Stage 15.

"We considered several ideas," said Harold Ramis of the scene.[32] "One had the Hindenburg arriving with flaming passengers getting off carrying luggage that was also on fire. Another was the precursor to the ghost train that is now in the film. We also had a cemetery scene where the gravestones start taking off like rockets."

Lorne Peterson reveals that the film's *Titanic* was only half-built. "We didn't have to do both sides, just one side and a bit of the bow," he says. "The shot was low so you didn't see the deck. It was under three feet tall and maybe twelve feet long, built in plastic on a wooden frame. We also took iron powder and blew it on a layer of matte spray while it was still wet and sticky, then hit it with an oxidizer. You could almost see the rust grow, making it look like it's been under the seawater for a long, long time."

Howie Weed helped conceptualize the *Titanic*'s undead. "I painted about twenty heads in various colors and in various forms of decay," he says. "Some were blue, some were green. I took streaks—like seaweed—and wetted them down with epoxy so they looked like they had been under water for years."

One effects-heavy scene—scratched during postproduction due to ILM's heavy workload—would have depicted a horde of ghosts stampeding from the bowels of the Manhattan Museum of Art. The moment would have finally convinced the mayor of New York that the ghostbusters were in the right. Its deletion required another explanation for the mayor's change of heart, accomplished through a boardroom scene and the mention of another mayor, albeit a deceased one. ("I spent an hour in my room last night talking to Fiorello LaGuardia, and he's been dead for forty years.")

"Right outside the old Customs House in New York, they had maybe four hundred, five hundred extras," remembers David Margulies, who played the mayor. "It was a tremendous number, and what was happening was that supposedly ghosts were bleeding through the walls. They had all the Industrial Light & Magic people—all of whom looked like young painters out of art school—and everyone was doing specifications. The scene really filmed well, it was a terrific, big scene.

"That was to be a big threat to New York, but in the time they had they couldn't get the technology right. They had to scrap that scene and write another one. And so I was flown out to California and did a scene where I'm talking about Fiorello LaGuardia. It was only about six weeks before the release of the movie, and they were working like demons."

GHOSTBUSTERS II
FINAL THEATER GHOST DESIGN
COLUMBIA PICTURES

LEFT Concept art for the theater ghost by Henry Mayo.

24. THE STATUE OF LIBERTY

If one of the script ideas for *Ghostbusters II* had remained intact, the Statue of Liberty would have appeared as an agent of destruction in Vigo's thrall. This cynical take—perhaps too similar in concept to the Stay Puft marshmallow man—evolved into Lady Liberty's star turn as the embodiment of New York optimism.

During the shoot, panicked pedestrians had been filmed in New York City along with the ghostbusters balanced inside a rocking crown on an LA soundstage. But the Statue of Liberty's big scenes were still missing, and all the work fell to ILM.

"We looked at doing the whole thing in stop motion," says Ned Gorman. "But we quickly dispelled that. Stop motion is painfully slow, and because the marshmallow man had been so wildly successful, it was, 'Let's not mess with a successful formula. Let's put a guy in a suit and build a miniature set.'"

But finding someone capable of fitting into the suit proved troublesome. "That statue is not designed to have somebody inside of it of any proportions," says Gorman. "We were looking at dancers and gymnasts until we realized most of them were not strong enough to actually hold the thing up."

Actor Jim Fye answered the call. "My agent sent me on an audition but couldn't tell me what the part was," he recalls. "She told me to go 'dressed for movement' and that I would need to walk like a statue."

Fye was soon in the studio with the effects team, finding additional work as the ghost jogger and the skinny Scoleri brother. "The Statue of Liberty was the last of my three shoots," he says, "but it was definitely the most difficult."

Because Lady Liberty wouldn't need to emote, a rigid, high-impact plastic mask, molded to match the statue's face, obscured Fye's features. Her crown, constructed of the same material, came equipped with lights and tiny figures representing the four ghostbusters.

"The fittings were challenging and took weeks," says Fye. "When [I was] fully costumed, it was like being wrapped up in a foam rubber mattress. Very heavy, very hot, and during breaks I couldn't sit down. I had one of those leaning boards that they use for actresses with big dresses so they don't wrinkle their costumes. The Statue of Liberty costume was glued onto me, and it took a lot of scrubbing to get that goo off every night."

OPPOSITE Statue of Liberty actor Jim Fye carefully makes his way through a miniature version of New York, while visual effects camera assistant Randy Jonsson and visual effects camera operator Terry Chostner capture the action.
BELOW Story illustration from an early draft of *Ghostbusters II* where the ghostbusters threatened to leave the statue in its prone position until the mayor dismissed all charges against them.

When the Statue lurches to life after a century of inertia, it wrenches itself loose from the bolts attaching it to its pedestal. "There was talk of, 'OK, what magic is happening here?'" says Gorman. "When they slimed the toaster, the toaster just bounced up and down. So if you slime a 110-foot statue, does the metal elasticize? How does she move without ripping apart? How do we animate that? Even in a wild, ghost-ridden world, you have to obey some sense of physics to keep it from looking absurd."

Howie Weed built a special foot for the Statue's first step, which Jim Fye wore like a boot. "I collected everything I could find that looked like understructure or rebar," says Weed. "The foot had all this stuff glued onto the bottom of it, including parts from model kits."

As with Stay Puft's rampage, the Statue of Liberty's giant-sized stroll occurred on a small-sized set. "We already had some of the big buildings, and we made more," says Lorne Peterson. "We also had little cables on the cars for making them move on the street, and the crowds were put in optically."

The miniature skyscrapers hemmed in Fye on either side while he took careful, deliberate steps. "I couldn't see where I was going very well," he says. "More than once in my walk down Fifth Avenue I bumped into the buildings."

During one scene, the statue steps on a police cruiser. ("Sorry, my fault!" shouts Ray.) To achieve the effect, a shot of an actual vehicle filmed on location was combined in postproduction with an eight-inch wax miniature car. As the shadow of Liberty's foot descended, technicians dissolved the fake car over the real one. ILM simulated the cruiser's blown-out windshield with a spray of margarita salt.

When the Statue of Liberty first sparks to life, a miniature of her torch explodes in a fireball. "On the first take, a piece of

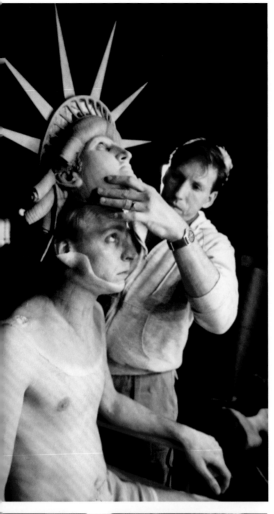

the rig—a circuit, or a ring that was retaining the explosion—flew up into the frame," says Gorman. "It was a mistake, but it looked good. We showed it to Ivan and he cut it in. That's the stuff that doesn't happen with CGI [computer-generated imagery]. You don't get those bits of serendipity."

The statue also needed to cross New York Harbor in neck-deep water. Lorne Peterson's crew built a shallow pool and partially submerged a model of the statue's upper torso. Two poles, attached to the bust and invisible beneath the water, allowed operators on either side of the pool to make lurching movements and transfer the same forward-step action to the model suspended between them.

"The shoulders were moving back and forth as if it was walking underneath," says Peterson. "Its hand was two or three times bigger than a human hand, and so the torch for that model was nearly three feet tall."

One scene that ILM never shot involved the Statue of Liberty lying prone outside the museum, with the mayor haggling with the ghostbusters over who should pay for her restoration. "It was like, 'Here's an American icon, and we're going to have it fall over,'" recalls Ned Gorman. The scene was soon excised from the film.

OPPOSITE TOP Storyboard illustrations of an angry Statue of Liberty, from an early draft of the script in which Vigo took control of the monument. **OPPOSITE BOTTOM** Ivan Reitman oversees construction of the head and arm used for the "wading in the water" sequence. **TOP LEFT** Jim Fye is fitted with the Statue of Liberty's headpiece by ILM creature maker Buzz Neidig. **TOP RIGHT** Fye prepares to swing the torch as ILM creature and make up designer Tim Lawrence looks on. **BOTTOM LEFT** ILM's Richard Miller sculpts the iconic features of Lady Liberty.

25. MUSEUM OF SLIME

Vigo hopes to be reborn at the stroke of midnight on New Year's Eve and takes steps to ensure no mortal meddles with his plans. The Carpathian erects a slime barrier and encases the Museum of Art in an impenetrable shell of goo.

Some shots of the sliming required actor participation, so a partial museum exterior took shape on a Burbank soundstage. Through tiny slits cut into the walls, Chuck Gaspar and his crew pumped eight thousand gallons of slime—enough to fill eleven dump trucks—to demonstrate Vigo's oozing takeover.

The remaining shots of the museum could be done at miniature scale by Lorne Peterson's model makers. "Our museum was somewhere between three and four feet tall and about five or six feet wide," says Peterson. "And we also did the banners in the front. They couldn't be cloth—they needed to be hard and rigid so they wouldn't move."

Surrounding the mini-museum, a clear plastic shell could be filled with water and injected with colors and glittering swirls of diamond dust. Only two takes could be filmed before the bright colors mixed into monochrome, requiring a complete draining and refill.

"Having that whole building covered with slime was a nightmare," says Dennis Muren. "How do you even design it to look like it's covered with stuff that has hardened? We did it with a clear plastic surface filled with liquid and bits of aluminum powder—that way you got little glints off of it, so it looked like it was living."

Cut from the film was a scene in which Hardemeyer, the mayor's aide, pounds his fists angrily against the museum's dripping skin. The slime promptly seizes him and sucks him inside, leaving only his shoes.

The ghostbusters ultimately breach the barrier by smashing the museum's skylight with the Statue of Liberty's torch, which required some precise glasswork from Peterson. "We made glass ceilings three feet across and then laid in really thin and brittle microscope-slide glass," he says. "We bought packets of it from a scientific supply store and used glass cutters to cut it to the size of the panes. We made three different ceilings, and then the guy broke through them."

A concept dropped early in development would have seen the slime acting as a catalyst for animating the museum's paintings. Discarded ideas for "fine art" ghosts included a geometric,

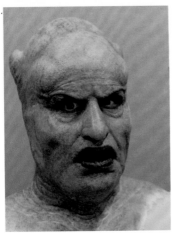

TOP LEFT Tim Lawrence and Howie Weed oversee a rejected ILM experiment involving Vigo's 3-D emergence from his 2-D painting. **TOP RIGHT** The crew films the severed heads used for the subway tunnel scene. **ABOVE** ILM artist Howie Weed dons heavy makeup to portray Ray Stantz under the influence of Vigo.

Escher-inspired creation and a nightmarish Hieronymus Bosch horror. But there was one painting that absolutely needed to disgorge its occupant: the portrait of Vigo. Without a face-to-face confrontation between Vigo and the ghostbusters, the movie had no climax.

"We were struggling, thinking, 'How are we going to make this painting come to life?'" says Ned Gorman. "The initial vision was that Vigo was going to carry himself physically off the canvas and step into the real world. The painting is larger than life, so if you had a twelve-foot figure rip himself off a canvas—like the stained glass knight in *Young Sherlock Holmes*—that could be a pretty menacing villain.

"We had done some tests with screens and optical filtration to create the look of the canvas and to see if we could put up gauze screens that Wilhelm could rip his way through. Ivan saw that but didn't understand that it was a pretty nascent test. He basically kind of hit the panic button and said, 'Game over, fellas, we're going to go a different way.' I think we had bitten off a little more than the schedule would allow. If we'd had another two or three weeks, we could have cracked it."

Howie Weed helped engineer Vigo's actual on-screen materialization. "You see the painting start to become three dimensional as the face of Vigo pushes away from it," he says. "I created a gigantic piece of rubber and projected an image of the actor onto the surface. I also had a face casting of the actor, and I pushed that through the rubber with a vacuum inside it so the rubber's surface would wrap around the head and give it more definition. Combined with the projection, we got this three-dimensional face. It was a pretty convincing effect."

But an early *Ghostbusters II* cut got mixed reactions from a test audience, prompting Reitman to rework the climax with a bigger role for Vigo. "The end of the movie was originally just going to be the boys rappel down on the ropes, slime Vigo, and boom, he blows up," says Ned Gorman. "But based on the audience preview they thought there wasn't enough of a confron-

tation." That meant a fresh round of filming in the museum's restoration room, but now the production had a problem.

"The restoration room set was struck [destroyed] at least a month before because they needed the stage for other movies," says Gorman. "Michael Gross had to get as much of the set rebuilt as he could to do the scenes of the baby floating and the guys getting knocked on their asses by Vigo. In some cases, if you were to pan a few inches to the right, you'd see they didn't have a wall."

In the new, upgraded showdown, Vigo undergoes a final transformation by possessing Ray Stantz and morphing into a distorted demon. "The design was something that [art director] Harley Jessup and I worked on together," says Howie Weed. "I took a clay casting of the actor's face and used a torch to melt and blister it, then made a casting of that and gave it a brown, veiny paint job. Harley added these drag-queen flourishes of makeup—red lips, blue under the eyes. It was like a potato meets Divine."

Ivan Reitman OK'ed the look, but Dan Aykroyd's schedule didn't allow him to play the demon-possessed Stantz. "I'm a big guy, so I asked Dennis Muren if I could do it," says Weed. "Because I was already there they didn't have to bring an actor in for fittings, and they could get on it right away."

Glass contact lenses covered the entire surface of Weed's eyes. To blacken his teeth, the makeup crew squirted his mouth with blasts of concentrated grape Kool-Aid. "The full makeup application took seven hours," says Weed. "When I got up, people had to hold on to me because my legs fell asleep."

EVERYTHING YOU ARE DOING IS BAD

Unfortunately, test screenings exposed gaps in the story structure that went deeper than the climax. Reitman discovered that audiences weren't connecting the menace of the mood slime with the evil of Vigo or even grasping the idea that the slime fed on negative human emotions.

Reitman scheduled reshoots in New York City for filming all-new, explanatory scenes. But that wasn't the only new pressure in the schedule. At the start of production, *Ghostbusters II* had a tentative release date of July 4, 1989. Since then, the target had moved up to June 23, but new information suggested Tim Burton's *Batman* planned to debut on the same date.

The studio opted for a new release date: June 16. It wasn't the news that ILM wanted to hear.

"It was not easy stuff at all, and it was down to the wire," says Dennis Muren. "Ivan said to me, 'The show has got to get done on this date, it has to, it can't be late.' That was the deal with the studio. He said, 'I don't want to see you getting an Oscar for this show, we're just talking about getting it done.' He said it with a chuckle, but that shows how serious it was that we do it."

As the schedule got tighter, the list of effects shots on ILM's plate kept getting longer. It started at 110, expanded to 130, and by the time of the *Batman* shuffle, the list had reached 180 shots. Muren finally declared that his at-capacity ILM simply couldn't finish the workload in time.

Since the timeline couldn't be extended, the remaining job list would need partial outsourcing. Among the effects shops available for a last-minute pitch-in on *Ghostbusters II* were Apogee, Available Light, and Visual Concept Engineering.

Apogee tackled one of Reitman's new scenes—written in reaction to the test screening—in which Ray, Egon, and Winston encounter a ghost train on an abandoned subway track. The dialogue clarified the nature of the threat ("Something's trying to stop us, we must be close," says Egon), and the shoot took place only three months before the movie's planned theatrical release.

These live-action scenes featuring Aykroyd, Ramis, and Hudson took place at Tunnel, a nightclub in New York's Chelsea district built above several hundred feet of unused tracks. Apogee production supervisor John Swallow tracked down an appropriately scaled model measuring twenty-five feet long to serve as the ghost train.

Added scares came with the addition of severed heads on poles, many of them rented from prop houses.

"[Visual effects coordinator] Pam Easley called me and said 'How many severed heads do you have?'" recalls Rick Lazzarini. "There's one in the left foreground in close-ups that we created and supplied. It was sculpted by Adam Jones, who ended up being the guitarist for Tool."

A rejected "frog ghost" would have hopped into view following the train's disappearance, displaying needle-like fangs and a long probing tongue.

"They told me, 'They're not going to use the frog ghost—Ivan doesn't think it's scary enough.' I thought, 'Well hold on, what's Slimer? This looks totally like it could be out of a Ghostbusters movie.' But they'd already made their decision."

One studio generated an ominous shot to convey the rising tide of Vigo's mood slime, only for the effect to go unused in the final cut. "In the opening you were going to see slime rising through forty feet of New York sediment—through layers of broken pipes and antiques and stuff—and then bubble through the cracks of the sidewalk," says Ned Gorman. "I think it was Colossal Pictures that did this shot, and it ran about twenty seconds. They basically built the set upside down and poured the slime in, and then flipped the shot."

Thanks to ILM's decision to pull in the eleventh-hour help from multiple effects studios, *Ghostbusters II* completed its post-production workload just in time for its scheduled release.

"We did pickups with the revised ending all the way until March, and we were on seven-day weeks from January all the way through the finish," says Ned Gorman.

Dennis Muren regrets the historical timing that prevented the movie from taking advantage of the benefits of the digital revolution. "That was the show where I really felt we'd reached the end of the line with traditional visual effects," he says. "It would have been great to have the digital tools ready two years earlier. I think *Ghostbusters II* could have looked a lot different."

TOP The ILM crew film a river of bubbling pink mood slime.
BOTTOM LEFT Rick Lazzarini and the rejected frog ghost.
BELOW Concept art by Henry Mayo shows how the frog ghost would have appeared in the sequence.

FROG-THING EMERGES FROM TUNNEL INTO PLATFORM AREA   9/28

26. ON OUR OWN

Randy Edelman composed an entirely new score for *Ghostbusters II*, independent of the familiar themes created by Elmer Bernstein for the first film. But in light of the success of Ray Parker Jr.'s "Ghostbusters," the prospect of creating another hit single seemed just as important to the filmmakers.

Ivan Reitman scoured the charts for an artist who seemed primed to deliver a hit. Bobby Brown, who learned the ropes as a member of New Edition, and who had recently launched a solo career with his number one single "My Prerogative," earned Reitman's nod.

Written and performed by Brown for *Ghostbusters II*, "On Our Own" peaked at number two on the Billboard Hot 100 following its release on May 30, 1989. In an ironic mirror of the larger battle of the box office, Prince's "Batdance" kept Brown's song from reaching number one.

In the film, Brown has a minor role as the mayor's doorman, asking Egon for a proton pack for his kid brother and prompting the response, "The proton pack is not a toy."

"On Our Own" anchored the official *Ghostbusters II* soundtrack album. It joined a second Brown song ("We're Back") and other tunes featured in the film, including "Spirit" by Doug E. Fresh, Glenn Frey's "Flip City," and Run-D.M.C.'s "Ghostbusters." Despite its importance to the plot, Jackie Wilson's "Higher and Higher" (which accompanied the dancing toaster scene) did not appear as a track. Instead, Howard Huntsberry's cover of the song—used in the film during the Statue of Liberty's walkabout—closed out the album as the final track on side B.

The music video for "On Our Own" debuted in June. With shots of Bobby Brown superimposed on billboards across New York City, the video made room for a grab bag of celebrity cameos intercut with scenes from the movie. The random star parade included Donald Trump, Christopher Reeve, Jane Curtin, Rick Moranis, and the Ramones.

RIGHT The packaging for the cassette single version of Run-D.M.C.'s "Ghostbusters."
OPPOSITE The cover for the sheet music edition of Bobby Brown's "On Our Own."

178

27. YEAH, BUT WHAT A RIDE

The teaser poster for *Ghostbusters II* intentionally mirrored that of the first film: no title, a black background, and a standout logo. This time, however, the classic No-Ghost symbol had been updated, its subject proudly holding up two fingers—interpreted as either a Churchillian "V for Victory" or (more obviously) as the universal sign of a sequel. The poster's tagline read, "Guess Who's Coming to Save the World Again?"

But 1989 saw multiplexes practically overflowing with movie sequels, making it tougher than ever for *Ghostbusters II* to distinguish itself from the pack. Other return engagements vying for ticket dollars included *Star Trek V: The Final Frontier*, *The Karate Kid, Part III*, *Lethal Weapon 2*, and *Indiana Jones and the Last Crusade*.

The Friday, June 16, launch date fell only one week before the opening of Tim Burton's *Batman*. *Ghostbusters II* opened big—breaking the box office record for the biggest three-day opening weekend—but the brooding superhero took a big bite out of the film's take over subsequent weeks. Ultimately, *Ghostbusters II* grossed less than its predecessor.

"We ran into a buzz saw called *Batman*," admits Ivan Reitman. "One of the things that happened is that the national zeitgeist changed. We hit it perfectly in the first movie—there was optimism in the mid '80s about America, and this remarkable 'going into business' story hit it perfectly for the whole world. Unfortunately, by the time the second movie came out, the country was in a more angry and depressed state of mind. Somehow the sweetness of the second *Ghostbusters*—and both movies have an interior sweetness—was out of step with the national mood.

"I think we had waited too long. We were right in the trough of interest for it, even though the movie ended up making hundreds of millions of dollars. More importantly, I was really proud of it. I thought it was good, but we had a problematic last act that we never solved."

Dan Aykroyd agrees with Reitman that the sequel works despite some flaws. "I don't think *Ghostbusters II* was better than *Ghostbusters*, but it certainly holds up as a companion piece," he says.

"I think part of the problem was that Bill got down on the second one and did it publicly," says Reitman. "He kept saying, 'There's too many special effects,' when in fact there were fewer. I think he just got a burr under his saddle about it.

"Fortunately, people are now starting to see it for themselves—away from all the hype and everything else—and are appreciating the second movie for what it is."

Reitman gives an honest accounting of his favorite and not-so-favorite moments: "I loved the stuff between Bill and the baby. I love Annie Potts and Rick Moranis babysitting. But I thought the painting thing, although it's cool and evocative, was almost a little bit too mundane considering what we had done in the first film.

"It didn't quite have the snap—the kind of world-dominating energy—that the first one had. It may not be the unique film that the first one is, but it's got plenty in it that is worth watching."

OPPOSITE The portrait of Vigo the Carpathian resolves into this humorously heroic painting, which is now stored at the Sony archive. **BELOW** The almost final version of the *Ghostbusters II* logo by Thom Enriquez. The team rejected a two-legged ghost as lacking visual simplicity.

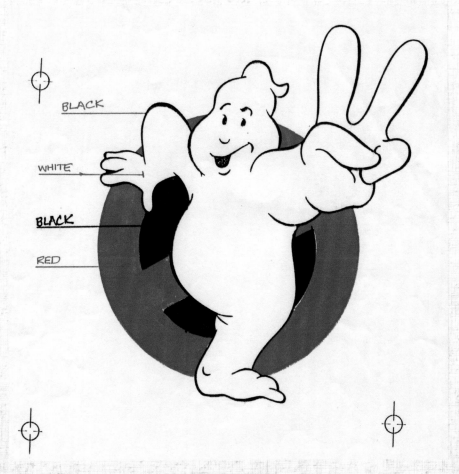

BLACK

WHITE

BLACK

RED

PART 3

THE EXPANDED
GHOSTBUSTERS
UNIVERSE

28. THE REAL GHOSTBUSTERS

While *Ghostbusters II* might have struggled to live up to its predecessor, the Ghostbusters franchise had been going from strength to strength in the five-year gap between the two films, most notably through the animated series, *The Real Ghostbusters*. The show starred an A-list of voice talents and expanded the universe in thought-provoking directions, despite the restrictions inherent in the medium of children's programming. The series even spawned a sequel, *Extreme Ghostbusters*.

To develop the *The Real Ghostbusters*, Columbia Pictures Television approached Burbank-based animation studio DiC Entertainment, the team behind the animated hit *Inspector Gadget*. A slot in the highly competitive Saturday morning network cartoon landscape was DiC's goal, with a separate mission to produce episodes that could air in syndication from Monday through Friday on local television stations.

"Columbia sold it to ABC as a weekly show and started doing it for syndication at the same time," says Joe Medjuck—who, with Michael C. Gross, ensured that the animated project retained the same appeal as the film. "Michael and I took over as executive producers to represent the filmmakers. We read every script and critiqued them to keep it in line with the movie." Under their supervision, *The Real Ghostbusters* would last a remarkable seven seasons, from 1986 to 1991.

It all started with a three-minute promo created to sell networks on the concept. Kevin Altieri storyboarded and directed the sequence alongside Eddie Fitzgerald, producing a dialogue-free reel that showcased ghost designs and ghost-busting tech and pushed the limits of cartoon physics (in one gag, the Ectomobile drove up the support wires of a bridge). The four main characters wore jumpsuits identical in coloring to those in the film, and bore facial features that resembled Aykroyd, Murray, Ramis, and Hudson.

A notable sequence from the animated promo featured a sheet-white ghost strutting down a sidewalk—an intentional homage to John Travolta in *Saturday Night Fever*—only to find himself trapped behind the red crossbar of the No-Ghost logo. This sequence proved so memorable it evolved into the intro of the main series.

PREVIOUS PAGES Peter Venkman looks on as Egon Spengler gears up in this image from *The Real Ghostbusters*. **BELOW** The Ectomobile can convert to a submarine in the animated Ghostbusters universe. **OPPOSITE** Lapping up the limelight, the four ghostbusters are once again surrounded by a crowd of cheering onlookers.

Impressed by what they had seen and excited by *Ghostbusters'* potential as a burgeoning franchise, ABC ordered a full season of animated episodes. DiC produced thirteen episodes for ABC, while simultaneously moving forward on a syndicated order of sixty-five episodes.

The Real Ghostbusters officially entered production under animation director Richard Raynis (*The Simpsons*) and story editor J. Michael Straczynski (*Babylon 5*). Though the series would star movie characters Peter Venkman, Ray Stantz, Egon Spengler, Winston Zeddemore, and Janine Melnitz, the medium of animation provided an opportunity to avoid likeness rights by going "off model."

"One of the big decisions was whether the characters should sound like the actors and also whether they could look like them," says Medjuck. "We thought we'd look at [the animated characters] as 'general representations.'"

Character designers, including Jim McDermott, Gabi Payn, Phillip Felix, and Everett Peck, reworked the characters' appearance, giving each ghostbuster a different color jumpsuit for better on-screen identification, and making clearer distinctions between body types and hairstyles. Ray became shorter and chunkier, Egon gained a whip-curl of blond hair, and Winston lost his mustache.

To fill the comedy sidekick role common in children's animation, the green Onionhead ghost from the first film became the team's mischievous mascot under his new name, Slimer. "People forget, Slimer didn't have a name in the movie," points out Medjuck. "He became much more of a character in the TV show."

The Real Ghostbusters had its characters, but it needed stories—seventy-eight of them at the outset. Story editor J. Michael Straczynski needed to hire writers fast.

Richard Mueller, no stranger to the Ghostbusters universe, became one of Straczynski's first acquisitions. In early 1985, Mueller had penned the paperback adaptation *Ghostbusters: The Supernatural Spectacular Novelization*.

In the pages of his book, Mueller had fleshed out the movie characters, revealing tidbits such as Egon Spengler's reading list (*The Mysteries of Latent Abnormality, Electrical Applications of*

the Psycho-Sexual Drive, and *Your Friend the Fungus*) and Peter Venkman's history as a carnival barker.

"I had great fun with it because I got to fill in the characters' families and backgrounds, and that became a playbook for the [animated] series," says Mueller. "For [series writers] wanting to know about Venkman's father or Ray's aunt or something like that, they could refer back to the book."

Mueller recalls how he joined *The Real Ghostbusters*: "Joe [Straczynski] called me because I'd known him from science fiction writing, and he knew that I'd written the novelization. He said, 'I have to turn out sixty-five [syndicated] scripts in four months. Will you please come?' I learned to work very fast—the first season I handed in eleven scripts. I wound up doing the show for six seasons."

Michael Reaves and Steve Perry also answered Straczynski's call. "I'd worked with Joe before, so when he got the green light, I was one of the first people he called," says Reaves. Adds Perry, "There were a lot of writers who wanted the work, but because both Michael and I were working on other shows, we only pitched a few stories." Straczynski liked their pitches and the duo became a core element of the story team.

Straczynski maintained tight control over scripts and penned many episodes himself, prioritizing consistent world building that paved the way for surprising sci-fi and supernatural concepts. Says Perry, "We were always looking for a way to spin a story scenario that had a neat hook and then deliberately went off in oblique directions."

The sixty-five episodes written for local syndication required less executive interference than the thirteen-episode batch for ABC. "With the notes from [ABC's] Broadcast Standards & Practices, it could take twice as long to write a network show," says Reaves. "With the afternoon package [the syndicated episodes], I would pitch an episode verbally, Joe would OK it, I'd write it, and boom—another paycheck.

"I wrote about nineteen or twenty episodes in all, which was as much or more than anybody else. But Joe was a goddamn machine. He was the Energizer bunny."

TOP *The Real Ghostbusters* employed simplified, stylized character designs: (left to right) Peter Venkman, Egon Spengler, Ray Stantz, Winston Zeddemore, Janine Melnitz, Louis Tully, and Slimer.
OPPOSITE CENTER Line work like this was inked and colored on an animation cel before shooting.
OPPOSITE BOTTOM RIGHT Egon, Peter, and Ray take aim.

Straczynski wrote a total of fifteen episodes in the first order, including "Citizen Ghost," which explained why the ghostbusters now wore multi-hued uniforms and how Slimer had joined the team. The episode "Take Two" served as a metacommentary on adapting original material for animation, ending with *The Real Ghostbusters* watching their live-action counterparts on a movie screen. "He doesn't look a thing like me," complained the animated Venkman, regarding Bill Murray.

As animation director, Richard Raynis worked with a team at DiC responsible for storyboarding the script directions into rough visual form and ensuring that the events would translate successfully into action. The bulk of the animation fell to KK C&D Asia, a Tokyo studio that enjoyed a close relationship with DiC. Each episode contained approximately four hundred background drawings and nearly thirteen thousand separate animation cels.

"We were all pretty knowledgeable about the ways that animation differed from live action—it all came down to movement," says Reaves, who remembers that sequences involving everyday scenes were often the hardest for the overseas studio to animate. "You could scale up something as cataclysmic as you wanted, which was why so many episodes ended with the equivalent of the Death Star blowing up real good.

"But to show a realistic crowd scene? That was just asking for trouble. This is why we tried to stage things out of town, or better yet, inside. In animation, New York is always a ghost town."

The voice cast for *The Real Ghostbusters* provided the final element that would help make the show such a success. "We had Lorenzo Music [*Garfield*] as the voice of Venkman for the first season," says Joe Medjuck. "Frank Welker [*Scooby-Doo*] played Stantz, but not necessarily sounding like Danny. And Maurice LaMarche was a very good mimic, and he sounded a fair amount like Harold." Frank Welker (*Scooby-Doo*) also voiced Slimer, with stand-up comic Arsenio Hall as Winston Zeddemore, and newcomer Laura Summer as Janine Melnitz. DiC's Marsha Goodman filled the role of voice director.

LaMarche didn't intend to imitate Harold Ramis when he auditioned for the part. "It was 1985, and the room was packed with every voice actor and every stand-up comic I knew," he recalls. "We were all told, 'Don't do the guys from the movie—don't try to do an impression.' But at that time, I was a stand-up comic at the Comedy Store whose act was 90 percent impressions. I got in the booth and all that came out was an impression, but strangely enough I got the job. Michael Gross later said, 'We don't want any more impressions. *He* gets to do it, but that's it. Nobody else.'"

Yet LaMarche put plenty of himself into the role of Egon. "I always viewed Harold's portrayal as my stepping-off point," he says. "I did the voiceprint, but it has to become its own thing and be infused with elements of the actor playing him. I never got to meet Harold, but by all accounts he was a spectacular human being and he brought some of that goodness into Egon. And I hope I did too."

Veteran voice actor Frank Welker admits he "didn't do a lot of internal thinking" when it came to voicing the straightforward, good-hearted Ray Stantz. But Slimer was another story.

"The producers and director let me ad lib a lot, and that helped," he says. "The writers would sometimes write suggested dialogue, and I would Slimerize all over it. When Marsha would say, 'Frank, do you think Slimer would do anything here?' was I going to say no? No way, blue jay! I would do something to create the proper Slimer moment. The usual comment from the booth was, 'Great, Frank—but can we shorten it a little?'"

For LaMarche—whose role as Egon was only his second major voiceover job—the show provided a rare opportunity to learn from a master. "I was still getting my feet wet, and I was lucky to sit next to Frank," he says. "Whether he wanted to be or not, he was my teacher. From Frank, I learned how to pull up a character from inside and how to cross-pollinate two different characters to make a unique sound. My own personal bumper sticker in my head was, 'What would Welker do?'"

The Real Ghostbusters provided Laura Summer with her first voice-acting gig. "[In auditions] they didn't have me do the character at all, they just had me read a monologue: 'Hello, Ghostbusters, please hold,'" she recalls. "Later, I got a call and they asked if I could do a New York accent. I said, 'Can I do a New York accent? That's where I'm from!'" Summer used her mother as a template for the inflections of Janine's line readings. "It was just in me," she admits.

Summer got a firm handle on the character right out of the gate. "She called it as she saw it, which is a very New York thing," she says. "And of course she was totally in love with Egon. Some writers didn't really write for her and just had her answer the phone, but in some of the episodes she was one of the boys."

Michael Reaves found Janine to be one of his favorite characters to write for, praising her "horn-rims that could double for a ninja throwing star, voice that could remove paint, and just [being] a well-seasoned 'sarcastinistrino.'"

The show's recording sessions had a light-hearted, playful vibe. "In the studio it was Lorenzo, Frank, Arsenio, Maurice,

TOP LEFT The animated Ectomobile design. The team also operated a flying gyrocopter dubbed Ecto-2. **TOP RIGHT** Stay Puft didn't need much redesigning to fit into the animated world. **BELOW** Slimer became the breakout star of *The Real Ghostbusters* and was eventually incorporated into the show's title. **OPPOSITE** Stay Puft looks less menacing than ever in this still from *The Real Ghostbusters*.

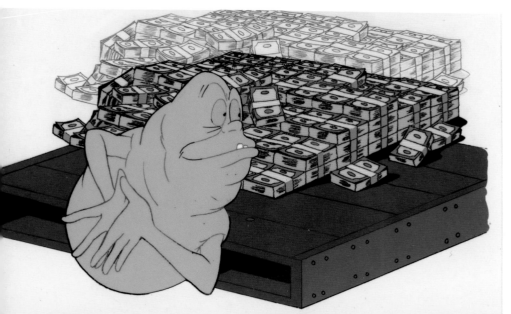

and myself," says Summer. "It was really relaxed—Arsenio might be giving me a massage! And there were so many laughs. I think the first show we did took seven or eight hours. I had nothing to compare it to, but the boys told me that was ridiculous—that you're supposed to do an episode in two hours. But we had a really fun rhythm."

Welker agrees: "I had worked with Lorenzo on many projects, and I knew Arsenio from stand-up, but we all got much closer on the show. Arsenio was never mentally in one place at a time. He was always in trouble with our director Marsha, because if he wasn't actually talking, his mind was elsewhere. You would hear all the actors working, dialogue flying, and then all of a sudden it would be absolute silence. We would turn and look at Arsenio, and he would be mentally traveling—visiting the Comedy Store, or buying a new car, or playing basketball with Kareem.

"We would laugh until we cried, because Arsenio would come up with the greatest excuses as to why he was not reading his lines. And no matter how hard Marsha tried to be mad at him, she would fall victim to his wit and charm."

Season one of *The Real Ghostbusters* aired in a half-hour slot during ABC's Saturday morning lineup from 1986 to 1987. The sixty-five syndicated episodes ran from 1987 to 1988, typically airing on weekday afternoons, but subject to varied scheduling from local TV stations.

Maurice LaMarche praised J. Michael Straczynski's influence over the initial batch of episodes. "It was Joe's philosophy that he wanted every script to be a twenty-two-minute version of what could be a sequel to *Ghostbusters* [the movie]," he says. "Each one had its own self-contained story and took the characters on a real arc into the supernatural."

MIDSTREAM RETOOLING

Unfortunately, this confidence in Straczynski's work wasn't enough for a network armed with focus-group findings. ABC, lagging behind rivals NBC and CBS in the overall Saturday morning ratings race, hired a research firm to come up with fixes. The aftermath of that decision led to an animation shake-up, a shuffling of the voice cast, and J. Michael Straczynski's peeved resignation.

Glendale-based Q5 Corp conducted the research on behalf of ABC. In their estimation, ABC's Saturday-morning lineup needed to appeal primarily to two- to eleven-year-olds, with a particular emphasis on the five to eight age bracket and a slight skew toward girls.

Q5's recommendations filtered down to the staff of *The Real Ghostbusters*. The backlash was strong and immediate. "All the writers, artists, and anyone involved with the show on a creative level was completely appalled," says Michael Reaves.

The company's suggestions for retooling *The Real Ghostbusters* included less reliance on sophisticated jokes, redesigning environments for maximum appeal to little boys, and putting the character of Ray Stantz on the back burner because he did "not appear to serve to benefit the program."

No character took more of Q5's criticism than Janine Melnitz. With the aim of making her a warmer, more supportive figure as suggested by the research, ABC dictated a host of changes that jettisoned Janine's spiky hair, pointed glasses, and barbed wisecracks in favor of soft features, circular specs, and a conservative, knee-length skirt.

"Janine was a strong, vibrant character," complained Straczynski to the *Los Angeles Times* in 1989. "They wanted her to be more feminine, more maternal, more nurturing, like every other female on television. [Q5] is a truly insidious orga-

nization, I make no bones about it at all. A lot of their research and theories are strictly from voodoo. I think they reinforce stereotypes—sexist and racist. I think they are not helping television, they are diminishing it."

The changes to Janine also meant the exit of Laura Summer. "They took away all her character and personality and wardrobe," recalls Summer. "And of course talking with a Queens accent meant 'tramp,' so they stopped with that too. She was a strong female character, and they dumbed her down and made her look like everybody else."

It was the end of the line for Straczynski. "I said, 'You're out of your mind. I will not do that, and if you try and push that through, I will leave,'" he recalled in a 2000 interview with IGN. "I always tell people that when I work for them, I have very few rules: I don't lie, I don't bullshit, and I never ever bluff. If I say I'm going to go, I'm going to go. And I went."

Len Janson and Chuck Menville stepped in as the new story editors. Elsewhere, Will Meugniot replaced Richard Raynis as animation director. And more changes occurred among the voice cast.

"As the show went along, apparently Bill Murray watched it and said, 'Hey, how come Harold's guy sounds like him, but my guy doesn't sound like me?'" says Maurice LaMarche. "And that was the end of Lorenzo as Venkman."

Full House's Dave Coulier filled Music's shoes as the new Peter Venkman. Kath Soucie voiced Janine Melnitz after the departure of Laura Summer, and a short time later, Buster Jones took over from Arsenio Hall in the role of Winston Zeddemore.

"That's just the way show business works," shrugs Coulier. "I mean, the original father on *Full House* was replaced by Bob

BELOW Blackie was a ghost cursed by an Egyptian artifact in the episode "The Long, Long, Long, etc. Goodbye." **BOTTOM LEFT** The Boogieman was a recurring villain introduced in the episode "The Boogieman Cometh." **BOTTOM RIGHT** Janine Melnitz as she appeared in her first incarnation, prior to her network-mandated character softening. **OPPOSITE TOP LEFT** Character model sheet for Slimer. **OPPOSITE TOP RIGHT** Ray and Slimer share a moment. Slimer started out as a mascot and later became an integral member of the team.

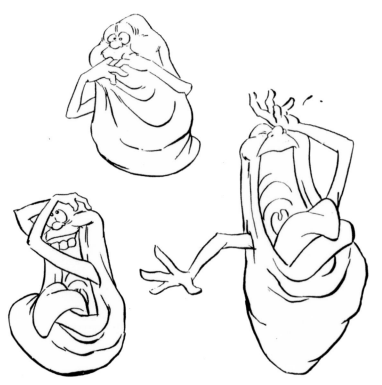

Saget. As an actor you have no power over it—they can just change in midstream."

Dave Coulier tailored his Venkman voice to sound more like the original actor. "Joe Medjuck said he wanted the character to sound more like Bill Murray," he recalls. "They loved Lorenzo's performance, but they wanted a sound that was truer to the movie. That's what I gave them, basically doing my impression of Bill Murray, but more of his *Caddyshack* character and not so much from *Ghostbusters*. When I went in to audition they liked what they heard."

Maurice LaMarche and Frank Welker remained in their roles and quickly made Coulier feel at home. "I had worked with Maurice and Frank on other projects, and I felt very comfortable with those guys," he says. "When the three of us were in a room, we were constantly doing voices to make us laugh. Frank would go into Bob Hope, and I would go into Tony Curtis. It was a blast.

"The scripts were challenging to a voiceover actor. There were lots of tones you had to bring to a character—it wasn't just me doing Bill Murray. That became a big challenge to me— to retain the character, but act through what we were doing with the story."

In the role of Slimer, Frank Welker had more to do than ever. In 1988 the show was rechristened *Slimer! and the Real Ghostbusters*, expanding into an hour-long format consisting of two fifteen-minute *Slimer!* cartoons with a standard *Real Ghostbusters* episode in the middle.

It was a clear sign of the show's kid-friendly renovations. In the *Slimer!* shorts, the green ghost took center stage—interacting not with the ghostbusters but with a new cast of low-stakes antagonists including Manx the alley cat, Bruiser the dog, the hapless Professor Dweeb, and Scareface, the comical head of the ghost mafia.

Sandwiched between *Slimer!* bookends, *The Real Ghostbusters* kept on chugging. EPA agent Walter Peck dropped in as a guest villain, and the Stay Puft marshmallow man frequently reared his puffy head. The release of *Ghostbusters II* in 1989 allowed the show to make references to the new canon, and in "Partners in Slime" Peter coats himself with Vigo's mood-sensitive ectoplasm and gains the ability to levitate. Nerdy accountant Louis Tully finally joined the cast (voiced by Rodger Bumpass), displaying a puppy-dog attraction for Janine Melnitz.

"We had good writers, and Chuck Menville and Len Janson were great story editors," recalls Richard Mueller. "We're especially proud of the animation on seasons three and four because it was beautiful, absolutely gorgeous. And we got to tell good stories."

Yet the focus on Slimer and the incorporation of focus-group tweaks failed to yield a ratings bonanza. Straczynski declined an offer to return as story editor, but did write a handful of episodes later in the show's run. His 1990 outing, "Janine, You've Changed," deconstructed Q5's softening of Janine Melnitz as the in-universe work of a wish-granting demon.

"After their first round of notes had been implemented and had met with resounding failure, [Q5] slunk away into richly deserved oblivion," says Reaves, who recalls an in-joke shared among crew members behind the scenes. "I was giving notes on a storyboard and I saw something in one of the panels—just a bit of background paint, and hardly noticeable unless you knew the story. But for those who did know, it provided a nice bit of closure: an exit sign on an expressway that read, 'EXIT Q5.'"

By the time *The Real Ghostbusters* ended its run in 1991, the show had produced a remarkable 140 episodes over seven seasons—not to mention a toy line, a series of fast-food tie-ins, and even a branded breakfast cereal. For kids growing up in the era, *The Real Ghostbusters* had a huge impact on playground pop culture.

"For many fans, the continuing adventures of the ghostbusters on the cartoon show were just as important to them as the movie," says Maurice LaMarche. "Each episode was like another movie."

29. EXTREME GHOSTBUSTERS

Extreme Ghostbusters debuted in 1997. Taking place in the same universe as *The Real Ghostbusters*, it acknowledged the six years that had passed since the cancellation of the original series—and in world-building terms, that meant a whole new cast of characters. "All the stories about knights don't have to be about Sir Galahad," says producer Joe Medjuck. "And all the stories about the ghostbusters don't have to be about our original guys."

Talks about reviving the Ghostbusters property in licensed animation began in 1995, and by January of the next year Columbia TriStar Television announced the new series in the industry trade press. Richard Raynis, Jeff Kline, and Bob Higgins would be leading the operation, with Joe Medjuck and Dan Goldberg as producers and a tie-in toy line from Trendmasters appearing on shelves. One wrinkle: the name of the upcoming series was listed as *Super Ghostbusters*.

"Trendmasters really wanted us to call the show *Super Ghostbusters*," explains Jeff Kline. "We felt it was too much like *Super Friends* or super heroes—a little too soft for us.

We wanted something that said, 'If you watched the previous cartoon, this is different from the Ghostbusters you're expecting.'"

That resulted in *Extreme Ghostbusters*, a name that exemplified the edgy zeitgeist of the 1990s. The new distributor for the show, Bohbot Entertainment, came up with an apt catchphrase for their promotional website: "Extreme ghosts call for *Extreme Ghostbusters*!"

Bob Higgins, Columbia's head of development for kids TV, saw *Extreme Ghostbusters* as a smart rebranding of the Ghostbusters property. "We wanted to trade on the [*Ghostbusters*] brand recognition, but introduce the franchise to an audience who largely was not familiar with it," he says. "The movies were popular in the '80s, but we were talking to an audience where *Ghostbusters* was not part of their culture. We wanted to create something that spoke specifically to them."

Producer Audu Paden had a similar take. "The thesis was that, if the kids loved it when they were ten, you give them another show when they're fourteen to fifteen and edge it up a little bit, so you retain them a bit longer."

BELOW An early promotional piece showcasing the cast of *Extreme Ghostbusters*. The "riveted" No-Ghost logo would not be used in the final design. **OPPOSITE** A Fil Barlow illustration of an insect-like ghost (from the episode "Fear Itself") that makes its victims experience their deepest terrors.

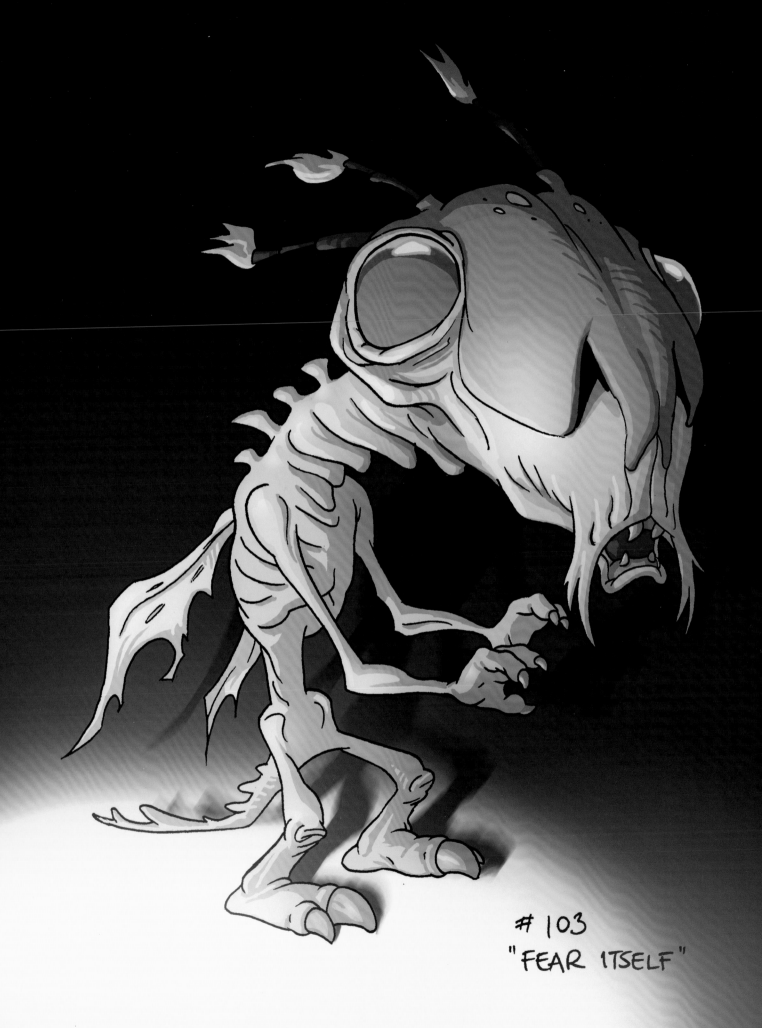

\# 103
"FEAR ITSELF"

The show took place in the same continuity as *The Real Ghostbusters*, but only Egon Spengler, Janine Melnitz, and Slimer would carry over into the new cast. Under *Extreme Ghostbusters'* premise, a precipitous drop in paranormal activity had driven the original ghostbusters into other avenues of employment, leaving Egon to monitor the firehouse's containment unit while teaching classes at a local college. When ghosts unexpectedly return to New York, four of Egon's students take up the mantle previously held by himself, Venkman, Stantz, and Zeddemore.

The success of *Extreme Ghostbusters* would hinge on the appeal of its four new leads. Australia–based artist Fil Barlow helped craft their looks by faxing illustrations across the Pacific to Richard Raynis in Los Angeles. "Back in 1987, when Richard was working on *The Real Ghostbusters*, he'd asked me to design a character—the Grundle—and now he wanted me to do conceptual stuff for the main characters [on *Extreme Ghostbusters*]," he recalls.

Many of Barlow's early designs, including Egon Spengler as a bearded, war-weary wizard type, exemplified the far-out limits of *Extreme Ghostbusters'* brainstorming. "I was just trying a lot of concepts and seeing what hit," says Barlow. "We were talking ideas and I said, 'What if there was a war between ghosts and demons?' Richard said that demons weren't a good thing to have on TV in America, so we nixed that."

Directives from the top required *Extreme Ghostbusters* to be relevant to a new and diverse audience, which shaped the conceptual casting. "One of the first decisions we made was to make sure we had a girl in the team," says Higgins. "When you're trying to appeal to a broad kids demographic, creating a show that's all guys is cutting off your nose to spite your face. We wanted to have a strong female presence who was part of the team and not a tagalong."

That character became Kylie Griffin, a moody genius obsessed with studying the occult, and her design underwent constant evolution. "We sketched an idea of her having this huge vacuum cleaner thing on her back," says Barlow. "I wanted her to be more goth, so I was doing trench coats and things like that to try and be less traditional with the concepts.

"Richard wanted to put her in more of a football uniform, with protective padding. He sent me Polaroids of a young lady who was about the right size, and he'd actually put her in man-sized shoulder pads. I took that as reference, and that became Kylie's final look."

Tara Strong (*X-Men*) provided the voice of Kylie. "I knew that she had to be very real—it wasn't your typical over-the-top cartoon," she says. "They were smart at picking actors that were versatile enough to give authentic acting beats during crazy situations. Kylie was a really cool girl who had this dead grandmother and a diary, but all sorts of other levels to her."

Fil Barlow pushed for more female representation among the four main leads, though Kylie was as far as it went. "When I was working on shows in the '80s, the main lead always had to be a blonde Caucasian guy," he says. "I'd always be throwing in different racial mixes and I also noticed there was always one token female. I sort of teased Richard a bit: 'What if we had *more* females?' Every time he said to make a character, I'd show him a female version, just to give him a choice."

Though the remaining leads would be male, they came from a variety of ethnicities and life situations. "In kids entertainment you want to not make everybody white, and to try to appeal to as many six- to eleven-year olds as you can," says Bob Higgins. "In that group there are white kids and black kids and Asian kids and Hispanic kids, so we diversified our team away from the original."

Eduardo Rivera, a lanky, goateed Latino slacker, became the next ghostbuster. The character provided a cynic's perspective on ghostly happenings while nursing a serious crush on Kylie. Rino Romano provided his voice.

"Spiritually, and I know this sounds stupid, but I thought I was born to play that role," Romano says. "Eduardo was basically the lovable fuck-up. He's in love with the girl but he's too much of a wuss to admit it. He's both the comic relief and the antihero, and the romantic foil. [*Extreme Ghostbusters*] was the best-written show, because it wasn't just about the ghostbusting, it was about the characters."

The next ghostbuster, Garrett Miller, originally bore the name Lucas but was always conceived as someone working with a disability. "Richard originally proposed that he wanted one of the characters in a wheelchair," recalls Barlow. "I found references for people who were disabled, who had wheelchairs and calipers [forearm crutches]. I just kept sending him designs, like a smorgasbord."

To ensure Garrett's situation didn't come across as exploitative, the producers hired Kirk Kilgour—a star volleyball player paralyzed by a spinal cord injury—to consult. Armed with Kilgour's insights, the team wrote Garrett with both care and honesty, later winning honors from the Los Angeles Commission on Disabilities.

"What sets Garrett apart from his peers isn't his physical issues but his personality," says Kline. "He's way over the top and kind of arrogant. Once we hit upon that—and that we weren't going to do the 'afterschool special' of the kid in the wheelchair—it became much easier to write. We didn't have to be as precious with it."

The show avoided making Garrett's wheelchair into a gimmick. "Wheelchairs don't have jetpacks," says Higgins.

"We wanted to play as close as we could to what's possible. It wasn't a vehicle, or a fun toy, it was a part of his character."

Kline laments the fact that the wheelchair prevented Garrett from making it into the first wave of Trendmaster action figures. "The toy company really didn't want us to do Garrett in the wheelchair," he says. "They didn't think any kid was going to want to aspire to be a hero in a wheelchair. Richard Raynis, Bob Higgins, myself, and Sandra Schwartz [at Columbia] really pushed back. But I don't believe there was a Garrett toy." Though Trendmasters went as far as making a prototype toy of Garrett and his wheelchair, the figure went unproduced.

The final spot in the ghostbusters quartet went to Roland Jackson, an easygoing African American gearhead. Roland exhibited a special reverence for the under-the-hood workings of the team's classic Ectomobile. Alfonso Ribeiro (Carlton from TV's *The Fresh Prince of Bel-Air*) provided his voice.

"We were throwing together four teenagers who wouldn't choose to be together otherwise, and then putting them in a

ABOVE Fil Barlow's illustrations of the new ghostbusting crew: (left to right) Roland Jackson, Eduardo Rivera, Garrett Miller, and Kylie Griffin.

BIKER GHOST
#103 GHOSTBUSTERS

TOP LEFT Janine Melnitz, as well as Egon Spengler and Slimer, provided a link to the earlier continuity of *The Real Ghostbusters*.
TOP RIGHT A Fil Barlow concept for an undead biker ghost, complete with tattoos and spiked helmet. **OPPOSITE** A gaggle of ethereal ghost designs cooked up by Fil Barlow for the opening credits sequence of *Extreme Ghostbusters*.

situation that required them to form a family," explains Jeff Kline. "Nothing has more drama—and potential comedy—than family."

Egon Spengler would be the patriarch for this ersatz brood, played again by Maurice LaMarche. "There always has to be a passing of the torch, so I was thrilled to be that guy," says LaMarche. "I guess Egon had the most mentor-ish personality. I was glad because we got a bunch of new ghostbusters and a new team of talented actors."

In the years since the last episode of *The Real Ghostbusters*, Egon's life had passed in real time. "His hairline had receded," says LaMarche. "And real time passed for me too—I'd become a father. Egon was a little too old for this kind of thing; he was tired and a little less patient. I had a screaming baby keeping me up at night. That helped form the more fatigued Egon."

Janine Melnitz returned too, as did her romance with Egon that had previously provided character tension in *The Real Ghostbusters*. This time Pat Musick played Janine, becoming the third performer to voice the animated version of the character after Laura Summer and Kath Soucie.

"I was thrilled to be playing Janine, and Moe was thrilled to be playing Egon," says Musick. "Those characters are set in stone when it comes to the ghostbusters. Janine, of course, wanted Egon very badly—that was the undercurrent, that she

was totally nuts for Egon. And Egon cared about Janine, but his big thing was ghosts and ectoplasm."

Janine had undergone a notorious midstream softening in response to focus-group research on *The Real Ghostbusters*, but times had changed, and *Extreme Ghostbusters* had the freedom to strike out in the opposite direction. "They said, 'We want her sexy. We don't want a wacky Janine, we want a hot Janine,'" recalls Musick. "And they drew her hotter than they used to. While she wasn't the babe-ella of all babe-ellas, she was still pretty cool. And she was also a real wiseass."

Also returning was Slimer, the firehouse's mascot ghost. (A companion for Slimer, a mischievous goblin named Gnat, was considered but never materialized.) Though Frank Welker had voiced the character on *The Real Ghostbusters*, this time the role went to Billy West.

"I really had no idea why I was doing Slimer," admits West. "I was new in town and I didn't even know Frank. I've always felt bad about that, because I didn't create that character and all of a sudden I'm doing him. I had to go by a template that was created by somebody else, and I felt that was not such a great thing."

Extreme Ghostbusters debuted on September 1, 1997, with a two-part premiere written by Dan Angel and Billy Brown—kid-friendly terror veterans who had worked on the *Goosebumps* TV series. Story editors Dean Stefan and Duane Capizzi helped set the tone for the rest of the run, trying to squeeze out as many frights as possible within the limits of the medium.

"We pooled a bunch of our writer friends together, sat around a big table, and spent the better part of a day just spitballing story ideas," says Kline. "The original movie is remembered as a raucous comedy, but it actually has some scary stuff in it. We wanted to have moments of real scares—to do a little bit of a horror show for kids."

Romance was on the table too, even when served with a side of innuendo. "We went a little further with the relationships," admits Kline. "There's a moment where Eduardo is having a fever dream about Kylie. There's sexual subtext to that that probably would have never gotten by a network censor."

The show wore an air of nighttime grittiness and didn't shy away from reminders that comparing past successes to current realities can sometimes be discouraging. "It's interesting that that show took place in the '90s with the downturn in the economy," says LaMarche. "The Reagan era was over. It was scraped together from the ashes of the *Ghostbusters* era, of franchise rights and big business."

Making *Extreme Ghostbusters* proved to be a high-wire act, and producer Audu Paden found himself in the spotlight. "We did forty half-hour episodes in less than a year," he says. "At a certain point we were delivering five episodes a week. Originally we were going to have two producers, but I realized four months in—as I was on the toilet and people were sliding drawings under the stall for my signature—that I alone was going to be seeing this thing through to the end."

By design, the look of the animation would not have the same stylistic hallmarks developed on *The Real Ghostbusters*. "We were in the '90s, so the style was a little sharper and less

BONDY

SPINEY

FLYER

LIZARD

EYEBAD

OPENING SEQUENCE
FLYING GHOSTS
GHOST TRAIN)

Art by Fil Barlow Extreme Ghostbusters © Copyright 1997 Columbia Tristar

THE SPHINX
XGB #102
Sc: 02-102-01

Art by Fil Barlow Extreme Ghostbusters © Copyright 1997 Columbia Tristar

SAMHAIN

TOP LEFT Grundel, a villain introduced in *The Real Ghostbusters*, returned in the *Extreme Ghostbusters* episode "Grundelesque." **TOP RIGHT** The Extreme Ghostbusters meet this Egyptian terror in the episode "The Sphinx." **BOTTOM LEFT** The pumpkin-headed Samhain is a genuinely threatening foe. **OPPOSITE** The ghost train featured in the *Extreme Ghostbusters* opening credit sequence.

rounded—a little more MTV," says Higgins. "We wanted something that felt hip and urban because the show was set in New York City."

But redesigns only added to the challenges facing the two South Korean animation studios working on the show, Hanho Heung-Up and Koko Enterprises. "We were getting material in from Korea—just an insane amount of stuff—that just wasn't working," says Paden. "In a show that had probably seven hundred cuts in twenty-two minutes, we would have to do two hundred retakes. We were building scenery as the curtain was rising. It was as close to a 'live' cartoon as I've ever been exposed to."

By contrast, the voice actors enjoyed a laid-back, warmly sociable environment. Notably, their recording sessions occurred at night, with performers encouraged to deliver true-to-life performances that reflected their mutual rapport.

"It was one of the first animated series where they had everybody perform fairly naturally," says Pat Musick. "Up until that point [in animation], everybody had been over the top. One of the things they stressed about this show is that they wanted everybody to be as real as possible with the roles—to underplay them. At the time, it was a bit revolutionary.

"And the other great thing was that the whole cast was there for the sessions. In animation, lots of times they record you separately and put it together later on. We were all in the room together live, and it was just amazing fun. Most of us had been running to different sessions all day, so the evening was usually a time to go home. So to have an evening recording session—people initially were leery. But when we got there they had great food, it was a great atmosphere, and we all just ended up liking each other."

Billy West recalls a similar atmosphere. "Night sessions are weird, because it's like the *Enterprise*—you don't know whether its day or night out," he says. "Time gets lost, so you just wind up having fun. There's a synergy in the room among actors when they're ensemble performing. Tara Strong and I used to go out for coffee afterward just to talk about the world. After being in New York for so long I felt kind of lost being in Los Angeles, but things like that pull you through."

For Tara Strong, *Extreme Ghostbusters* is a succession of happy memories. "It's the only animated series I've ever done at night, and it was like a party," she recalls. "We all clicked, and we all genuinely loved each other. We would all experience each other's lives: marriages and divorces and boyfriends and girlfriends. I remember Maurice eating pizza with peanut butter."

Adds West, "Mo was working a lot of jobs back then. I'd have to poke him when it came time for his lines, because he'd be asleep."

Meanwhile, away from the recording studio, the stress of producing the show's animation led to some unorthodox, impromptu fixes behind the scenes. "The price it took on the teams and their health is one of the most extreme that I've experienced in thirty years of making animation," says Audu Paden. "But there was an advantage to having to work quickly—I found myself going out to some of the most extreme places and giving guys a shot. Guy works in a video store one day, he's a storyboard clean-up the next."

Sadly, scaring up ratings proved difficult, and *Extreme Ghostbusters* only ran for a single season. "Bohbot Kids Network was a syndicated block, which means we were competing against the big boys: ABC, CBS, NBC, and Fox," says Higgins. "The show was syndicated on a channel-by-channel basis, and it was hard to get many eyeballs. But we were able to sell a lot of merchandise, so that means somebody was looking at it."

Pat Musick points out the contrasts between the series and its forerunner. "It was almost the exact opposite of where the original show had to go," she says. "They wanted to be cool and

hip and edgy and yet not have *Ghostbusters* fans look at it and go, 'What the hell did they do to the show?'"

"It was the '90s, it was a young, cooler, hipper *Ghostbusters*," says Rino Romano. "It was *Extreme Ghostbusters*."

Audu Paden wasn't surprised when the show wasn't picked up for a second season. "I think we sort of knew we had forty episodes and then done," he says. "It was very unusual on that kind of show to get a new order. That would involve *Simpsons*-esque ratings, and we knew we were going to be in—to be blunt—the ghetto of programming time when only the stoners, the insomniacs, or those who had night jobs were going to watch it. I don't think they really had the fuel to get into orbit and stay there."

Despite the short run of *Extreme Ghostbusters*, Maurice LaMarche believes the episodes have staying power. "It's a show about a family," he says. "None of them were related by blood, but they faced death together and faced peril with humor.

"We all want that, that some extension of us will go on. Even atheists I know say, 'I wish it were true, I wish I believed in the afterlife.' I think that in the show's affirmation—as goofy as that afterlife might be—people find comfort in that."

30. GHOSTBUSTERS VIDEO GAMES

By the time *Ghostbusters* hit theaters in 1984, the home video game industry had suffered its first big crash. With sales at an all-time low, gaming developers sought out big-name properties that might bring some additional audience appeal.

Only one *Ghostbusters* game, Activision's 1984 tie-in, materialized during the era. David Crane (creator of the hit *Pitfall!*), wrote the game in six weeks, borrowing elements from the incomplete *Car Wars* game to provide a jump start for the Ectomobile driving sequences. The game emphasized entrepreneurism, giving each player a new Ghostbusters franchise and $10,000 in the bank and encouraging business purchases such as antighost suits, marshmallow sensors, and ghost bait.

"If you want to design a game around a license, you have to be very careful," Crane told *Edge* magazine in 2007. "The best strategy is to design an original game that would stand alone even without the license. Our original theory was that a licensed game should be a great game first, and a licensed game second. The success of the *Ghostbusters* game reinforced our belief—that was clearly the right way to go."

Though the basic mechanics remained the same across all platforms, *Ghostbusters* appeared for the Commodore 64, the Atari 2600, the Sega Master System, and the Nintendo Enter-

tainment System. The NES version by Japanese studio Micronics ended with an awkwardly translated victory message:

CONGLATURATION !!!

YOU HAVE COMPLETED
A GREAT GAME.

AND PROOVED THE JUSTICE
OF OUR CULTURE.

NOW GO AND REST OUR
HEROES !

Ghostbusters sold well and became Activision's most ported game across various platforms. But it was only one game. The prospects for *Ghostbusters II* looked a little brighter in terms of variety, thanks to the third-generation console renaissance buoying the video game industry in 1989. Two *Ghostbusters II* tie-in games bore the same title but came from completely different studios and featured unrelated gameplay and visuals.

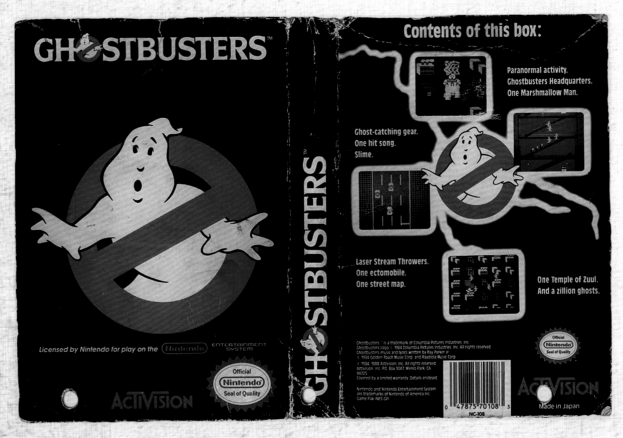

OPPOSITE Stay Puft on the rampage in 2009's *Ghostbusters: The Video Game*. **BELOW** The original packaging for the *Ghostbusters* Nintendo Entertainment System game from Activision.

The first, developed for consoles by Imagineering, was a side-scrolling shooter with a Galaga-style sequence in which the player shot fireballs from the Statue of Liberty's torch at dive-bombing ghosts. The second, more leisurely, game came from Dynamix, in which players could opt to earn money by shooting at ghosts or by going on slime-sampling missions prior to their showdown with Vigo.

A third game based on the movie sequel, 1990's *New Ghostbusters II* (from Japanese company HAL Laboratory) never appeared in North America due to licensing disputes, but stood out for its inclusion of Louis Tully as a playable character. Featuring cutesy characters and an overhead perspective, the game took in familiar locations from the movie such as the courthouse and the art museum. The same year, SEGA's *Ghostbusters* launched on the company's popular consoles. A platform shooter, with squat, cartoonish representations of our heroes, the story culminated with the ghostbusters going head-to-head with Janna, Goddess of Darkness.

Other games focused on the ghostbusters' animated incarnations. Appearing in arcades, 1987's *The Real Ghostbusters* (Data East) permitted cooperative play in an overhead shoot-'em-up. The 1993 Game Boy version of *The Real Ghostbusters* bore a curious pedigree—in Japan, a virtually identical game was released as *Mickey Mouse IV: Mahou no Labyrinth*, with lead character Peter Venkman replaced by the Disney character; meanwhile, in Europe, Venkman was replaced by Garfield the cat and the game was retitled *Garfield Labyrinth*.

The animated series *Extreme Ghostbusters* led to a trio of games from Light and Shadow Productions, including a 2001 Game Boy Color release bearing the same title as the show and a follow-up (*Ghostbusters: Code Ecto-1*) for the Game Boy Advance. *Extreme Ghostbusters: The Ultimate Invasion*—a

first-person shooter similar to *Time Crisis*—appeared in 2004 for the PlayStation.

The games had their fans, but tech limitations couldn't reproduce the unique science of 'busting. It took next-generation hardware—and the participation of the movie heavyweights—to make an immersive game that could go head-to-head with the films in terms of pure entertainment.

GHOSTBUSTERS: THE VIDEO GAME

"The intent was to make a game that felt like it was a potential sequel to the series," says Mark Randel, president and chief technology officer of Terminal Reality. "The game takes place after the second movie and wraps up a storyline that was in the background of both films."

Though Terminal Reality released *Ghostbusters: The Video Game* in June 2009, the earliest hints of a new Ghostbusters game came three years earlier from a completely different studio. Slovenian developer ZootFly produced a demo reel of in-game footage in May 2006, despite not having secured a Ghostbusters license. Fans who saw it were excited.

"Back in 2006, we had gotten money from Vivendi Universal to do a demo in order to get a full game greenlit," recalls Randel. "We did our prototype, which turned out to be the ballroom sequence with Slimer. But around the same time, this company in Europe came out with their demo and put out a video. They inadvertently helped us, because it put to the forefront how popular the franchise still was, and helped us get the money secured for the full game."

Randel's team didn't want to make a disposable tie-in. But to achieve their ambitious vision, they needed the participation of the people who had turned the movies into megahits. "Dan Aykroyd was looking for ways to get *Ghostbusters III*

BELOW LEFT AND CENTER A variety of *Ghostbusters II* video games appeared on shelves at the same time for various platforms. **BELOW RIGHT** *The Real Ghostbusters* for GameBoy proved to be a modified version of an unrelated game. *Extreme Ghostbusters* for GameBoy Color was one of several games created for the new animated series.

made," says Randel. "We showed the demo of capturing Slimer in the ballroom to Dan, and he brought Harold in."

The story for *Ghostbusters: The Video Game* was written as a high-stakes supernatural epic by Aykroyd, Ramis, and the team at Terminal Reality. "It was definitely collaborative," says Randel. "Dan and Harold were involved from the start. They gave structure and ideas for the plotline and had a small team to figure out the gags and other fun things we could do. Harold and Dan had the final say to make sure it fit within the Ghostbusters universe."

Aykroyd viewed the game as another chapter in the adventures of Venkman, Stantz, Spengler, and Zeddemore. "I thought it was almost like a third movie," he says. "It was a great piece of writing because the team really got it. They understood what the bible was, and who the characters were. They followed the rules and even expanded on the concepts. Harold and I wrote for it, but they came up with the story. It's always great to get new creative voices, because once we turned the designs over to the teams, they came up with beautiful executions—the way the Ectomobile looked, the way the packs looked, the uniforms, the whole thing."

In addition to writing duties, Aykroyd and Ramis returned to voice their characters. With the two of them on board, securing the rest of the *Ghostbusters* cast picked up steam. Soon both Bill Murray and Ernie Hudson had signed on—reuniting the four ghostbusters for the first time in two decades.

"I loved being part of it," says Ernie Hudson. "I was happy to get back together with the guys because I thought it was long overdue. Bill Murray, when he was asked, said 'Are all the guys there? Is Ernie Hudson going to be there? Because I'm not doing it without Ernie.' That kind of loyalty you don't get in Hollywood."

Murray admitted similar feelings in a 2009 David Letterman interview: "I got really back into the ghostbusters thing, and it was fun being Dr. Peter Venkman. I was laughing and I was improvising. It was just like being in the movies—a lot of fun."

Other returning actors included Annie Potts as Janine Melnitz and William Atherton as Walter Peck. Bill Murray's brother Brian Doyle-Murray (who had played a skeptical psychologist in *Ghostbusters II*) played the mayor of New York, while Max von Sydow once again voiced Vigo the Carpathian—trapped in his painting as an interactive object inside the ghostbusters' firehouse.

"Somebody actually flew to Europe to record [Sydow]," says Randel. "They recorded something like a hundred lines. You can [interact with the painting] many times and you'll probably never hear everything he can say."

Due to the participatory nature of video gaming, every player who picked up a controller starred as the fifth ghostbuster. Nicknamed "rookie" by the other members of the squad, the player protagonist was effectively a blank slate.

"The character never even talked," says Randel. "He was kind of a nodder. We did that because the essence of the ghostbusters is the timing and the camaraderie between Dan,

ABOVE The four ghostbusters as they appear in *Ghostbusters: The Video Game*, voiced one again by Ernie Hudson, Bill Murray, Harold Ramis, and Dan Aykroyd.

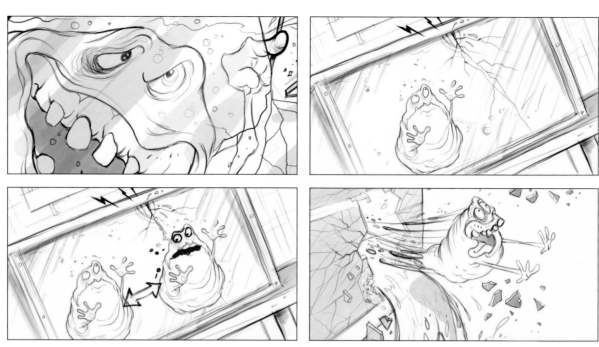

Bill, and Harold. The only way to re-create that was to make you watch them."

Set on Thanksgiving Day 1991—two years after the events of *Ghostbusters II*—the game centers on a new threat that combines the demon-worshipping architect Ivo Shandor from the first film and the underground river of mood slime from its sequel. EPA agent Walter Peck is now the head of the newly formed Paranormal Contract Oversight Committee (P-COC), giving him governmental authority over the ghostbusters' operations. While investigating a fresh outbreak of supernatural activity, the ghostbusters revisit old haunts (including the

Sedgewick Hotel and the New York Public Library) and bust some familiar ghosts.

"We took the iconic stuff that people remembered, like Slimer and Stay Puft, so people would be drawn right back into the universe," says Randel. "A lot of people might not have seen the movies in years, so that was done to have a really fun opening."

The mechanics of capturing spooks and specters were replicated accurately, with entangling proton beams that must be wrestled into position above a glowing ghost trap. Throughout the game, upgrades to the player's gear are presented as

cutting-edge paranormal developments. "Constantly having Ray and Egon invent new things was almost a video game in itself," says Randel. "Egon is like, 'That's the right piece of equipment to get you through the next section of the game at just the right time.'"

The game's climax involves a battle with a giant sloar (from Louis Tully's *Ghostbusters* line, "Many Shubs and Zuuls knew what it was to be roasted in the depths of a sloar that day, I can tell you!") and a showdown with the Destructor inside the spirit realm. "At the end of the first movie, they went through the portal when they were fighting Gozer," points out Randel. "Our idea was to expand on that and imagine what the ghost world would be like. They go through these portals and get stuck there, and wind up having to get back to the real universe."

A few of the team's ideas didn't make it into the final release. "There was a sequence that took place on Thanksgiving Day, where the Thanksgiving Day parade floats came alive," says Randel. "But we couldn't get the gameplay quite right."

After three-and-a-half years of development, *Ghostbusters: The Video Game* launched on June 16, 2009. "We spent countless numbers of hours and late nights rewatching the movies just to make sure that the feel was right," says Randel. The team's dedication paid off when it met the passion of *Ghostbusters* fans.

"The game was a big success," says Randel. "We were concerned that something using a licensed property would get a bad review, but that didn't happen. It got glowing reviews everywhere. According to the charts it sold over three million

units across all systems. But Atari was the publisher, and then Atari fell into bankruptcy. We had lots of concepts for a sequel, and had a few levels scripted, but a sequel never materialized."

A follow-up from a different studio, titled *Ghostbusters: Sanctum of Slime*, dropped two years later, but *Ghostbusters: The Video Game* remains unique as both a compelling story and a remarkable cast reunion. "We all grew up when *Ghostbusters* came out, so it was a labor of love," says Randel. "We made something that we were really, really proud of."

31. GHOSTBUSTERS IN COMICS

When *The Real Ghostbusters* hit television screens in 1986, it created an entire animated universe that soon spawned toys, merchandise, video games, and other spinoffs—including comic books. A bifurcated strategy saw separate comics released in North America and overseas.

Marvel UK got things going in March 1988, five months before the U.S. comic made it to shelves. A new issue of the UK version of *The Real Ghostbusters* comic appeared every week, featuring short adventures starring the ghostbusters and Slimer, intermixed with prose stories (framed as entries in Winston's diary) and pages from Spengler's Spirit Guide providing ghostly facts. The series ended in 1992 after an impressive 193-issue run.

In the United States, NOW Comics published its own tie-in title beginning in August 1988. NOW's *The Real Ghostbusters* ran for twenty-eight issues, while a separate *Slimer!* comic book series (labeled "fun for the whole family!") was published at the same time. The company produced a comics adaptation of *Ghostbusters II* in 1989, but substituted the animated versions of the characters to avoid licensing issues. A bankruptcy filing in 1990 put the comics on ice, but they briefly returned under the NOW banner in 1991.

BELOW Interlocking covers for the "Mass Hysteria" story arc. Pencils by Dan Schoening and colors by Luis Antonio Delgado. **OPPOSITE** Cover for the *Ghostbusters: Haunted America* trade paperback. Pencils by Dan Schoening and colors by Luis Antonio Delgado.

By 1992 the *Real Ghostbusters* animated series had run its course, and so had the comics. Canadian company 88MPH acquired the Ghostbusters comics license a decade later, releasing the four-issue *Ghostbusters: Legion* in 2004. Set shortly after the first film but updated to a contemporary environment (complete with references to cell phones and Cameron Diaz), the miniseries became a one-time curiosity when 88MPH collapsed later that year.

Later, a 2008 anomaly—Tokyopop's manga-style anthology *Ghost Busted*—featured black-and-white tales with a Japanese artistic influence, but failed to make a big splash. Although *Ghostbusters* comics seemed to be on shaky ground during this period, the same year saw IDW snap up the Ghostbusters comics license, leading to a renaissance in four-color storytelling.

"I think there's a lot of really good stuff in those early, pre-IDW comics," says IDW editor Tom Waltz, who views the company as the heir to a legacy of strong *Ghostbusters* comics. "As far as I'm concerned, you can never have enough 'busting, and it's always fun to see the boys in gray interpreted by creators who love and cherish the property as much as we do."

IDW tested the waters with a string of one-shots and a 2008 miniseries, finally launching an ongoing *Ghostbusters* series in 2011.

"The reaction was extremely positive," recalls Waltz. "First issues for any big licensed title tend to get decent pre-orders, so the initial excitement from retailers wasn't much of a surprise. However, it's also true that those early numbers don't mean anything if the comic isn't up to snuff—sales will tank pretty fast

LEFT Janine Melnitz bags a big one in *Ghostbusters*, vol. 2, issue #3. Pencils by Dan Schoening and colors by Luis Antonio Delgado. **ABOVE** Dan Schoening drew this variant "artists edition" cover for *Ghostbusters*, vol. 2, issue #10.

if fans aren't happy. As it turned out, fans loved what we were doing, as proven by multiple printings of various issues and great sales numbers for the first arc."

The first *Ghostbusters* volume produced sixteen issues, and a relaunched second series ran for twenty. IDW helped keep the mythos fresh by introducing new characters, including scheming Ron Alexander and his competitive business, the Ghost Smashers, and FBI Agent Melanie Ortiz who teams up with the ghostbusters in Roswell, New Mexico.

"Nothing makes me happier than knowing characters we thought up in our own brains worked out so well," says Waltz. "It's hard to think about the ghostbusters without Mel and Ron in the mix. It's like our little babies went out into the world and done real good—or in sneaky Ron's case, real bad."

Nods to the larger tapestry of Ghostbusters fandom include appearances from Kylie Griffin (*Extreme Ghostbusters*) and "the rookie" (*Ghostbusters: The Video Game*). Secondary characters from the films, such as Walter Peck, Jack Hardemeyer, and Janosz Poha, appear in supporting roles. But at its core, IDW's ghostbusters saga is still about the four 'busters who started it all.

"We see Peter, Ray, Egon, and Winston not only as co-workers and friends, but as a family of sorts," says Waltz. "Along with their supporting cast, especially Janine, we strive to tell stories that revolve around their quirky relationships and even quirkier personalities, staying as true to the movies as we possibly can. All of the supernatural antics and action? That's the icing on top."

OPPOSITE TOP LEFT Pencils by Dan Schoening for *Ghostbusters*, vol. 2, issue #16. **OPPOSITE TOP RIGHT** Egon and a rival are buried in paperwork in the cover for *Ghostbusters*, vol. 2, issue #6. **OPPOSITE BOTTOM** Interlocking covers for the four-part "Happy Horror Days" story arc, running through *Ghostbusters*, vol. 2, issues #9–12. **TOP LEFT** A ghost shark is an unexpected sight in Chicago in *Ghostbusters*, vol. 1, issue #13. **TOP RIGHT** Ray has an arachnophobic encounter in *Ghostbusters*, vol. 2, issue #18. **ABOVE** Dan Schoening's pencils for *Ghostbusters*, vol. 2, issue #4.

THIS ROOM PROTECTED BY...

THE REAL GHOSTBUSTERS™

Collect all *TheReal Ghostbusters*™ Toys.

Peter Venkman™ and Grabber Ghost™

Ray Stantz™ and Wrapper Ghost™

Egon Spengler™ and Gulper Ghost™

Winston Zeddmore™ and Chomper Ghost™

The Stay-Puft Marshmallow Man™

The Green Ghost™

Bug-Eye™ Ghost

H₂Ghost™ (squirts water!)

Bad-to-the-Bone™ Ghost

ECTO-PLAZM™ Play Gel. Proof of a ghostly encounter, ghost figure included in each. Collect all four.

Stage your own supernatural battles!

GOOPER GHOSTS™ Figures. *Squisher™ Banshee Bomber™ Sludge Bucket™* The GOOPER GHOSTS each come with a can of ECTO-PLAZM. Goop THE REAL GHOSTBUSTERS with these whimsical ghosts.

GHOSTPOPPER™ Toy Weapon. Pop the soft foam "ghostpops" at all the ghosts in your neighborhood!

GHOST ZAPPER™ Toy Weapon. A unique light and sound toy that lets you enter the world of THE REAL GHOSTBUSTERS!

ECTO-1™ Vehicle. Get ready to roll into your own ghostly adventures. Comes with the GHOSTWINDER™ winch! (hero figures sold separately)

Kenner

32. GHOSTBUSTERS TOYS AND MERCHANDISE

Ghostbusters broke box office records in 1984, but at first, only the bootleggers were benefitting from the merchandise.

"Literally the first week there were T-shirts on the street with the No-Ghost symbol," says Ivan Reitman. "But they were all counterfeit. There were no toy deals, there were no T-shirt deals, there was nothing. But there was extraordinary demand."

It wasn't until the animated series *The Real Ghostbusters* landed on TV screens that toymakers saw potential in Ghostbusters as a perennial licensed property.

"Companies like longevity in a product," says Michael C. Gross. "It takes them a long time to tool up to make toys, especially for a movie they're not even sure is going to be a hit. That's why there was no merchandising from the first movie. And so [Columbia] said, 'Fine, we'll back the cartoon up with a toy line.'"

That was Kenner's *The Real Ghostbusters* line, which debuted in 1986 in conjunction with the show's first season. "It was the number one boys' toy line for a year," says Gross, "and it did about $200 million overall, I think."

The animated versions of Peter Venkman, Ray Stantz, Egon Spengler, and Winston Zeddemore looked different from the actors who had played them, and so did their action figures. "The cartoon characters have been immortalized in plastic, so a lot of kids only know us as the cartoon characters," said Harold Ramis at the time of the release of *Ghostbusters II*.[33] "They look at me and they go, 'Your hair isn't blond.'"

The initial wave of Kenner's *The Real Ghostbusters* action figures featured the four heroes, each wearing a proton pack and packaged with a small ghost figure. Some of the more famous ghosts, including Stay Puft and Slimer (referred to on

BELOW *The Real Ghostbusters* Fire Station playset, which came with a containment unit and pole. **OPPOSITE** Promotional room sign that advertised Kenner's The Real Ghostbusters line of figures, toys, and vehicles.

THE REAL GHOSTBUSTERS. FIRE STATION PLAYSET
HEADQUARTERS FOR THE REAL GHOSTBUSTERS ACTION FIGURES

After a long hard day of hunting ghosts, there's no place like home! "Ghost Central" has been recreated here for THE REAL GHOSTBUSTERS heroes and the ECTO-1 vehicle. It includes the "Ghost Pursuit" firepole which THE REAL GHOSTBUSTERS can slide down, a "Goop Grate" with a 5 oz. can of ECTO-PLAZM play gel, a "Ghost Containment Unit" for storing those menacing ghosts, opening and closing garage doors, and THE REAL GHOSTBUSTERS logo sign. It's hauntingly familiar—seen every week on TV and loads of fun!
Ages 4 and up. One 5 oz. can of ECTO-PLAZM play gel included. Hero figures not included.

FIRE STATION

NO. 80580
PKD. 4, WT. 17 LBS.
CUBE: 5.59 CU. FT.

58   59

THE REAL GHOSTBUSTERS.
GHOST ZAPPER, TOY WEAPON
A UNIQUE LIGHT AND SOUND TOY

Kids get to rid their own house of ghosts when they use this versatile role-playing weapon to project and eliminate six different ghost images. Pull the trigger and an animated ghost is projected onto a flat surface. The eyes and mouth of each ghost can be made to move up and down mysteriously. Pull the trigger to its second stage and one of four electronic zapping sounds will be emitted. Release the trigger and the projected ghost image disappears. Two C batteries and one 9-volt battery not included. Ages 4 and up.

NO. 80200
PKD. 6, WT. 11½ LBS.
CUBE. 1.06 CU FT

64

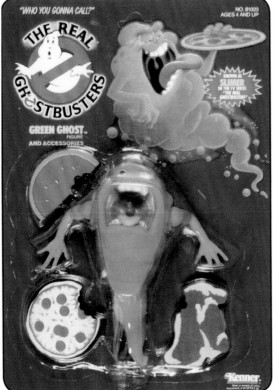

ABOVE Kenner's promotional materials for the ghost zapper projector toy. **RIGHT** Slimer, identified on this action figure card simply as "Green Ghost," came packaged with multiple foodstuffs.

the toy's card back as "Green Ghost"), received separate releases as standalone figures.

Many of the toy ghosts had no relationship to either the animated series or the movie. Gooper Ghosts such as Banshee Bomber had huge mouths to swallow the heroes whole and coat them in slime (branded Ecto Plazm, and available in pink, yellow, blue, and purple). The Monsters line brought Dracula, Quasimodo, Frankenstein, and more into the Ghostbusters universe.

In 1988, the four heroes appeared on toy shelves sporting some new advancement in toy technology. Fright Features figures changed their expressions with a squeeze, while the following year's Screaming Heroes figures made a whistling sound when wound up.

"What was novel about the vintage line was that it had kind of all those cool scare features," says Scott Neitlich, former marketing manager for Mattel's Matty Collector division. "Every year they had to find new and innovative ways of getting their A-list guys out there in order to get a second or third purchase. That meant refreshing with a new gimmick.

"And a toy company isn't just selling to consumers. The first stop is, you have to sell it to retailers, who want to see what's the new innovation, what's the new packaging. Toys have to have some new innovation every year, if not every season."

The 1990s Power Pack Heroes line was notable for its inclusion of Louis Tully in action-figure form. The Slimed Heroes came with heat-sensitive paint that changed colors when squirted by icy water. The Ecto Glow Heroes figures—which featured glow-in-the-dark facial masks—marked the end of Kenner's *The Real Ghostbusters* line in 1991.

After an absence of six years, Ghostbusters toys returned to shelves when Trendmasters picked up the license to the animated series *Extreme Ghostbusters*. The line only lasted for a single season in fall 1997.

Of the four extreme ghostbusters, three of them (Roland Jackson, Kylie Griffin, and Eduardo Rivera) appeared as action figures, as did their mentor, Egon Spengler. Left out was the wheelchair-using Garrett Miller due to the cost of adding a wheelchair accessory. The pumpkin-headed ghost, Samhain, appeared in the *Extreme Ghostbusters* line as a villain, despite only appearing in the show's opening credits.

Movie-accurate Ghostbusters toys first appeared in 2004 from Neca. Unfortunately the company only received partial likeness rights for its reproductions, which didn't include the cast of the *Ghostbusters* movies. "Neca didn't have rights to

the humans, only the ghosts," explains Neitlich. "It was cool to get the Terror Dogs and the rest, but they couldn't legally offer the humans, and no line is really complete without them." During the Neca run, the company produced figures of Gozer, Stay Puft, Slimer, and both Terror Dogs (Zuul and Vinz Clortho).

It wasn't until the twenty-fifth anniversary of the original film's release that the movie heroes received plastic immortalization. In 2009, Mattel unveiled a lifelike line of twelve-inch *Ghostbusters* heroes, and soon added a six-inch series.

TOP The 2009, nostalgia-heavy Retro-Action line from Mattel featured multicolored jumpsuits and *The Real Ghostbusters* facial styling: (left to right) Spengler, Stantz, Zeddemore, and Venkman.
ABOVE LEFT The Janine Melnitz and Samhain firehouse set from the Retro-Action line.
ABOVE RIGHT The Retro-Action figure of Egon Spengler, complete with vintage-style packaging.

Each release in Mattel's first wave of six-inch two-packs came with a removable proton pack and detachable proton stream. The other items included with the figure varied quite a bit—Egon came with Slimer, Winston with a smoking ghost trap, and Ray with a reproduction of the famous No-Ghost sign.

"It was the first time any characters from the movie had been done, period," Neitlich points out. "The main cast, the secondary characters, the villains, anything. We pretty much had universal rights to both of the movies, but with some of the actors we had to get likeness approvals. Bill Murray took longer than the others, which is why the Venkman figure was maybe the fifth or sixth in the line."

To fill out the ranks, Mattel released figures including Walter Peck, Dana Barrett in her Zuul dress, and Louis Tully possessed by Vinz Clortho.

"Movie-based toys were always one of those golden eggs out there as far as brands that deserved toys but never got them," says Neitlich. "When the opportunity came around to add them, that was beyond a dream come true. It was like, 'Wow, we're actually going to make Ghostbusters toys—that's amazing!'"

The twenty-fifth anniversary of *Ghostbusters* in 2009 provided new outlets for movie merchandising and proved that the franchise had retained every ounce of its pop culture power. "When I first started at Sony, Ghostbusters wasn't a property that anyone in merchandising was focusing on," says Greg Economos, Sony's senior vice president for global consumer products. "But we did some research and found that the logo and the film itself were classics."

Economos helped shape a wide-ranging twenty-fifth anniversary licensing program that extended far beyond the high-profile releases of *Ghostbusters: The Video Game* and Mattel's action-figure line.

"It really was the first time we said to the studio, 'Here's a property that has merit in the consumer products world, and we're going to see what we can do with it,'" he says. "There was pent-up demand. It became really successful in all categories of merchandising, everything from toys to apparel. Since then, we've done close to $250 million at retail in Ghostbusters business."

Among Economos' favorite products is IGT's Ghostbusters slot machine. "It really allows you to experience *Ghostbusters* by putting in a couple of bucks," he says. "There are a lot of creative elements in there that give you a good sense of the movie, while having fun at a casino."

The thirtieth anniversary of *Ghostbusters* in 2014 brought about an even bigger merchandising splash from Economos and his team. "We asked, 'How do we really get consumers engaged?'" he says. Among the year's cross-promotional surprises was a partnership with Krispy Kreme, where customers could buy donuts themed after Stay Puft and Slimer.

OPPOSITE TOP LEFT The six-inch Egon Spengler action figure (plus Slimer) from Matty Collector's line of adult collectibles. **OPPOSITE TOP RIGHT** Four figures from the Matty Collector line: Venkman in classic uniform, Zeddemore with slime blower, Stantz with ghost sniffer, and Venkman in *Ghostbusters II* courtroom outfit. **OPPOSITE BOTTOM LEFT** Vinz Clortho and Vigo in packaging from the Matty Collectors line. **OPPOSITE BOTTOM RIGHT** A two-pack of Egon Spengler (in his *Ghostbusters* costume) and Ray Stantz (in his *Ghostbusters II* costume) from Matty Collector. **TOP LEFT** Slimer and Stay Puft were popular subjects for T-shirts released through Sony's licensing division. **ABOVE** IGT's popular Ghostbusters slot machine.

ABOVE AND RIGHT Japanese icon Domo came to life through Funko vinyl toys, appearing as Stay Puft, Slimer, and a ghostbuster. BELOW The Ecto-1 LEGO set came with minifigs of each of the four ghostbusters. OPPOSITE Specially commissioned art from Gallery 1988: (clockwise from top left) Stay Puft looms over a subway map of Manhattan in Anthony Petrie's "Metroplasm"; "We're Ready to Believe You" by Dave Perillo features some vintage-flavored advertising; "Are You a God?," a horror-themed work by Dan Mumford; and Mark Englert's piece entitled "The Flowers Are Still Standing."

Custom, eye-catching thirtieth anniversary art prints came to life through Jensen Karp (founder of the Los Angeles–based Gallery 1988) and the talents of more than seventy artists. "Jensen really has the pulse on the fans," says Economos. "We commissioned him to create pieces of original art that traveled to different cities—there were lines around the block. The gallery in LA is on Melrose Avenue, and the day it opened there were over a thousand people in line."

Exhibitions of these unique Ghostbusters art pieces also appeared in Chicago and New York before finishing the tour at San Diego Comic-Con. "We did limited-edition lithographs and T-shirts based on that art," says Economos. "Everything sold out."

Other items produced to mark 2014's special event included a LEGO Ecto-1 set, packaged with four LEGO mini-figures depicting the Ghostbusters team. "The set was only supposed to be sold online and at LEGO parks, but it did so well they ended up selling it in mass-market stores," says Economos.

"We also did collectible vinyl products with Funko that look really cool," he adds. "And we did a mash-up with Domo—the Japanese brand mascot—allowing Funko to create a Ghostbusters/Domo mash-up brand."

Through consumer products, Economos has demonstrated that the franchise is as vital as ever and that the fans still hunger for new ways to enjoy the Ghostbusters universe.

"Showing that the franchise is still viable, that it still has its pulse on consumers, that's something that merchandise does," says Economos. "Merchandising is a way to show that the content is still an important part of our culture."

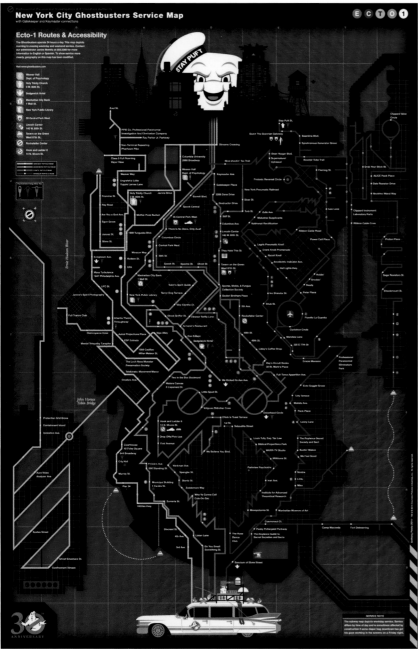

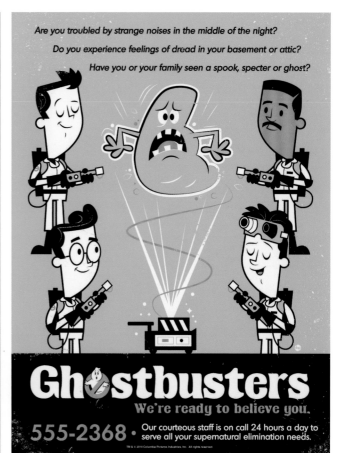

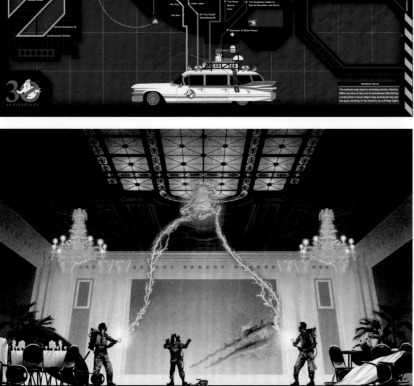

GHOSTBUSTERS FANDOM

Fans of *Ghostbusters* numbered in the tens of thousands during the summer of 1984. Within a month of the film's release, the most dedicated fans had already established a means of showing their allegiance.

The official Ghostbusters Fan Club began on July 3, 1984, under the direction of Swissvale, Pennsylvania, residents Mark Lister and Jim Garvey. The pair paid Columbia an estimated $10,000 for the rights, and the club collected more than forty thousand members across the world in a little over a year.[34]

The $8.95 registration fee paid for a membership kit that included a Ghostbusters metal badge, a Certificate of Anti-Paranormal Proficiency, a membership card, stickers reading "This Property Protected by Ghostbusters," a sticker of the Ectomobile, a Ghostbusters logo patch, and a one-year subscription to the Fan Club's quarterly newsletter.

"People loved *Ghostbusters*," recalls Ernie Hudson. "And then the cartoon came out, and kids were both watching the cartoon and watching the movie. But then around 1995, I started to see guys dressing up in ghostbuster jumpsuits. And that started to grow."

Wearable ghostbusters gear wasn't anything new. The Kenner toy line had included dress-up items, including a proton pack, a Nerf-like ghost popper, and a neutrona blaster with a crank-operated rotating proton stream. A ghost trap with air-triggered doors could be opened by stomping on a foot pedal.

Kids who had grown up on the plastic toys, however, had entered adulthood and forged friendships with other lifelong *Ghostbusters* fans. Many possessed expertise in engineering and gadgetry, and their pursuit of authentic-looking ghostbusters gear became a passionate, shared project.

"By the time I realized that there was a ghostbusters prop-making community, around 1998, they were already a sophisticated group of researchers," says Adam Savage, former movie prop builder and host of TV's *MythBusters*. "The Ghostbusters group was incredibly thorough about sharing what they had found out about the nuts and bolts—someone might figure out that a tiny heat sink is a transistor from a radio from World War II, or something. That way, everyone is included."

Though proton packs can be tricky to reproduce in a movie-accurate state, Savage points out that 100 percent fidelity is never required.

"With a pair of khaki coveralls, a hundred fifty bucks at a hardware store, and a little bit of ingenuity, you could make a reasonable ghostbusters costume," he says. "Having a low threshold to entry is deeply within the ethos of the ghostbusters themselves. It's the 'everyman' fantasy, and I think that the openness of the prop community comes straight from the sweetness of the movie and its characters."

Ernie Hudson has seen practically every type of fan costume, including ones that surpassed the gear he wore in the films. "I was at a convention and a guy had a pack with a wand that would shoot steam and a laser beam that would cut through the steam," he says. "These are working-class people, and they loved the movie enough to invest in it."

Mattel even got into the prop replica business, releasing a PKE meter reproduction targeted at adult collectors in December 2010. "The PKE meter was the smallest, and it sold very well," says Scott Neitlich. "That was followed up by the ghost trap, then the ecto-goggles, and finally the proton wand."

Adds Savage, "Costuming is a chance for fans to put themselves into a story they love. There are some franchises where you put on the costume and *become* that character. But not with the ghostbusters. Everybody who puts together a costume makes sure that it's *their* name that's on that nametag."

ABOVE Adam Savage of TV's *MythBusters* with his own ghostbusters gear (photo by Norman Chan). Savage, who admits to flaws in his first version of the costume, says he is currently working on a new, more accurate one. **OPPOSITE** "They're Here to Save the World," a Ghostbusters thirtieth anniversary print by Joshua Budich from Gallery 1988's collection.

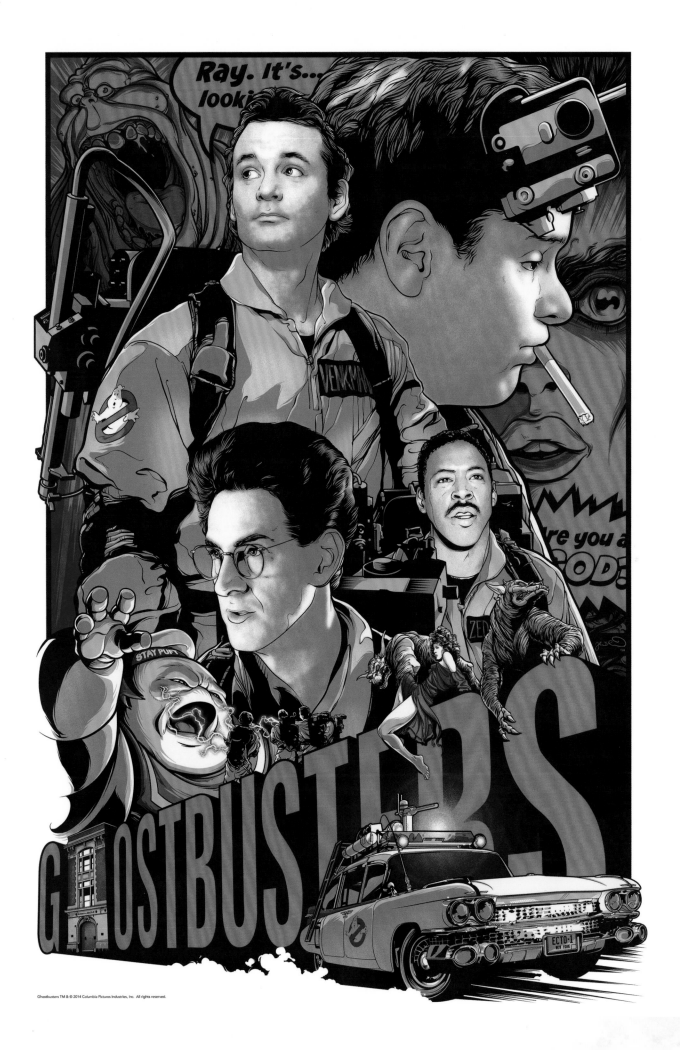

33. SEE YOU ON THE OTHER SIDE

The idea of a third Ghostbusters movie starring the original cast went through countless half-starts and reconceptions throughout the 1990s and 2000s. With the passing of Harold Ramis in 2014, the prospect of a *Ghostbusters III* seemed increasingly unlikely.

"For a while the concept for the third movie was that we'd cleaned up all the ghosts in New York and the ghostbusters were out of business," says Aykroyd. "But that's not where we should be going. We should have new ghostbusters doing their thing, being handed the torch by the old. Once people start thinking along those lines, we're going to be able to keep it alive."

That's where the Ghostbusters franchise is now. Multiple films are in the pipeline that will reboot the original 1984 concept, while honoring its comedy DNA. In a move that made global headlines, it was announced that 2016's *Ghostbusters* (directed by *Bridesmaids*' Paul Feig) will star an all-female ghostbusting team of Kristen Wiig, Kate McKinnon, Leslie Jones, and Melissa McCarthy.

Both Ivan Reitman and Dan Aykroyd are closely involved with the film, as well as with other Ghostbusters projects still on the horizon. Their production company, Ghostcorps, is dedicated to reinvigorating the supernatural premise and uncovering new branding opportunities.

"We want to expand Ghostbusters in ways that will include different films, TV shows, merchandise, all things that are part of modern filmed entertainment," said Reitman.[35] "It's just the beginning of what I hope will be a lot of wonderful movies. My primary focus will be to build Ghostbusters into the universe it always promised it might become. The original film is beloved, as is the cast, and we hope to create films we will continue to love."

For Aykroyd, the opportunity to tell a bigger, wilder, more inclusive supernatural success story just makes sense.

"Whenever I see kids, female and male, no matter how old they are, if they're interested, I always say, 'Welcome aboard. You're one of our cadets.'"

BELOW Phantom City Creative's "Spooks, Specters, and Ghosts" from Gallery 1988's collection.
OPPOSITE Anthony Petrie's thirtieth anniversary print "Ghostbusted" from Gallery 1988's collection.

INSIGHT
EDITIONS

PO Box 3088
San Rafael, CA 94912
www.insighteditions.com

 Find us on Facebook: www.facebook.com/InsightEditions

Follow us on Twitter: @insighteditions

All BOSS Film Ghostbusters photos by Virgil Mirano, courtesy of Richard Edlund.

Ghost Trap prop on page 56 courtesy of Brandon Alinger and Prop Store (www.propstore.com).

Library of Congress Cataloging-in-Publication Data available.

ISBN: 978-1-60887-510-8

Publisher: Raoul Goff
Acquisitions Manager: Robbie Schmidt
Art Director: Chrissy Kwasnik
Designers: Chrissy Kwasnik & Chris Kosek
Executive Editor: Vanessa Lopez
Senior Editor: Chris Prince
Production Editor: Rachel Anderson
Editorial Assistant: Katie DeSandro
Production Manager: Anna Wan

ROOTS of PEACE   REPLANTED PAPER

Insight Editions, in association with Roots of Peace, will plant two trees for each tree used in the manufacturing of this book. Roots of Peace is an internationally renowned humanitarian organization dedicated to eradicating land mines worldwide and converting war-torn lands into productive farms and wildlife habitats. Roots of Peace will plant two million fruit and nut trees in Afghanistan and provide farmers there with the skills and support necessary for sustainable land use.

Manufactured in Hong Kong by Insight Editions

10 9 8 7 6 5 4 3 2 1

INSIGHT EDITIONS would like to thank everyone who helped make this book a true celebration of the Ghostbusters universe by contributing their time, memories, photographs, and art: Brandon Alinger, William Atherton, Dan Aykroyd, Fil Barlow, Richard Beggs, Suzy Benzinger, Peter Bernstein, John Bruno, Bill Bryan, Norman Chan, Brian Chanes and Profiles in History, Randy Cook, Dave Coulier, Lori Cowley, David Crane, Ron Croci, Katie Cromwell, Gary Daigler, Stephen Dane, John DeCuir Jr., Tom Duffield, Greg Economos, Richard Edlund, Gilbert Emralino, Thom Enriquez, Michael Ensign, Andrew Farago, Jim Fye, Ned Gorman, Gloria Gresham, Michael C. Gross, Bob Higgins, Ernie Hudson, Harley Jessup, Steve Johnson, Slavitza Jovan, Jensen Karp, Virginia King, Jeff Kline, Gene Kozicki, Maurice LaMarche, Dan Lanigan, Rick Lazzarini, Peter MacNicol, David Margulies, Henry Mayo, Michael Maxwell, Kimberly McCauley, Jim McDermott, Joe Medjuck, Mark Morse, Richard Mueller, Dennis Muren, Bill Murray, Pat Musick, Steve Neill, Scott Neitlich, Alex Newborn, Audu Paden, Ray Parker Jr., Steve Perry, Lorne Peterson, Annie Potts, the Harold Ramis estate, Mark Randel, Richard Raynis, Michael Reaves, Eric Reich, Ivan Reitman, Rino Romano, Paul Rudoff, Adam Savage, Dan Schoening, Robin Shelby, Mark Siegel, Mark Stetson, Chris Stewart, Tara Strong, Laura Summer, Tom Waltz, Sigourney Weaver, Howie Weed, Bo Welch, Frank Welker, Billy West, Mark Wilson, Terry Windell, Ramin Zahed, and Stuart Ziff.

Sony archive photography by Ethan Boehme.

NOTES
1. *Entertainment Tonight* (1989), 14.
2. Bob Costas, *Later with Bob Costas* (1989), 14.
3. Don Shay, *Making Ghostbusters* (New York: Zoetrope, 1985), 14.
4. *Cinefex 17* (June 1984), 16.
5. Shay, *Making Ghostbusters,* 18.
6. Shay, *Making Ghostbusters,* 18.
7. Shay, *Making Ghostbusters,* 18.
8. Shay, *Making Ghostbusters,* 19.
9. Shay, *Making Ghostbusters,* 24.
10. Harold Ramis, Ghostbusters DVD commentary track (Columbia/TriStar Home Video, 1999), 36.
11. Shay, *Making Ghostbusters,* 53.
12. Shay, *Making Ghostbusters,* 53.
13. Shay, *Making Ghostbusters,* 83.
14. Shay, *Making Ghostbusters,* 84.
15. Shay, *Making Ghostbusters,* 88.
16. Ramis, Ghostbusters DVD commentary track, 115.
17. *Starlog* (March 1989), 118.
18. Patrick Goldstein, *Rolling Stone* (June 1, 1989), 53–61, 118.
19. Kim Masters, *Premiere,* vol. 2, no. 11 (July 1989), 75, 120.
20. Leeza Gibbons, *Hollywood Insider* (USA, 1989), 120.
21. Goldstein, *Rolling Stone,* 120.
22. Adam Eisenberg, *Cinefex 40* (November 1989), 120.
23. Goldstein, *Rolling Stone,* 121.
24. Arsenio Hall, *The Arsenio Hall Show* (1989), 121.
25. Chris Connelly, MTV's The Big Picture (MTV, 1989), 122.
26. Lorianne Crook and Charlie Chase, *Crook & Chase* (TNN, 1989), 126.
27. Chantal Westerman, *Good Morning America* (ABC, 1989), 128.
28. Lorianne Crook and Charlie Chase, *Crook & Chase* (TNN, 1989), 129.
29. Eisenberg, *Cinefex 40,* 138.
30. Eisenberg, *Cinefex 40,* 163.
31. Eisenberg, *Cinefex 40,* 166.
32. Eisenberg, *Cinefex 40,* 169.
33. Eisenberg, *Cinefex 40,* 213.
34. *The Pittsburgh Press* (Oct. 7, 1984), 220.
35. Mike Fleming Jr., *Deadline* (Mar. 9, 2015), 222.